Power
Eighteenth Century India

Power and Conflict in Eighteenth Century India

The Life of Solomon Earle

Dr ROBERT ADAMS

© Robert Adams, 2019

Published by Robert Adams

All rights reserved. No part of this book may be reproduced, adapted, stored in a retrieval system or transmitted by any means, electronic, mechanical, photocopying, or otherwise without the prior written permission of the author.

The rights of Robert Adams to be identified as the author of this work have been asserted in accordance with the Copyright, Designs and Patents Act 1988.

A CIP catalogue record for this book is available from the British Library.

ISBN 978-1-9996926-0-5

Book layout and cover design by Clare Brayshaw

Prepared and printed by:

York Publishing Services Ltd
64 Hallfield Road
Layerthorpe
York YO31 7ZQ

Tel: 01904 431213

Website: www.yps-publishing.co.uk

Contents

1.	Introduction	1

PART ONE : BEGINNINGS : 1751-1768

2.	Ashburton and Gujarat	5
3.	To London : 1767	13
4.	A Passage to India	20

PART TWO : INTRODUCTION TO INDIA

5.	Mughals and Marathas	35
6.	The Honourable East India Company	43
7.	The Rise of the Gaekwads and the start of the Anglo-Maratha War	54

PART THREE : EARLY YEARS IN INDIA : 1768 – 1778

8.	Bengal & the Company Army : 1768 to 1772	63
9.	Warren Hastings	74
10.	India : 1772 to 1778	83

PART FOUR : CROSSING THE PENINSULAR : 1778-1780

11.	The Crossing I : Antecedents.	91
12.	The Crossing II : Kalpi to the Narmada	96
13.	The Crossing III : Battle of Wadgaon, January 1779	106
14.	The Crossing IV : Hoshangabad to Surat	112

PART FIVE : BARODA AND BENGAL : 1780-1785

15.	Campaigning in Gujarat : 1780	120
16.	The Duel and the Thunderbolt of Mars	133
17.	Resident at Baroda : 1781 to 1783	145
18.	Return to Bengal : 1783 to 1785	160

PART SIX : THE COLERIDGE CONNECTION

| 19. | 1774 to 1783 | 169 |
| 20. | 1784 to 1792 | 179 |

PART SEVEN : HOME : 1785 – 1821

21.	Back in England : 1786 to 1804	199
22.	To the Isle of Wight	209
23.	The Letter Book	217
24.	Coda	240
25.	Conclusions	257

NOTES	260
SELECT BIBLIOGRAPHY	291
GLOSSARY	297
ACKNOWLEDGEMENTS	304

1. Introduction

On the 21ˢᵗ March 1768 a young man set sail for India on board the *Salisbury*, a 657 ton East Indiaman. He did not return to England for another eighteen years. He had left his home in Devon the previous year carrying letters of introduction to the East India Company (EIC) headquarters at Leadenhall Street in the City of London. Fortunately for us he left a record of his time in India. His name was Solomon Earle.

This book is an account of his life but I would like to think it is much more than that. As well as accompanying Solomon on his voyage to India we will look at what was happening in Britain and India at the time. Britain was just starting on its route to dominating the world for the next century or more. India was in turmoil with the disintegrating Mughal Empire and with various contenders vying to step into the vacuum left behind. And just as the *Salisbury* arrived off the coast of Bengal, Captain Cook set off from Portsmouth on another voyage, his first in the *Endeavour,* in search of the fabled southern continent of *Terra Australis*.

Seventeen-year-old Solomon left Ashburton, Devon, on the long road to London in 1767. At the time London was the largest city in the world, teeming with life and fraught with danger. He had letters of introduction to join the EIC at Leadenhall Street. By the time he left India in 1785 he had taken part in an epic march across India, risen to the rank of Captain in the EIC army and been appointed Resident to the Maharaja of Baroda, Fatesinghrao Gaekwad. Residents were representatives of the British, rather like ambassadors. After his return to England he was appointed as adjutant to the newly developed recruiting depot at the Isle of Wight. Meanwhile the Napoleonic Wars were just getting underway.

But why would it be of interest to people to read a book about a comparatively ordinary man from the newly developing middle classes of England?

1. Introduction

Because he was present during a crucial time in history, crucial for both India and Great Britain, and because we can use his short account of his life as a lens to examine and understand how and why things evolved the way they did. This is of value when we look at Great Britain and India in the present day. As I wrote this account Britain was in turmoil about whether to leave or stay in Europe. In the eighteenth century Britain was very much out of Europe. Trade was sought outside Europe, in competition with other countries, particularly Holland, France, Portugal and Spain. At the same time, in India, a group of Hindu warriors from a mountainous area around Pune were in the process of taking over much of Northern India from the Mughals. They were called the Marathas. It was inevitable they would come into dispute with the British, which they did, in a conflict known as the First Anglo-Maratha War of 1775 to 1783. The two sides were evenly matched and the outcome was, as you will see, by no means clear.

For the British in India the late eighteenth century was a time of consolidation rather than conquest. Robert Clive's acquisition of Bengal from the Mughals in 1757 had been completed and there was a need to clear up the mess left behind. The newly appointed Governor-General, Warren Hastings, was the man to do this. However world influences, notably the war in America and the eventual involvement of the French, sparked conflict in India. Wars were triggered to the west with the Marathas and to the east with the Sultan of Mysore. Warren Hastings decided to send a contingent of the Bengal army right across the peninsular of India to Bombay. Solomon's account of this epic march is one of only two available today.

Over in Gujarat Solomon took part in the siege and capture of the city of Ahmedabad and then spent over two years in Baroda as Resident. During his time in the EIC army he got to know the two elder brothers of Samuel Taylor Coleridge, John and Frank. As part of the story of India we will follow the life and eventual tragic death of these two brothers. I was able to read a series of letters written by the two brothers that give a first hand account of life in the EIC army at the time. There is no doubt their experiences in India had a major influence on the poetry of their younger brother.

On his return to England Solomon married Rose and they produced a large family. Solomon took up post as adjutant to the Isle of Wight recruiting depot in 1804. He remained there until his death in 1824. Life at the depot is explored through a series of letters that Solomon and the Commandant, John Gillespie, sent to Leadenhall Street.

Throughout this book I have introduced the key players of the time, both Indian and English. I have also outlined the background history of the Mughals, the Marathas and the EIC. As Warren Hastings had such a major influence on the history of India at the time I have devoted a separate chapter to exploring his life, his early influences and the difficulties he faced in Bengal.

I have a personal interest in Solomon's life and travels. My mother was born in India and when I first began investigating my own family history I had no idea what I would find. When I sat down with my mother and went through what she could remember about her family history we could only go back to the late nineteenth century. Her father had ended his time in India as Archdeacon to the Afghan Memorial Church in Colaba, Bombay. The family returned to England in 1937. When I was a child my mother had entertained us with stories about India. She talked about ayahs, plates that could be eaten and memories of the voyage home at the age of seven.

My mother was not aware that her ancestor, Solomon Earle, had gone out to India 170 years before that. When I started looking into things a bit further I was able to link up with a distant relative in Australia, Rick Desmier, who had traced our family history back to the Earles. He had also published Solomon's account and many other documents, on line. Solomon's granddaughter, Harriet Tytler, had also kept an account of her time in India and this account had been published in 1986.[1] Harriet had escaped from Delhi in 1857, during the outbreak of the Indian Mutiny, known in India as the First War of Independence. Mount Harriet, in the Andaman and Nicobar Islands, is named after her.

As I researched my family history I wanted to know more about what the British were doing in India in the first place, and why and how they had eventually managed to take control of the whole sub-continent. I therefore read as much as I could about the history of the time, reading historical accounts and deciphering original manuscripts at the British Library. I also wanted to visit as many places as I could that were mentioned in Solomon's account, both in England and India. I followed, as far as possible, the route

1. Introduction

taken by the Bengal Army across India. Plans came to fruition in 2016 when I set out with a friend to travel across India by train.[2] Like Solomon I ended my journey at Baroda where I was able to meet the current Maharaja, His Excellency Samarjitsing Gaekwad.

This book is the result of my three years of investigation into life in late eighteenth century India and England. My hope is that by reading it you will learn and discover as much as I have about how and why the British gained prominence in India. You will learn about life in the EIC army, life at the Court of Baroda and gain some understanding of the complex politics of the time. My aim is that by reading this book history will be brought alive for you, at a time when the future path of British dominance over India was neither inevitable nor predictable. You will surely see parallels with the history of our present time and life in Britain and India today.

I have provided a bibliography if you wish to explore the history of this time in more detail.

A NOTE ON THE TEXT

Language in India has changed over time. To add to the complexity the British interpreted some Indian words in their own peculiar way. For example Raghunathrao and Fatesinghrao were called Ragoba and Futty Sing respectively. In this book I have used place names in their historical context, for example Bombay instead of Mumbai, when referring to the eighteenth century (see glossary).

PART ONE : BEGINNINGS : 1751 – 1768

2. Ashburton and Gujarat

ASHBURTON

Ashburton is situated on the eastern edge of Dartmoor, on the main road between Exeter and Plymouth. The countryside is typical of Devon, in other words rolling hills cut by narrow, sunken lanes. Just to the west of the town the land rises, past old mine workings and hill forts, to the granite uplands of Dartmoor. Arthur Conan Doyle visited the area to gather material for his novel, the Hound of the Baskervilles. The town was named in the Domesday Book (1086) as *Essebretone*. The Norman word comes from old English *Aes* meaning ash tree and *burra* meaning a stream. *Ton* is a farmstead or settlement.[1] The area was prosperous due to tin mining. By 1305 Ashburton was one of four official stannary towns. Stannary towns are recognised centres where tin can be weighed, checked and stamped. But by the seventeenth century the industry was in decline and prosperity at this time came from the wool trade and the fact that the town was situated on the road to Plymouth.

Unfortunately in 1757 this road was in a sorry state of repair. We know this because Solomon Earle's grandfather, also called Solomon, had been named in a bill to the House of Commons in a petition for funding to make repairs.[2]

In the mid eighteenth century several Turnpike Acts had been passed enabling local entrepreneurs to develop a much faster road network throughout the country, and charge road users accordingly. It was a time of free enterprise with many innovations in new design taking place, such as the spinning jenny (1764), steam engine (1769) and threshing machine (1784). These new inventions started the process that made the modern world, heralding quick and efficient transport, communication and industrial manufacture.

2. Ashburton and Gujarat

In 1750, the year of Solomon's birth, England had only just survived a major shock when the Scots invaded the country during the '45 Rebellion. There was competition with other countries for trade. However Britain was fast becoming a major contender, having more opportunities as a result of the rising middle-classes and reduced control by the monarchy.

Ashburton had close links with the East India Company because of the local production of woollen goods, or serge, which was then exported to the east. However there was little demand for wool in hot climates and the Company had to find other more valued exports, such as glass, weapons and gold and silver bullion. In the early part of the nineteenth century the EIC gradually lost its charter and eventually its monopoly on trade, so the export of woollen products declined. This had an effect on the prosperity of the town and may have explained why Solomon later relocated elsewhere.

Several well-known Ashburtonians were involved with the EIC. For example, in 1762, John Dunning, who later became Lord Ashburton, was employed to draw up a legal defence of the EIC against complaints by the Dutch East India Company. However the most significant Ashburtonian with Company links was Sir Robert Palk (1717 to 1798).

Robert Palk came of yeoman stock and was educated at Ashburton Grammar School. He was sponsored to attend Wadham College, Oxford, and then entered the church. He served as a naval chaplain and eventually ended up in Madras. When the preceding chaplain, Francis Fordyce, was sacked after publicly insulting Robert Clive, Palk was appointed in his place. Palk later served as paymaster to Stringer Lawrence's army and started to amass a fortune. He eventually became Governor of Madras from 1763 to 1767. On his return from India he became MP for Ashburton and was made a baronet in 1782. As a consequence of his good fortune he sponsored others, including Solomon Earle. He supported Solomon's entry to the EIC army as a cadet and also provided him with a letter of introduction to use when he arrived in Calcutta. It was not possible to enter the EIC army as a cadet without sponsorship, usually from a member of the governing body in London, as well as a significant other.

Solomon's grandfather was born in 1700 in Ashburton. It is not clear what his occupation was, but in 1751, together with John Tapper and William Bastard, he had a licence to fell timber at *Woodleys Lott Wood, Buckland in the Moor*.[3] In 1752 there is a record of a William Bickford being apprenticed to a master tailor called Solomon Earle. The Sherborne Mercury gave notice of his death in 1777 and recorded his occupation as a *Proctor of Tythes*, in other words a collector of tithes, or taxes. He clearly had many occupations.

Solomon's father John (born in 1725) married Eleanor Mills (born in 1730) in 1746 and they were both buried at Ashburton. His occupation is not recorded.

Solomon's will (published in 1824) listed the ownership of *freehold farm lands and Estate called Whiddon situate near Ashburton*. Whether this was family land, or land Solomon purchased after returning from India, is not known. The current Ordnance Survey map records *Higher and Lower Whiddon Farms* in the same place. The Exeter and Plymouth Gazette of 1828 contained an advert about the sale of Lower Whiddon Farm, *by direction of the executors of the late Solomon Earle Esq.* and a tithe map of 1840 makes record of a *Captain Earle's Field,* complete with location map.

The Earle family of Devon are thought to originate from a branch of the de Erleigh family from Earley, near Reading. They owned various plots of land around Ashburton, but strangely seem to disappear from records after the early 1800s.

Lower Whiddon farm still exists just a few miles up the valley from Ashburton.

Lower Whiddon Farm, Ashbuton. Photo 2017

2. Ashburton and Gujarat

John and Eleanor Earle had four children: John (1746), William (1748), Eleanor (1750) and Solomon (1750). It is highly likely that he attended the local grammar school, also known as the *free school* at the St. Lawrence Chapel, in Ashburton.

We know nothing about Solomon's childhood but there is an interesting contemporary account of a childhood in Ashburton published in a biography of the life of Richard Carlile (1790 to 1843). It is unlikely that things would have changed much in Ashburton between the 1750s and 1790s. Richard Carlile became a well-known political agitator for the establishment of universal suffrage and the freedom of the press. He attended the grammar school from the age of nine until twelve and was then apprenticed to a tinsmith. Carlile was present at the Peterloo Massacre in 1819[4] and published an eyewitness account. His daughter published an account of his life entitled *The Battle for the Press*, published in 1899.[5] The first chapter covered his early life and included a verbatim account of his schooldays written by Carlile himself in the form of a letter. Rather than précis this account, extracts are included below:

At twelve years of age I left school, with a knowledge of writing, arithmetic, and the Latin language, and a pretty good knowledge of words and the tact of spelling them, I was wholly ignorant of grammar. I remember well when my severe old writing and ciphering master was told that I was about to leave him to learn Latin, he said, 'Hi, hi! you had better learn English first'. This old man never gave me a chastisement without saying, 'There, you larned rascal, take that! You will thank me for it by the time you are twenty years old.' For my part, I had no more idea of school education than that it was a pastime for boys, and I sought an exchange from old Hanaford's to the Latin school with no idea but that of more play and less punishment, and because all the better dressed boys were there; but I found after that this smattering of Latin gave me everywhere an air of superiority, and among such company as I was able to keep I passed for a scholar. The very vanity and flattery attached to this state of mind, I believe, induced me to seek further knowledge.

I jumped in! and on a Sunday, too! The stile of the first meadow was a leaping bar, and in the church-yard you cannot see a tomb or headstone, forty years old, but I have jumped over it. Should you see the centre of the town flooded in its drains, you may see my picture as a boy beating through it. I have bathed and fished in every brook, and stolen apples from every tree within a mile of the town.

In the chapel of Lawrence Lane, where, from nine to twelve years of age, I got some Latin, you will probably find my name cut in the boards, if it be worth looking for. At Lads-Well, at the bottom of that lane, you will see the scene of some early exploits of mine, one of which was, with a new suit of clothes on, trying to jump over this well.

It is a singular circumstance, but I can trace both the Quarterly Review and the Republican to the free schools of Ashburton. Wm. Gifford and Dr. Ireland, the Dean of Westminster, both received the rudiments of their education at these free schools, and I came after them to undo, I hope, all the mischief that they as politicians have done. These free schools of Ashburton were not so free for the poor as for the rich; one of them was a school for Latin and Greek wholly, free by endowment, and here only the children of the richer people were admitted. Here, also, I followed Dr. Ireland and Wm. Gifford.

The aforementioned William Gifford was born in 1756 and spent eight years at the Free School, apparently making *wretched progress*. After his parents died, a local surgeon sponsored him to go to Oxford. In later life he became a famous satirist and first editor of the *Quarterly Review*.[6] He was buried in Westminster Abbey. John Ireland was born in Ashburton in 1761 and was the son of a butcher. He went on to become Dean of Westminster and was also buried in Westminster Abbey, in the same grave as his great friend William Gifford.

Solomon presumably did well enough in his education, judging by his command of English evidenced in later correspondence. He must have left school at around the age of fifteen before leaving for London to seek his fortune.

The grammar school at St. Lawrence Chapel closed in 1938. The chapel is now open to the public and does have the names of several pupils carved into its benches, but sadly there is no sign of Richard Carlile or Solomon Earle. You can however see a carving by one of its most famous pupils, William John Wills who, together with Burke, became the first westerners to cross the Australian continent. Both Burke and Wills perished on their return journey in 1861.

2. Ashburton and Gujarat

GUJARAT

We will now travel 4000 miles to India to enter Maratha territory just south of Gujarat. Around the time Solomon was growing up in Ashburton the future Maharajah of Baroda, Fatesingh Gaekwad, would have been living at Songhar, the Gaekwad family stronghold. The Gaekwad capital moved to Baroda soon afterwards. Baroda (Vadodara) is a city in Gujarat, a province on the north west coast of India, north of Mumbai and south of Rajasthan. Fatesingh will be introduced as this stage as he is destined to become a key player later in our story.

Fatesingh's father, Damaji, was in the process of securing his kingdom around Baroda. In 1755 Damaji finally succeeded in taking the city of Ahmedabad from the Mughals. He was supported by Raghunathrao, a gentleman who we will also come across later. Raghunathrao was a rival to the overall ruler of the Maratha Politic based in Pune, known as the Peshwa.

We do not have any information about the exact date of birth of Fatesingh, except that he was born before 1751. We do know that he had five brothers and, like Solomon, was not the first-born, or even the second born son.

The period from 1751 onwards was a very unsettled time for India with internal struggles for territory and invasions by Afghans and Persians from the west. If we look at just a small part of India, Gujarat, not only were the Marathas in conflict with the Mughals, they were also in conflict with each other.

The overall Maratha leader, the Peshwa, had demanded a half share of all the acquisitions made by the Gaekwads in Gujarat. Damaji Gaekwad was not happy with this. In 1751 he sent a force of 15,000 men to Satara to join other dissenters. However his men became trapped and Damaji ended up having to come to terms with the Peshwa to avoid total defeat.[7] He was taken prisoner and sent to Pune where he remained for two years. When Damaji was released he joined with Raghunathrao to secure Gujarat. The Gaekwads now became official rulers of the province.

There followed a brief period of peace while the young Fatesingh was growing up with his brothers. All this changed in 1761 with the holocaust of Panipat (described in more detail later). Briefly the Marathas sent a huge army to the north of Delhi to take on the invading Afghans, on behalf of the Mughals. They were defeated with terrible slaughter at the Battle

2. Ashburton and Gujarat

of Panipat. Damaji survived the battle and returned to Gujarat with his troops intact. It is not known whether Fatesingh was old enough to have accompanied his father to the battle.

In 1767 the Peshwa, Balajirao, died and was succeeded by his son Madhavrao. Raghunathrao was not pleased as he wanted to succeed himself. Things came to ahead in 1768 when Damaji agreed to join Raghunathrao in another campaign against the Peshwa. He sent his second eldest son Govind. The two forces met at Dhodap. Raghunathrao and Govind were defeated and taken prisoner. Soon after this Damaji died. Unfortunately for the Gaekwads his death created a vacuum into which the rivalry between Govind and Fatesingh fermented, turning into a dispute for succession.

The oldest son, and rightful heir to the Gaekwad throne, Sayajirao, despite being *feeble-minded,* was backed by the *resourceful and energetic* Fatesingh to refute his brother Govind's claim.[8] Fatesingh travelled to Pune and managed to win over the Peshwa's court. As a result Sayajirao was declared successor, with Fatesingh as his *mutalik* (or agent). But the terms were severe and, as his namesake explained in his 1989 account, the inability to pay this tribute *ultimately drove the Gaekwads to seek an alliance with the British East India Company as a means of breaking loose from the stranglehold of the Poona Court.*[9]

And when they did this, the Company representative who was sent to Baroda to secure the alliance was none other than Captain Solomon Earle from Ashburton. How all this came about will be explored in later chapters.

We will now return to rural Devon, a place of relative calm in comparison with India. It is doubtful whether Solomon would have known much about the politics of India. Even the British in Bombay were ignorant of the intricacies of Maratha politics. The directors of the EIC in London had little idea either. The aim of the directors at this time was to continue to run a profitable trading company and their aim was not to acquire land and the responsibility of ruling another country. However the Presidency at Bombay Island were casting greedy eyes on the successful campaigns of Robert Clive and others in Bengal, 1200 miles to the northeast. After the battle of Plassey (1757) and Buxar (1764) the Company had taken over the government and revenue collection in Bengal. Robert Clive finally returned to England in 1767 a very rich man.

2. Ashburton and Gujarat

Solomon would certainly have been aware of the fame and fortune of Robert Clive and, more locally in Ashburton, Robert Palk. Both had returned from India in the same year. In that year Solomon departed for London. He may not have realised at the time that he would not be returning to his hometown for another eighteen years. We can only imagine the tearful farewell to his family as he boarded the Exeter stage in the main street of Ashburton. There were, and still are, several coaching inns situated along the main street. His chest would have been secured on the roof and he would be keeping safe on his person his letters of recommendation.

3. To London : 1767

By the late eighteenth century London was well on its way to becoming the greatest trading and financial centre ever known.[1] Great Britain's success in the world market and the establishment of empire had brought in tremendous wealth. The population had expanded from half a million in 1700, to approximately 750,000 by 1750,[2] and to roughly a million by 1800. After the eighth Gin Act[3] had been passed in 1751, London was gradually becoming less brutal and violent.[4] A cosmopolitan area had developed around Covent Garden, between the City and the West End, centred on a square called the Piazza. More wealthy people had moved up from the country to settle in Westminster, attracted by the social activities on offer and the parks and pleasure gardens at Vauxhall and Ranelagh. International trade was situated more in the City and towards the expanding dock and shipbuilding areas to the east. The Seven Years War had finally ended in 1763 with a resounding victory for Britain.[5]

In the autumn of 1767 Solomon would have boarded the London stage from Exeter, to start the second leg of his journey to the great metropolis. He wrote in his journal that *in 1767 Mr Sullivan, one of the Directors of the E. I. Company, a very particular friend of our family, proposed to send me to India, as a writer in the Honourable Company's service.*[6] As the youngest of four siblings he would have had to find ways of supporting himself without the backing of family money and, with little inheritance to expect, would have needed to make his own way in the world. Employment as a writer in India would have been an exciting, if rather risky, way of achieving this.

Travel in the eighteenth century was not an easy prospect, although the establishment of turnpike roads was beginning to improve things. Between 1751 and 1772 there was a massive expansion of turnpike trusts and road improvement, the period being described as one of *turnpike mania*.[7] But travel was still very slow, dangerous and uncomfortable, with stagecoaches covering a maximum of between four to six miles each hour. The poor found it easier, and cheaper, to walk.

3. To London : 1767

One alternative to travel by stagecoach was the post-chaise, rather like a shared taxi. James Boswell hired a post-chaise in 1762 to travel from Edinburgh to London. It took him four days, with overnight stops at Berwick, Durham, Doncaster and Biggleswade.[8] The journey had cost Boswell eleven pounds, a considerable sum in those days, with additional costs for overnight stays and tips.[9] Solomon was more likely to have taken the cheaper stagecoach. There would have been room for eight passengers inside, with second-class seats in a basket at the back, and the rest on the roof with the luggage. Travellers on the roof ran the risk of being hit by passing branches, or simply 'dropping off,' if they fell asleep. The faster mail coaches were not introduced until 1784, so the journey of around 200 miles would have taken Solomon five days or more.

On arrival in London, probably at the turnpike at Hyde Park Gate, it is likely Solomon would have transferred, with his luggage, to a hackney carriage. Hackney carriages were the equivalent of buses today. They followed set routes and cost sixpence per half mile. He could have walked and sent his luggage on later, but in doing so could easily have got lost. Street signs were in the early stages of being introduced in 1767 and London, particularly the part of the City that had survived the Great Fire of 1666, would have been a complex maze of streets.

Where would he have gone? Unfortunately he did not inform us, but it would have been sensible to head somewhere in the direction of the headquarters of the East India Company at Leadenhall Street in the City. At the time this building had an imposing classical façade, built in 1729. The building was demolished in 1861, after the Company had been wound up. The space age Lloyds Building (completed in 1986), now occupies the site.[10]

Temporary lodgings could have been found at an inn, but a cheaper and longer-term lodging would have been arranged with a family, or a relative. Ten per cent of England's population lived in London at the time. Solomon spent five months in London and it is not known where he stayed. He must have liked the place as he chose to live there after his return from India.

On calling at Leadenhall Street he was informed that no writers were to be appointed for that season and, instead, it was proposed to send him out to India as an army cadet. The alternative would have been to wait for another year. He recorded, *not knowing the advantage of the Civil Service over the Military, and having taken leave of my friends in the country, I preferred the*

3. To London : 1767

THE EAST INDIA HOUSE AND PART OF LEADENHALL STREET, 1726-1799.
From an original drawing in the East India House.

East India House, Leadenhall Street. Print from Beveridge, 1862

former. He was appointed as a cadet on the 29th December 1767. He finally set sail for India on the 21st of March 1768.

To get some idea what life was like in London for a young man in the 1760s, one of the most well known sources is James Boswell's London Journal.[11] Boswell later wrote the famous biography of Samuel Johnson.[12] William Hickey also wrote about his experiences in London at the same time.[13]

It must have been an incredible adventure for a young man from the country to arrive, on his own, in such a place. You can only imagine the stench from drains, sewers and horse-manure, and from the dunghills at places such as Whitechapel, where waste was piled up. He would have heard the clatter of carriages over cobbled streets and the cacophonous cries of street sellers coming from all angles. In those days London was in the throes of a building boom. There would have been scaffolding and shuttering everywhere. The New Road, across fields from Paddington to Islington, was almost complete and infill developments were under construction, extending out to the New Road and beyond. The Strand had

3. To London : 1767

been paved in 1765. Before 1750 London had only one bridge, London Bridge. Its narrow arches supported rows of houses, treacherous for river traffic. Westminster Bridge had been completed that year and the houses on London Bridge were in the process of being demolished to widen the bridge.

There was little street lighting and all sorts of goings on took place in alleys after nightfall. St. James Park was a particularly risky place after dark, although the gates were locked at 10pm. Between 7 and 10pm the park would have been packed with all classes of people promenading about. One visitor from abroad could not understand how *the first quality blended with the lowest populace,* and furthermore, why this was allowed.[14]

James Boswell arrived in London in 1762. He been to London before and had always wanted to return. As his father, the Laird of Auchinleck, would not support him, he had to wait until he reached maturity at the age of twenty-one before he could afford to return. Unlike William Hickey, Boswell initially resolved to be temperate and to avoid, *whores and card games*. These temptations proved impossible to resist, at least the former.

William Hickey, on the other hand, had no such qualms, so much so that by the age of nineteen, in 1768, his expenditure well exceeded his funds. London was, and still is, an expensive place to live. At the time Hickey was an articled clerk. He ended up mixing office funds with his own money until a deficit of £500 had been accrued. His father, a lawyer, bailed him out and decided that the only way to deal with the matter was to get him out of the country. Like Solomon, he was enrolled as a cadet in the EIC but, whereas Solomon was sent to Bengal, Hickey opted for Madras. He left for India a year after Solomon, in December 1768. As far as I am aware they never met.

Both young Boswell and Hickey were in a different situation to Solomon. To start with they were both a few years older but, more importantly, both had the funding to make the most of London life. Solomon would have had several months to observe life in a cosmopolitan city, even if he could not have afforded to take a full part.

In the 1760s life for the idle young man of means revolved around the theatre, taverns, coffeehouses, chophouses and, in some cases, the bordello. In addition to the Royal Opera House, there was a theatre at Drury Lane, Covent Garden and the Little Theatre in the Haymarket, run by Samuel Foote (1720-77). In 1772 Samuel Foote put on a play parodying the nabobs (men returning from India with great wealth). David Garrick (1717-79) was also acting and producing plays at this time. Boswell described watching Garrick in a performance of Shakespeare's Henry the Fourth Part Two.[15] Theatres were open from 4pm with the play starting at around 6pm. The audience sat on benches and often joined in with the performances, heckling and catcalling. In fact the level of disturbance in the pit could be so great that a row of iron spikes were installed along the front of the stage to protect the actors from theatre mobs.[16] In 1772 Boswell attended a play where two Highland officers, newly returned from fighting for the British cause in Havana, were pelted with apples. Boswell wrote, *my Scotch blood boiled with indignation. I jumped up on the benches, roared out, "Damn you, you rascals."*[17]

Boswell also spent his time in coffeehouses where he read the papers and listened to, and wrote down, the conversations he overheard. He took his meals in steak or chophouses when he could afford it. These institutions were generally places where men ate on their own at shared tables. It is entertaining and informative to note his entry for Wednesday 15th December 1762:

The enemies of the people of England who would have them considered in the worst light represent them as selfish, beef-eaters, and cruel. In this view I resolved today to be a true-born, Old Englishman. I went into the City to Dolly's Steak-house in Paternoster Row and swallowed my dinner by myself to fulfil the charge of selfishness: I had a large fat beef-steak to fulfil my charge of beef-eating; and I went at five o'clock to the Royal Cockpit in St. James's Park and saw cock-fighting for about five hours to fulfil the charge of cruelty.

He then went on to describe the steak-house in more detail:

A beefsteak-house is a most excellent place to dine at. You come in there to a warm, comfortable, large room, where a number of people are sitting at a table. You take whatever place you find empty; call for what you like, which you get well and cleverly dressed. You may either chat or not as you like. Nobody minds you, and you pay very reasonably. My dinner (beef, bread and beer and waiter) was only a shilling.

3. To London : 1767

Boswell then described his visit to the Cockpit. He did not find this experience so pleasant and mentions feeling sorry for the poor cocks. The cocks were equipped with silver spurs and had to fight to the death. Boswell described seeing a lack of pity on the countenances of the spectators.

Because of previous debts Boswell resolved, successfully, to stay away from card games. This was difficult as he was invited to social engagements where card playing was the main activity. William Hickey got a *severe shock* on seeing the body of a certain Mr Nunez after he had shot himself as a result of accruing gambling debts of near £10,000. *He had put a small pocket pistol into his mouth, and actually blown off the entire upper part of the skull, blood and brains being scattered round the room.*[19]

James Boswell spent the first few months of his time in London trying to have his way with Louisa, an actress. He eventually succeeded after many weeks of wooing, and considerable expense. Hickey was introduced to the delights of the fair sex by his nurse (Nanny Harris) who shared a bed with him when he was a child. He spent his early years seeking sexual encounters, an activity that, as mentioned previously, eventually resulted in him being packed off to India. He described visiting the pleasure gardens at Ranelagh where he ate *capital stewed grigs* (small eels) and played field tennis.[20] In May 1768 he witnessed a riot when up to seven Londoners were killed by a Guards regiment, consisting *principally of Scotch men*, who opened fire on the mob when they refused to disperse after a reading of the Riot Act.[21] This incident took place at St. George's Fields in Southwark, outside the Kings Bench Prison. The crowd had gathered to protest at the imprisonment of John Wilkes, who had criticised King George III and was the editor of an anti-government newspaper called *The North Briton*. James Boswell was a colleague of John Wilkes, having first met him in 1762 at the Beefsteak Club, a dining club in Covent Garden.

William Hickey was called to see the Directors of the EIC in November 1768 for his interview. Presumably Solomon had a similar interview. Hickey wrote that he was called into the committee room:

after waiting nearly two hours in the lobby, at which my pride was greatly offended, I saw three old dons sitting close to the fire, having by them a large table, with pens, ink, paper, and a number of books laying on it. Having surveyed me, as I conceive, rather contemptuously, one of them, in such a snivelling tone that I could scarcely understand him, said:

3. To London : 1767

"Well, young gentleman, what is your age?"
I having answered "Nineteen," he continued:
"Have you ever served, I mean been in the army? Though I presume from your age and appearance you cannot."
I replied I had not.
"Can you go through the manual exercise?"
"No, sir."
"Then you must take care and learn it."
I bowed.
"You know the terms upon which you enter our service?"
"Yes, Sir."
"Are you satisfied therewith?"
'Yes, Sir."[22]

This comprised the full extent of Hickey's interview. After being enrolled as a cadet he wrote that he was given *twenty guineas for clothes and bedding etc.* It does not take much thought to work out what Hickey then spent that sum of money on.

Solomon was likely to have received a similar amount of money the year before. This was actually a considerable sum in those days given that the average annual income for a working family was in the region of forty pounds. Presumably Solomon spent his money more wisely than William Hickey. Perhaps he had some spare cash to attend the theatre, or visit one of the pleasure gardens.

He may have walked through the old streets of the City, or taken a boat down the Thames to witness the hive of activity taking place in that part of London. In December that year the ship on which he was to take his passage to Calcutta, the *Salisbury,* was being loaded and re-fitted at Blackwall. The river would have been over-crowded with ships loading and unloading onto lighters and barges. Cargoes from the East were brought to the 'legal quays' at Blackwall, then taken under armed guard by road to the Company's warehouses to the east side of the City.[23] Most business was conducted in the coffeehouses.

4. A Passage to India

Getting to India in 1768 was a hazardous undertaking. It took on average five to six months and involved sailing down the west coast of Africa, around the Cape of Good Hope, then across the Indian Ocean, usually picking up supplies at one of the Islands off the east coast of Africa. When Robert Clive sailed to India in 1743 his ship was blown off course. The *Winchester* ran aground and Clive ended up spending some time at Pernambuco in Portuguese South America, while his ship was repaired. In 1769 the frigate *Aurora,* carrying new members of the Bengal Council to Calcutta, was lost with all hands.

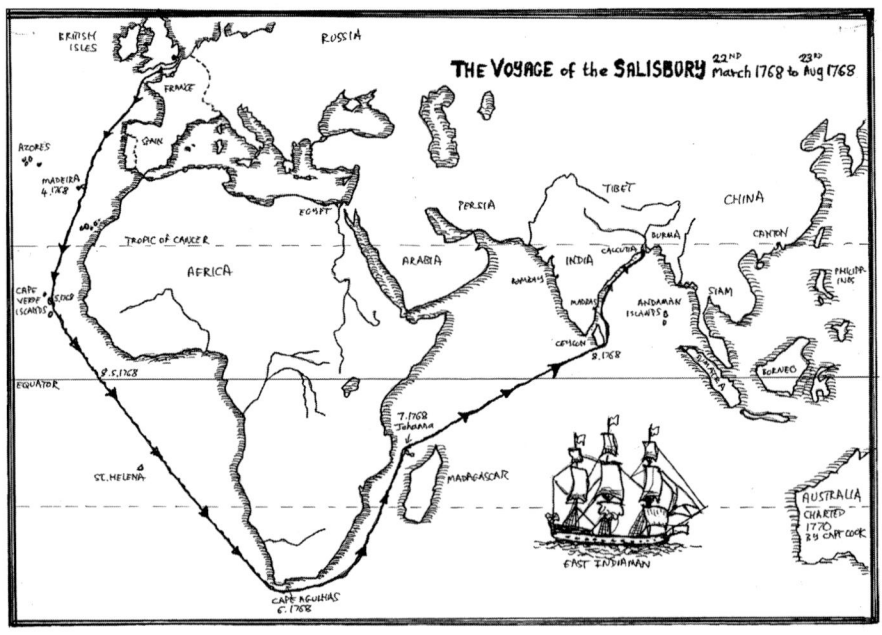

The Voyage of the Salisbury. March to August 1768

4. A Passage to India

In the 1760s it was not possible to accurately measure a ship's position when out of sight of land. The north/south position (latitude) could be estimated by measuring the angle of the sun at midday (or the North Star at night) but only on a clear day. Measuring the east/west position (longitude) was much more problematic. As a result of the inadequate measurement of longitude, a major disaster occurred in 1707 when four warships of the British Fleet, under Admiral Sir Clowdisley Shovell, went down in fog off the Isles of Scilly with the loss of over two thousand men.[1]

Each degree of longitude equates to $1/360^{th}$ of a circle; in other words each hour is equivalent to fifteen degrees of longitude. It is therefore theoretically possible to compare times to measure longitude. But in the eighteenth century it was not possible to measure time accurately while at sea. The pendulum clock (invented in 1657) was inaccurate at sea due to the movement of the waves. In 1714 the British government set up the Board of Longitude and offered a huge reward to anyone who could come up with an accurate method of measuring it.

There were two possible methods, (1) comparing the position of the moon with the stars, a sort of astronomical clock, and (2) inventing a clock that told the time accurately at sea. At the time producing such a clock was felt to be impossible, so most research went into developing accurate astronomical tables.

In 1761 Yorkshireman John Harrison managed to perfect an accurate clock (which he called a chronometer) but the Admiralty were reluctant to give out the prize. At the time astronomical methods were thought to be more suitable, particularly with the invention of the sextant that could measure accurate angles. There was also distrust of the concept that a clock, as small as that invented by Harrison, would be effective – not to mention the expense of manufacture. So it was not until the 1820s that chronometers became available for general use. Harrison was eventually awarded the prize, but the final amount was not released until 1776 after an appeal to King George.[2]

In 1767 the first Nautical Almanac was published. The Almanac included various tables denoting the positions of the moon and stars. This method was accurate up to less than a degree. But a degree covers approximately sixty nautical miles at the equator, reducing towards the poles. The Captain of the Solomon's ship would have been using the relatively inaccurate Nautical Almanac method.

4. A Passage to India

Because of the widespread use of the Nautical Almanac, the Greenwich Meridian was later accepted as zero longitude and Greenwich Mean Time (GMT) or Universal Time (UT) became the time standard worldwide. The almanac method gradually went out of use during the nineteenth century when chronometers became more widely available

Thanks to Solomon's journal it has been possible establish the exact ship he took passage on. This ship was an East Indiaman called the *Salisbury*. And, even better, the actual Captain's log of this voyage has been preserved in the East India Collection at the British Library.[3] The log started a few months before the ship sailed and detailed the loading and rigging of the vessel at Gravesend. Every day of the five-month voyage was logged. In view of the availability of this fascinating record, the passage is described in detail.

Solomon (then aged seventeen) joined the *Salisbury* at the Downs on the 21st March 1768. The Downs are an area of the English Channel, off the East Kent Coast, near Deal. Solomon would have travelled down from London by coach. In those days there was no training for cadets prior to arrival in India. The Addiscombe Military Seminary was not opened until 1809.

The *Salisbury* was a three-decked, 657-ton East Indiaman. Its Captain was John Wyche, who later became mayor of the city of Salisbury. A painting of him still hangs in Salisbury's Guildhall, attributed to John Hoppner RA. It was painted in 1783 when he was somewhat older, complete with red face and jowls. In 1768 he was clearly well on his way to making a fortune as he shipped up to £4,660 worth of private goods to sell in the east consisting, amongst other items, of stationary, hats, clocks, drugs (three chests), gold and silver lace, hosiery, saddlery and wine.[4]

Wyche's Log revealed that the ship was moored in the Thames for some months, at least from December 1767. At this time ocean going ships were constructed at various yards along the Thames, eastwards of the Isle of Dogs, the area that later became East India Docks. The *Salisbury* was launched in 1764 and made a total of four voyages to the East Indies and China. Each voyage lasted approximately two years. The vessel was owned by Sir Charles Raymond, a retired sea captain and now 'ship's husband,' or 'managing owner'. Raymond had made his fortune in private trade, which had enabled him to build up enough capital to invest in ships transporting goods for the EIC.

4. A Passage to India

A previous incarnation of the *Salisbury* is worth mentioning as it was on a Royal navy ship, *HMS Salisbury*, that James Lind in 1747 carried out one of the first controlled experiments in the history of medicine. Lind administered cider, vitriol, vinegar, oranges, lemons and other substances to a group of twelve sailors with scurvy. The ones who received the citrus fruits recovered. [5] But it was not until 1794 that citrus fruits were fully accepted by the Admiralty as a preventative treatment for scurvy. *HMS Salisbury* saw action in the East Indies and was eventually broken up at Bombay in 1761.

While the *Salisbury* was moored at Blackwall, from the 7th Dec 1767 until the 11th March 1768, Captain Wyche recorded the daily weather and various works that had to be carried out to prepare the ship. This included *staying* the masts and rigging, loading various stores and receiving passengers.

During this period cargo taken on board included coal, 720 *pigs of lead* (essentially oblong blocks), candles, copper, pitch, cables and anchors. Water butts were filled and the lower masts were stayed and rigging was set. The yards were *blacked* and the gun deck was *scraped*. Then the topmasts were set up and the sails were *bent*. Surveyors from the *Honourable Company* came on board to check the timbers and the roundhouse was *caulked*. Caulking is a method of sealing the gaps between timbers to make them watertight, using oakum, a mixture of hemp and tar.

On the 19th January 1768 the ship was taken down to Gravesend by a pilot, a certain Mr Dorman, and anchored in *mid channel*. This took around six hours, presumably on the ebb tide. Captain Wyche recorded that he *found Mr Hunter, one of the surveyors, dead in the guest cabin*. There is no information about this incident, or what might have led to Mr Hunter's death.

At Gravesend the serious business of loading armaments began. This included: *109 barrels of gunpowder, 100 shells, 2 ten-pounder and 2 twelve-pounder cannons, 2 brass royals, 50 chests of arms, 1 lay of musket balls and 10 chests of stationary*. At around this time soldiers started coming on board. Captain Wyche recorded that a total of sixty-nine soldiers boarded over several days.

Food started to be loaded including: *thirty-five pork hides, small beer and other stores*. More ordnance came on board consisting of: *20 brass guns, 1 mortar, 20 nine-pounders and 14 four-pounders complete with carriages*. Brandy,

4. A Passage to India

for the use of the military, was loaded.

Mr Haffy came on board and paid the Company soldiers. Other passengers started to board together with their luggage. Throughout this time Captain Wyche described the loading of *private trade*. There seemed to have been quite a lot of this. At this time employees of the EIC were allowed to take part in private trade to supplement their income. In India private trade was known as 'country trade' and was the main way that employees of the Company supplemented their income and made their fortune.

On the 11th March the pilot, Mr Wheatly, came on board. Then the anchor was weighed and the *Salisbury* began to move out of the Thames Estuary and down the north coast of Kent towards the Downs. This took four days. Pilots with local knowledge were needed as this part of the coast has many shallow areas of sand. The Captain recorded that the ship initially anchored by *Blacktails Beacon*, and then again off the *North Foreland*, which is just off the northern tip of the Kent Coast.

The final anchorage was three miles off Deal with a *WSW bearing to Walmer Castle* (we can therefore accurately determine its position). The ship was anchored there for a week while final preparations were made for sea and to wait for the wind to blow in a favourable direction. There were likely to have been many other ships waiting in the same place for a fair wind. This was when Solomon boarded the vessel. We do not know exactly when, as several passengers boarded at this time and Captain Wyche does not name them.

As Solomon's journal is brief, other contemporary accounts of voyages to India are described below. The most detailed of these accounts is the diary of the aforementioned William Hickey.[6] Others include the diaries of Fanny Parkes [7] and Harriet Tytler, Solomon's granddaughter. [8]

Almost a year after Solomon, William Hickey set forth on his first voyage to India on the *Plassey*. Hickey boarded in December 1768 at Gravesend, but got off again when his ship reached Margate as he suffered from seasickness. He actually went back to London to meet up with one of his many women before coming back to Deal to rejoin his ship. But when he got there he had a shock as he spotted the ship in full sail. He was however reassured to discover that the sails were merely being dried. He settled in at the *Three Kings* [9] and had a *merry* day. Just as he was retiring to bed he heard a gun being fired and realised that the ships were about to sail as the wind had turned to the northeast. This led to a mad dash to hire boats. Hickey wrote that he had previously contracted a boat for a guinea, but was laughed at by his friends at the time for being over-cautious. However they then had to pay between three and five guineas, so he had the last laugh. After boarding he described retiring to his cot and waking the next day to find that he was setting out with a convoy of thirteen ships bound for the East. He wrote that they made a *grand and interesting spectacle*.

On his second voyage, this time to the West Indies in September 1775, Hickey gave an account of a huge storm that hit when his ship, the *New Shoreham,* was anchored in the Downs. They were blown towards the coast of France and nearly wrecked. On sailing back he disembarked. Most of the waiting ships had dragged their anchors and some had smashed into each other, while others had been wrecked. Hickey described walking to Sandwich from Deal (a distance of about eight miles) and seeing the beach *covered with pieces of wreck, dead bodies of the unfortunate persons that had perished, and hundreds of sheep and hogs from Government transports.* At the time the American war had just started and the majority of ships were bound there.

You can get a good idea what it must have been like on board a sailing ship at the time by visiting *HMS Trincomalee* at Hartlepool Heritage Dock. The *Trincomalee* is the oldest warship still afloat. It was built in 1817 and, although just over 1000 tons, has a similar design to the *Salisbury,* with three masts, twelve square sails, eleven fore and aft sails and a set of 'studding' sails. Like the *Salisbury* it also has thee main decks. There were several 'orlop' decks, or platforms below the mess deck and below the waterline. Heavier cargo was stored below these decks. The powder magazine was situated aft and was protected by a copper lining and brass fittings, to avoid sparks. The soldiers, passengers and officers were all quartered on the lower, or mess deck, below the gun deck. The sailors slept in removable hammocks on both decks. The officers and cadets were situated at the bows in tiny cabins. Live animals were kept aft. It is unlikely that Solomon would have had a cabin to himself. The quarters would have been very cramped and it must have been rather unpleasant, and certainly very odorous, especially in bad weather.

4. A Passage to India

HMS Trincomalee, Hartlepool Heritage Dock 2016

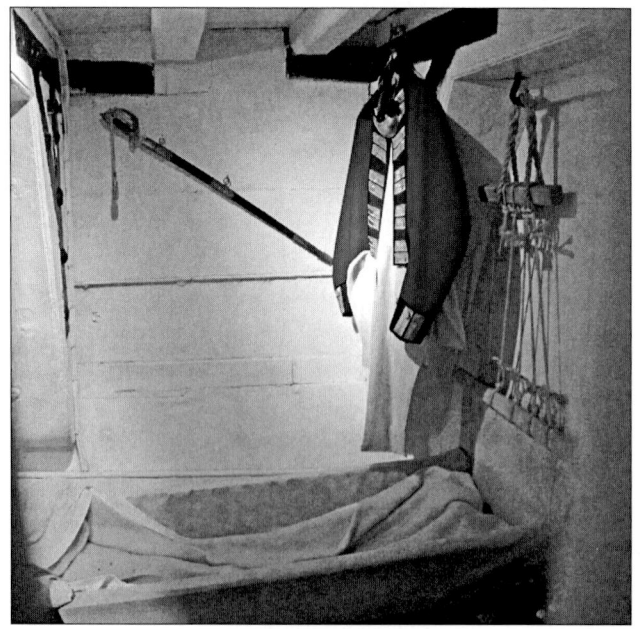

One of the cabins

4. A Passage to India

While at the Downs Captain Wyche recorded that he mustered the ship's company. Fresh provisions were taken on board and the *Salisbury* finally set sail on March 22nd 1768.

Solomon's brief account gives us an outline of the voyage. It was usual at the time to call in at Saint Helena, a remote island off the West African coast (later to be the final resting place of Napoleon). But instead the *Salisbury* called in at Madeira and then sailed on to anchor off St. Jago, one of the Cape Verde Islands. They stayed there for ten days before heading for the Cape and on to *Johanna (*now Anjouan), one of the Comoros Islands in the Mozambique Channel.

The Captain's Log (see photograph) has two entries for each day on every page. The log was only recorded over a twelve-hour period, during the day. A regular record was kept of the distance travelled. Incidentally the origin of the word 'log' comes from an actual log that was let out on a rope behind a boat to measure the distance travelled. This distance was of course measured in knots, or nautical miles per hour. The word knot originally came from the knots that were tied in the 'log' rope at regular intervals.

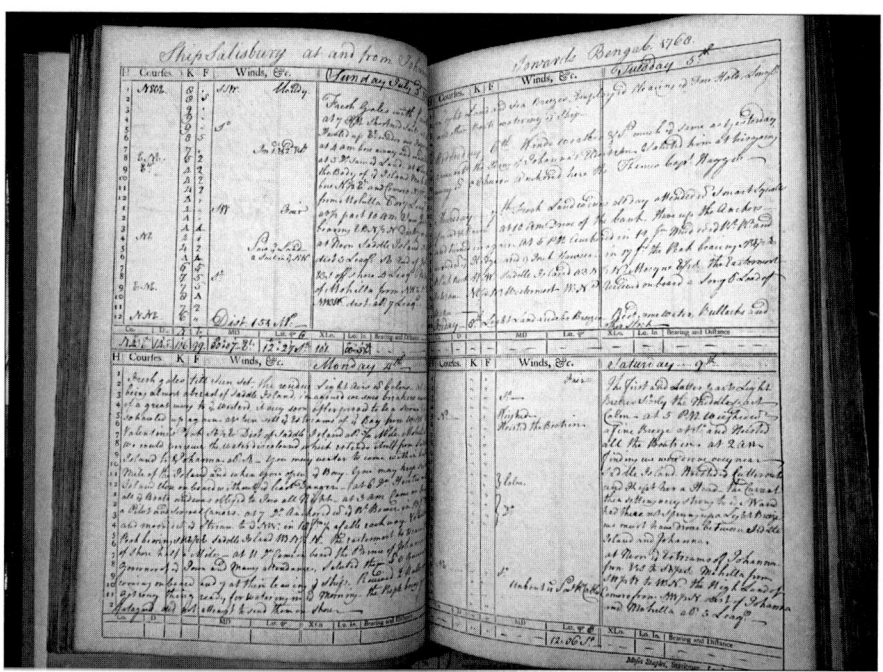

Photograph of the Captain's Log of the Salisbury. British Library

4. A Passage to India

The captain recorded the distance travelled each hour. This generally varied between zero and seven knots, depending on the wind strength and direction, which was also recorded. The latitude was generally measured each day at noon, when possible, from the height of the sun. At times the draught was taken, especially when reefs and shallow water were suspected. The total mileage each day was totted up. This generally varied between 50 and 120 nautical miles every twenty-four hours. General observations were made in the final column.

For the first few days the *Salisbury* sailed on a WSW bearing heading straight down the English Channel into the Bay of Biscay. On the second day the captain recorded observing Portland Bill from a distance of about six leagues (eighteen nautical miles). It then took sixteen days to reach Madeira where Solomon wrote that they *took in wine*. Madeira is a fortified wine that, like port, keeps for long periods and is therefore a useful cargo for India, given the heavy drinking that was prevalent amongst the English at the time. They left the next day (8th April).

On Thursday 14th May the log entry reads:

AM, called a Consultation of the Officers there being many people ill. ……Complaints which has occasioned a vast consumption of water, it was the opinion of the whole that it was highly necessary for the good of the Hon[ble] Company's Military and People on board to refresh at St. Jago and fill up our water.

St. Jago (or Santiago as it is now known) is the largest of the Cape Verde archipelago. It is much further north than Saint Helena and, at the time, was a Portuguese colony and slaving base. It can perhaps be assumed that the Captain consulted all the officers as it was not usual, or perhaps even safe, to anchor off a Portuguese island.

While at St. Jago the longboat was sent ashore several times to collect water. The Captain recorded that John Seam, a soldier, *departed this life*. Then *bullocks, hogs, sheep, goats, turkeys and fowls* were taken on board. There was no breeze on Sunday 24th April, but the ship was able to sail the next day. Latitude was recorded as 14 degrees.

The ship crossed the *equinoctial* on Sunday May 8th 1768. Neither Captain Wyche nor Solomon made a note of any celebrations. This is perhaps

4. A Passage to India

unusual as the voyages of William Hickey (1769), Fanny Parkes (1822) and Harriet Tytler (1839) all made reference to huge celebrations. Hickey recorded the practice of *ducking and shaving*, or else the customary forfeit of a gallon of rum to the ship's crew. Parkes described showers of water being poured from the main top, a flaming tar barrel being thrown overboard and Neptune and his lady being dragged around the deck on a chariot made from a gun carriage. Harriet (then aged 11) was fascinated to see the 'line' of the equator through a telescope. But she had been tricked, as a hair had been placed within the telescope to fool the children. By 1832 'celebrations' had became more extreme when those who had not crossed the line before were tarred and feathered, unless the crew got extra grog. Perhaps it is not surprising that some of these rituals faded out of use in later years.

On several occasions during the voyage Captain Wyche recorded that the soldiers were engaged in *picking oakum*. As previously described, oakum was a mixture of tar and fibre used to plug gaps between the timbers. Picking oakum involves recycling old ropes by pulling them apart fibre by fibre. In Victorian times 'picking oakum' was a common task for prisoners or inmates of workhouses.

On the 30th May hammocks and chests were cleared out of the gun-deck so it could be washed. This was necessary on a regular basis.

The journals of Hickey and Parkes outline how the passengers amused themselves during the long voyages. Parkes described the activity of fish-spotting. She spotted flying fish, schools of dolphin and whales. She wrote that the curious birds and fish they saw relieved the tedium of the voyage. Parkes also described passengers shooting at albatross and other birds such as *Cape-hens, Sea Swallows and Pintado*. Had they not read the 'Rime of the Ancient Mariner,' (published in 1798)? She also recounted boxing matches, the playing of pitch and toss for money and many games of chess and backgammon. Hickey described a wager to eat a ship's biscuit in less than four minutes with no water – not an easy task.

On the 15th June 1768, Captains Wyche's log recorded that land was sighted from the masthead and recorded as possibly being *Cape Lagullas*. This was presumably Cape Agulhas, the demarcation line between the Atlantic and Indian Oceans. It is situated 110 miles south east of present day Cape Town. In those days the Dutch occupied Cape Town. Hickey described being very disappointed when a *glorious breeze* appeared and his captain decided to sail on without stopping.

4. A Passage to India

He wrote, *the " glorious breeze " however in no way consoled us for our disappointment, and we were rather sulky during a couple of days, at the end of which time we were reconciled to passing our favourite port, and good humour was restored.*

The next part of the voyage was through the dangerous Mozambique Channel. Captain Wyche described keeping a close lookout and taking soundings on a regular basis, particularly at night. Sounding leads were hollow so they picked up shells and corals from the seabed. Wyche added that he *saw a light on shore* and conceded that this was *a very dangerous place to make land in the night.*

William Hickey described seeing some rocks:

I looked into the sea, where to my great terror and surprise I beheld the rocks, as they appeared to me, close to the ship's bottom but Rogers assured me they were at least forty fathoms below us. In a few minutes after, however, he exclaimed, "Damn my eyes if I like this," and instantly ran into the Round house. Captain Waddell, returning with him upon deck, ordered the course to be altered three points, and the lead to be cast, which being done, they found only four fathoms, so that if there had been any sea the ship would have struck. These rocks it seems were not properly laid down in the charts, at the time we were over them, not being in sight of land and the Charts making them within five leagues of Madagascar, whereas we were upwards of twenty off shore. By standing off an hour we lost sight of the rocks, and were once more in deep water.

On Sunday 23rd June the Island of Comero was spotted NSW, and on the 4th July the *Salisbury* anchored at the *saddle* of the Island of Johanna, about half a mile offshore. Johanna (Anjouan) and now forms part of the Comoros Group, after an invasion in 2008. Looking at the map of Anjouan you can see a very obvious saddle shape along its northern shore where the capital Mutsamudu is situated.

The Island of Johannah must have appeared like a paradise after the long voyage. Solomon described it as a *delightful little island, situated between the African coast and the North of Madagascar; it is about the size of the Isle of Wight and abounds with cattle. And delicious fruits, such as Pines' Oranges, Bananas &c., all growing spontaneously; the country is hilly and well watered, abounding with game.*

4. A Passage to India

William Hickey also landed at Johanna and described it as *one of the most luxuriant and picturesque scenes it is possible to conceive*. On arrival his ship was surrounded by outrigger canoes sellig fresh meat, fish and fruits. He outlined the marketing approach of the islanders:

> *They spoke a strange jargon, intended as English, frequently repeating these words, "Johanna man, Englishman, all a one brother come. Englishman man very good man, drink ee de punch, fire de gun, beatee de French, very good fun."*

On arrival Captain Wyche received on board the *Prince of Johanna, the governor of the town and many attendants*. They were saluted with *five guns*. Two bullocks were taken on board. He described the ship's company as being fatigued so no shore parties were sent until the next day. They stayed at Johanna for five days and had to change anchorage on a number of occasions, possibly due to the strong winds.

William Hickey had much more to say about Johanna, but thankfully recorded nothing about any women he might have encountered. He described the capital as having *streets only about four feet wide*, and the habitations being constructed out of *clay and wicker*. He wrote that the natives *amuse themselves with bull fighting*. About five of them bait a bull, much smaller than European bulls, with a cloth and then run around it trying to avoid its horns. He described an excursion to visit a *stupendous cascade* reported to be 500 feet high. Later on the ships company were entertained by a duel between two cadets from another ship. The two *foolish lads* had been gambling with cards. They ended up having a quarrel that turned into a fight. The officers on the ship advised that, as gentlemen, they should settle their dispute *in the field*. But what the opponents did not realize was that their pistols had not been loaded with ball. There was an argument about the number of paces. Eventually both fired at the same time. One of them dropped down, but it was only a faint. Honour was therefore satisfied.

On the way back to his ship Hickey nearly drowned when his outrigger overturned. By his description it was clear that he had never learnt to swim. One of his companions grabbed him by the hair, which came off in his hands. It was a wig! Hickey had been advised to shave his head before going to sea.

4. A Passage to India

The voyage of the *Salisbury* continued on the 9th July 1768 after, as Solomon wrote, *supplying ourselves and the ship's company with necessaries as well as luxuries*. They sailed across the Indian Ocean to the Island of Ceylon, now Sri Lanka. On Monday 25th July Captain Wyche recorded that, at two o'clock in the morning, the mizzenmast was lost during a gale. He described this as *a mistake of the helm*. It was all hands on deck to clear the rigging and what was left of the mast. Presumably the hapless helmsman was chastised in some way, but Captain Wyche does not describe what happened to him. Perhaps Solomon slept through this incident, as he does not mention it.

On the 4th August the island of Ceylon was sighted on a bearing of NNW at a distance of six leagues. At the time the coastal part of Ceylon was occupied by the Dutch, after taking it from the Portuguese. The Sinhalese still occupied the Kingdom of Kandy, in the centre of the island. The British took Ceylon from the Dutch in 1796 and finally conquered the whole island in 1815. Harriet Tytler stopped off at Ceylon on her voyage back to India in 1846. She wrote that her ship, an early version of a P&O paddle steamer, lost part of its paddle wheel in a storm. She described Galle, the town on the southern tip of Ceylon, as a *lovely spot full of tiny islands covered with coconut trees growing right down to the water's edge*. But it was *so hot and muggy*.

After passing Ceylon the *Salisbury* continued north up the Coromandel Coast, the east side of India. The Captain took bearings on the flagstaffs at Pondicherry, the French colony, and Madras, before anchoring off Vizagapatum on the 11th August 1768. The next day a Lieutenant Dupont was sent on shore as he was *much disordered in his senses*. It is interesting to conjecture whether this Lieutenant Dupont might have become the Colonel Dupont who surrendered to Arthur Wellesley after the Battle of Burhanpur in 1803.

The *Salisbury* weighed anchor on the 13th August and continued on its voyage to arrive at Balasore Roads three days later. Balasore is the capital of Odessa, the state just south of Bengal, where the British had a factory. The ship stayed there for at least two days waiting for a pilot to guide the vessel to Culpee, opposite Fulta, in the mouth of the Hooghly. Calcutta is situated about sixty five miles up-river from there. A Dutch pilot came on board but he would not agree to take the ship. The first and third mates were then sent out in the cutter to search for another pilot and cannons were fired. It must

4. A Passage to India

have been frustrating after so many months at sea. Eventually they must have been successful as they arrived half a mile off the *Pagoda* at Culpee on the 23rd August. On the 25th the *long boat* was sent to Culpee.

Solomon's long voyage was nearly over.

In 1822 Fanny Parkes wrote that her ship, the *Marchioness of Ely*, was becalmed for eighteen days and ended up at Carnicobar, one of the Nicobar Islands. She described seeing *naked men in canoes* and was thankful that she had not landed at the Andaman Islands as she had been told that the inhabitants there had a *fondness for strangers of a nature different to the Carnicobarbarians*. In other words she had been told they had a fondness for human flesh. Fanny's ship was re-provisioned and they soon arrived at Ganga Sagar Island, in the mouth of the Hooghly.

Solomon wrote that on landing at Calcutta he heard the sad news that his uncle, Captain Mills, and also his cousin, Captain Adams of the Engineers, had died. He described these being *heavy losses*, being only *fifteen years* (his actual age was seventeen). He remained at the Presidency, *but a few days*, and was then ordered to join the First Brigade stationed at *Moaghip* where he was appointed as an ensign.

His lot was very different to that of William Hickey who lived it up in Madras before returning to England via China as he felt there was no future for him as an ensign in the Company army. On arrival in Calcutta, Fanny Parkes found a *sufficiently large house* in Park Street, Chowringhee, and had a very sociable time attending a number of balls.

Before leaving this part of the story it is interesting to see how different it was when Harriet Tytler returned to India at the age of seventeen in 1846. In 1825 the first steamship sailed to India via Cape Horn in just 113 days. P&O started operating steamships in 1842 and ran two routes. The first was the usual route around the Cape. Harriet took the second, much quicker route that involved traveling to Alexandria by steamship, then up the Nile to Cairo and then overland to Suez (18 to 20 hours in a horse and carriage). She then took another steamship to India. This sounds complicated but when Harriet took this route it took only seven weeks to make the journey, as opposed to five months. Aden was eventually acquired by the British and used as a coaling station as the steamers needed to refuel frequently. The Suez Canal was not opened until 1869.

4. A Passage to India

Harriet received some sad news when she arrived at Aden, which she described it as a *God-forsaken place*. The news was that her father had died. And when she got to Calcutta she found that her mother and sisters were in the process of returning to England. She had to stay on in India because, if she had left, her father's EIC pension would apparently have been lost. Harriet's father was Solomon's son, John Lucas Earle (1791-1845). John Lucas took ship to India at the age of sixteen in 1817. But that is another story.

I travelled overland to India by public transport in 1979. It took me nine weeks to get from London to Delhi. When I travelled to India again in 2016 in order to research this book, the flight to Delhi from Heathrow took around ten hours.

PART TWO : INTRODUCTION TO INDIA

5. Mughals and Marathas

As the Mughal Empire gradually lost power, other competitors were vying for position and land. As Tammita-Delgoda described it: *like the tide, Mughal power gradually rolled back to reveal the rocks which now remained: rocks which were to prove the foundations of future states and nations.*[1] Some of these rocks were the newly independent Muslim states, like Oudh, Hyderabad and Bengal. Others were completely new contenders, notably the Marathas, the Sikhs and the new rulers at Mysore. And, in addition to the British, other European nations were competing for influence, notably the Portuguese, the Dutch and the French. It was a huge melting pot.

MUGHALS

By 1768 the Mughal Empire had virtually become a spent force. The Emperor, Shah Alam II, was under the control of the Marathas. In 1761 Shah Alam had asked the Marathas to help him defeat the invading Afghans. Panipat, just north of Delhi, was a popular place for battles due to its strategic location on the main route from the Punjab to the rest of India. The Marathas lost the battle and the Afghans returned home, but Delhi remained under Maratha control. Shah Alam II was the Emperor who, in 1764, signed away the tax collection rights in Bengal to Robert Clive (the *Diwani*).

What needs to be understood is that India, before the conquest by the British in the nineteenth century, had never been a single country. India is vast and communication in those days was very slow. Many rulers came and went. The Mughals had nearly achieved total domination of the sub-continent under Aurangzeb, but they never conquered South India and there was much opposition to Aurangzeb's autocratic rule. Before the Mughals arrived, India had been composed of many different states.

The Mughal Empire had been prominent in India for over 200 years following the defeat of the Lodi Sultans of Delhi by Babur at the First Battle of Panipat in 1526. After taking Delhi, Babur went on to conquer the Rajputs to the south and Gwalior to the east. While there he ordered the destruction of some Jain sculptures as he was offended by their nakedness.[2] Generally though, the Mughals did not set out to impose their religion on states they conquered.

The Mughals were descendants of the Timurid Emperors and Genghis Khan, hence the name Mughal, the Persian word for Mongol, a native of Mongolia. Babur originated from Samarkand, a city on the Silk Road. They were Muslims ruling over a predominantly Hindu culture. Hamayun followed Babur. He was commemorated in a magnificent tomb in Delhi. The tomb was constructed of red sandstone and white marble and was a forerunner to the Taj Mahal. Hamayun's tomb was also the place where the last Emperor of the Mughals, Bahadur Shah Zafar II, surrendered to the British in 1857. This surrender finally ended Mughal rule in India.

Hamayun's Tomb. Delhi 2016

In just over 300 years the Mughals had achieved an awful lot. India is literally peppered by the remains of their spectacular buildings, including one that has been described as the most beautiful building in the world, the Taj Mahal. They were a cultured race. With the exception of Aurangzeb, the emperors were all poets and patrons of the arts. The official court language and script was Persian. They built up successful tax collection systems, without the need for land ownership.

After Hamayun (1530 to 1556) came the greatest of all Mughal Emperors, Akbar (1556 to 1605). Akbar encouraged religious tolerance and actually initiated weekly debates between Muslims, Hindus, Jains, Christians, Jews and Zooastrians.[3] As well as building Hamayun's Tomb, he constructed Agra Fort and the now deserted city of Fatepur Sikri. Fatepur Sikri, near Agra, was only occupied for ten years until the city apparently outgrew its water supply. Akbar also annexed Gujarat following the siege of Surat in 1572.

Akbar's son Jahangir followed (1605 to 1627). He was also a patron of the arts. He built the Shalimar Gardens next to Lake Dal in Kashmir. But there was a succession problem at the end of his reign. One of his sons tried to take over before his father had died. He was blinded as a punishment. Another son, Prince Khurram, murdered this son for good measure. Prince Khurram was later to become Shah Jahan. As prince he was resident in Burhanpur and Asirghar, both places we will return to later in this account.

Shah Jahan was famous for his buildings, and his favourite wife, Mumtaz Mahal. She died giving birth to her fourteenth child while staying at Burhanpur. The Taj Mahal was built as a memorial to her. The great Calcutta poet, Rabindranath Tagore, described the Taj Mahal as *a teardrop on the cheek of time*. Shah Jahan also ordered the construction of a new city at Delhi, called Shajahanabad. This city is now known as Old Delhi. Shah Jahan has been described as a rather aloof perfectionist [4] and a much more orthodox Muslim than his father and grandfather. But this this was nothing compared to his successor, Aurangzeb.

Any succession of a Mughal Emperor was not without incident and Shah Jahan's was no exception. He named his oldest son and favourite, Dara Shikoh, as his successor. But another son and rival, Aurangzeb, objected. Aurangzeb defeated Dara in battle near Agra and took his brother to Delhi in rags and chains. He then had him beheaded and sent the head to his father, at the time imprisoned at Agra Fort. When Shah Jahan died he was still a prisoner in Agra Fort, in full view of his masterpiece, the Taj Mahal.

Aurangzeb's rule (1658 to 1707) heralded the decline of Mughal power in India. He was austere and teetotal and aimed to create a strictly moral Islamic state.[5] The decline of Aurangzeb's rule can be compared to the decline of British rule in India, when the British also wanted to remain

5. Mughals and Marathas

aloof, failed to mix with the local population and, to a lesser degree, tried to introduce their own religion. Despite this Aurangzeb was an accomplished general and was responsible for expanding the Mughal Empire to its greatest extent.

But the Empire had become over-extended and Aurangzeb's intolerant policies triggered many rebellions. He lost the support of the Rajputs and stirred up the Marathas. But he did manage to capture Golconda (the fortress at Hyderabad) and its precious stones.

After his death the empire gradually disintegrated.

There were many changes of rulers and many invasions. The Marathas gained control of the Western Ghats and Gujarat. The state of Oudh and the city of Lucknow became independent with the Emperor ruling by name only. And of course the Europeans were there too, waiting and ready in the wings.

In 1737 the Marathas raided the suburbs of Delhi. However Delhi was to suffer far worse than this when, in 1739, the city was sacked by the Persian ruler Nadir Shah. Delhi never really recovered. The city was plundered and looted and thousands of the population were massacred. That great symbol of Mughal power, the Peacock Throne, was removed and taken back to Persia. One of the jewels on this throne was the famous Koh-i-Noor diamond.

There is really not much more to say about the Mughals in this brief overview. The Marathas took control of Delhi and the British followed. When the sepoy troops of the EIC army rebelled in 1857 they headed for Delhi seeking to re-instate the Mughal Emperor. The rebellion was unplanned and they needed a figurehead. The last Mughal Emperor (Shah Zafar, 1837 to 1858) reluctantly gave his blessing to the rebellion. When the British retook Delhi, Shah Zafar was taken into captivity, tried for 'treason' and banished to Rangoon in Burma. He died in 1862 and was buried in an unmarked grave.

The next contenders for power were the Marathas. They were a major power in central and western India, taking over territory formerly held by the Mughals.

But who were the Marathas and where did they come from?

5. Mughals and Marathas

MARATHAS

According to Tammita–Delgoda the Marathas were *a hardy, tenacious people who inhabited the parched, barren mountain ranges of the Western Ghats.* [6] The Western Ghats are the range of mountains running down the west side of India (ghat means step). The Maratha homeland is called Maharashtra and can be defined as the land where Marathi is the dominant language. They expanded from their mountain strongholds east to the *Desh* (the Deccan plateau) and west to the *Konkan*, the narrow coastal strip. They developed great skills in war, their modus operandi being fast raiding on horseback.

In 1768 the Marathas had territorial rights across India from Gujarat in the west, to Orissa in the east, and to Delhi, the Bundelkhand and Malwa to the north. Their base was the city of Pune (known as Poona by the British).

Let us go back to the beginning and look at how the Marathas came to be such great warriors and how they were able to achieve so much. It all started with a certain village chieftain called Shivaji (1627–1680).

Shivaji. Print from Beveridge, History of India. 1862

5. Mughals and Marathas

Nowadays Shivaji is revered in some circles almost as a divine figure, certainly a legend. If you visit Mumbai (Bombay) you will find that many public buildings have been renamed after him. In 1998 the Victoria Terminus, that magnificent emblem of the British Raj, was renamed the Chhatraparti Shivaji Terminus. The former Prince of Wales Museum of Western India is now the Chhatraparti Shivaji Mahavaj Vastu Sangrahalaya Museum. The airport has been renamed the Chhatraparti Shivaji International Airport. The historian Stewart Gordon is of the view that Shivaji has become what others want him to be. [7] To the British, he was a glorious rebel fighting against the superior power of the Mughals, but also a subversive figure. To some Hindus he is a symbol of Hindu dominance over the Muslims. To the socialists, he is a hero of class struggle, particularly of low caste people against high caste Brahmins. In reality he was none of those things, but succeeded in bringing the Marathas together into a single politic and without doubt remains a legend.

One of the famous legends about Shivaji is the story of his daring escape from Agra. He had to travel there to pay his respects to the Mughal court. He was warned that there was a plot to imprison him so he escaped, hidden in a basket of sweets. He then made his way back to the Deccan disguised as a Hindu priest with his face covered in ashes.

In the early seventeenth century there were two Muslims powers in the Maharashtra area; the Mughals in the north, extending to Ahmadabad and Surat, and the Adil Shahi kingdom to the south, based at Bijapur. On the coast there were the Portuguese. In 1659 Shivaji controlled the Pune region, right in the middle, and as such was in a vulnerable position. Like the Afghans, the Marathas survived by raiding outside their homelands and this behaviour would not be tolerated by the ruling powers. So they planned to crush him. But Shivaji had some success against the Bijapur armies and in a daring raid, sacked the wealthy trading base of Surat. The Mughal response was to send a 15,000 strong army to defeat him.

Shivaji developed the practice of fast, mobile, hit and run attacks. In other words to raid and then retreat back to the safety of inaccessible mountain forts. His armies also harried the supply chains of the vast invading armies, described by Gordon as moving cities. [8] The wars went on for years. It was notable that the Marathas continued to use the same tactics, with considerable success, against the British during the First Anglo–Maratha War of 1775 to 1783. But they then failed to follow up their advantage. It could be argued that the Marathas only became more vulnerable when, towards the end of the eighteenth century, they developed less mobile artillery regiments supported by foot soldiers.

The historical importance of Shivaji rests on the fact that he gathered many disparate groups of Marathas together into a *Polity* or confederacy, led by a *Peshwa,* or king, supported by the Brahmin leaders. He managed to carve a small kingdom out of a marginal frontier area and hold it against the vastly superior forces of the Bijapur and Mughal armies.[9]

After his death Shivaji was succeeded by his son Sambhaji. Aurangzeb then decided to conquer Bijapur and finally destroy Maratha power at the same time. In 1687 he succeeded in his aim to take Bijapur. He then turned his attention to the Marathas and took Sambhaji prisoner. Sambhaji was tortured, killed and his body was then hacked to pieces and fed to the dogs. But the Marathas continued the fight and Aurangzeb was getting old and tired, eventually dying in 1707. Then the Marathas gradually regained their power under the new Peshwa, Balaji Vishwanath.

In the 1720s, the Mughal state began to disintegrate with separate kingdoms developing in the Punjab, Oudh, Bengal and Hyderabad. The sacking of Delhi by Nadir Shah in 1739 did not help matters.

Around this time various Maratha families were becoming more powerful. In the north there were the Shindes, from Gwalior. In the west, the Gaekwads, at Songadh. In the east, the Bhonsles of Nagpur. And in the centre, the Holkars, from Indore. All these dynasties will become significant later in our story, particularly when the Peshwa, based in Pune, lost overall control of the Politic.

The Peshwa Bajirao Vishwanath died in 1740 and was succeeded by his son Balajirao. The wars against the Mughals continued with the Marathas gradually gaining ground. They continued to use their highly effective tactics using mobile horsemen and destroying the grain supplies of the large Mughal armies. In Gujarat the Gaekwads gained land, but had to share their revenue with the Peshwa. The Marathas were reliant on Europeans, particularly the British, for supplies of artillery and gunpowder.[10]

Meanwhile the poor peasants, the ryots, the farmers who toiled the land, had to pay taxes (tributes) to whoever happened to be in power. They were in effect paying protection money. This tribute was called a *jagir* and had to be paid under threat of force. The ryots were also at constant risk of armies passing through their lands and taking the fruits of their labour. As mentioned previously, under the Mughals, there was no ownership of land, but there was a highly organised system of taxation.

5. Mughals and Marathas

A turning point for the Marathas came in 1760, when Ahmad Shah Abdali invaded the Punjab from Afghanistan and threatened Delhi. The Mughals, now very weak, asked the Marathas for help. This was too good an opportunity for the Marathas to miss and they assembled a huge army of up to 80,000 men, including camp followers, at Panipat. Duff described the campaign as a *national cause of all Hindus*. The Afghan and Maratha armies were roughly equal in size, but the Persians had better artillery and a better command structure. The two great armies spent a few days skirmishing until the Marathas ran low on supplies. Eventually they were forced to attack or starve. Mass slaughter commenced. The tide of battle turned in the favour of the Afghans and by the end of the battle at least 50,000 people lay dead. Duff wrote that 200,000 Marathas died, presumably including the camp followers.[11] After the battle the Afghans took the women and children as slaves and cut off the heads of their male captives. They were apparently ranked in lines for this gruesome activity to be carried out.

And it was all in vain as after the battle the Afghans left for home. Their armies had not been paid and refused to continue. But this defeat left the Marathas weak and despondent and it took them over a decade to recover. And of course, this was just the time when the British were expanding their influence.

Like the Mughals, when Maratha leaders died there was often a struggle for succession. Madhavrao was declared Peshwa, but his uncle Raghunathrao (known as Raghoba by the British) was meant to share power. Battles ensued that ended with the murder of Madhavrao's successor Narayanrao by Raghunathrao's men in 1773. Raghunathrao assumed power, but not for long as we shall see later.

The British had learnt by experience during the campaigns in the Madras area that to gain influence and power against superior odds they needed to gain the advantage by supporting one rival against another. We will see later how they got things disastrously wrong in regard to the Marathas when the Bombay Presidency decided to support Raghunathrao while the Bengal Presidency tried to make an alliance with his enemy, the Bhonsles.

6. The Honourable East India Company

The English East India Company expanded from a few trading bases in 1757 to become rulers of most of India a few decades later. But their powers were finally taken over by the British Crown after the Indian Mutiny (or rebellion) in 1857. In practice the power of the EIC to control its own affairs in India was considerably reduced by William Pitt's India Act of 1784.

The story of the EIC is a salutary example of what can happen when free enterprise and massive business corporations take over the running of countries. Although modern multinational companies do not in the present day control their own standing armies, or take over whole countries, there is an argument that the political government of some countries are in the power of business corporations.

Throughout this book the East India Company will be referred to as the EIC, or the Company. The official name was the Honourable East India Company, often referred to as the 'Honble Company' in contemporary correspondence. Honour is defined as someone or something to be held in high respect or great esteem, to keep an agreement or to do something that is morally right. ^{OED} It is not always easy to justify this term when describing a company whose aim was to benefit its shareholders, often to the detriment of others.

The EIC was founded when a charter signed by Queen Elizabeth I gave the *Company of Merchants of London* the monopoly to *trade into the East Indies* for a period of fifteen years. The date was the 31st December 1599 and the charter was signed just before midnight on the dawn of a new century.

Around this time the advantages of improved marine design, and the development of navigational instruments, cartography and gunnery, had given Europeans the edge over their Asian rivals.[1] England had successfully defeated the Spanish Armada and merchant traders were turning their sights to the east for trade, as well as for easy pickings from raids against Spanish and Portuguese shipping.

6. The Honourable East India Company

In 1498 a momentous event in world history took place. The Portuguese explorer, Vasco da Gama, discovered the first sea route to India. Goods could now be brought to Europe by sea, instead of overland by the silk roads. From the 1500s an increasing number of ships made the voyage around the Cape of Good Hope, and trade in spices, particularly the much sought after pepper, became very lucrative.

The EIC established its own sea routes to the east, stopping for supplies at Saint Helena and then at either the Cape (Saldania) or one of the East Africa islands. To begin with trade was centred on the Spice Islands, situated around Sumatra, the Indonesian islands and the South China Sea. Trade centres, known as factories, were set up in various locations. The factories acted as storehouses where goods for trade could be collected and stored ready for shipment. Inevitably factories became at risk from attack and ships were vulnerable to pirates. There were also battles with rival trading countries, especially Spain, Portugal and Holland. This meant that standing armies and armed vessels became essential.

This explained why the Company needed to establish safe havens in various countries and why they set up treaties with local leaders and providers. There was no plan to take over the running of other countries. Factories were set up according to need, purely for the purpose of trade.

By the end of the seventeenth century the Company had developed three main bases in India: Surat (1612), Madraspatnam (1639) and Calcutta (1690). A triangular trade developed between England, India, China and the Spice Islands. Initially the Company wanted to trade English products, particularly wool, but the counties they wanted to trade with did not want wool. Instead bullion (gold and silver) was exported to India to purchase cottons. Goods were in turn taken further east to exchange for spices and other commodities to import back to England. A triangular trade also developed with Persia in which silks were exported to India in return for spices and cottons. Cohoo, or qahwa (coffee) was traded from Mokha, in Yemen. Coffee was first produced in Mokha from plants growing wild in Ethiopia. At this time Mokha was the only place in the world where coffee was available. It was only later that the tea trade developed with China, and the opium trade, transporting opium from India to China in exchange for tea.

In the 1600s the potential of the Cape was not recognised as a future trading base. The area was inhabited by a race called the Saldanians who, according to accounts at the time, adorned themselves with entrails.[2]

6. The Honourable East India Company

In 1615 an attempt was made to colonise the Cape using condemned prisoners. This small band of early colonists decamped to Robben Island, made famous later as the prison island where Nelson Mandela was sent. After this failed attempt by the English the Dutch took the initiative and were the first to colonise the mainland.

The Portuguese, who were well established on the West Coast of India, understandably objected to the arrival of Company ships. In 1612 things came to a head with a sea battle at Swally (Suvali) in the Gulf of Cambay, just off Surat. The EIC ships employed similar tactics used to defeat the Spanish Armada. Company vessels were lightweight and more manoeuvrable and were able to dart in, fire and retreat. The end result was a defeat for the Portuguese. From the shore, the Mughals watched. The EIC also had success against the Portuguese when they assisted the Shah of Persia to take the Portuguese fort at Hormuz (1619). After this the Portuguese largely retreated to their colony in Goa.

In 1661 the Island of Bombay was gifted to Charles II of England as part of the dowry of his Portuguese bride, Catherine of Braganza. The resident Portuguese initially refused to vacate the island. Charles II did not want the responsibility of governing the island so he sold it to the EIC. By 1690 Bombay had become the headquarters of Company affairs on the west coast. Each of the three main bases in India became known as 'presidencies.' And each presidency was separately controlled from London, now situated at the new offices on Leadenhall Street.

At around this time new rivals to the EIC, the French, were establishing themselves in Pondicherry.

As the seventeenth century drew to a close, the control of India by the Mughal Emperors started to decline. This meant that the hinterlands around the factory bases became much more unstable and unpredictable. Various small wars took place with local leaders. A Company agent (or factor) Job Charnock, got involved in various deals around the Hoogli River in Bengal. He eventually got permission to set up a factory on a fairly inaccessible bend of the river, further inland, at the village of Kalikata. Charnock was an abrasive but effective factor. He apparently snatched a young Hindu girl from her husband's funeral pyre and then took her as his bride. [3] At this time it was more acceptable to form relationships with locals, although this changed by the beginning of the nineteenth century. When Charnock threatened to leave, the Mughal ruler of Bengal, the

6. The Honourable East India Company

Nizam, requested his return. The Mughal rulers had become dependent on Company trade, selling silks and cottons to the English in return for gold and silver to fund their armies.

As factors in the EIC were very poorly paid it was acceptable for them to set up lucrative private trade agreements with the locals. This was allowed as long as the trade stayed local and did not interfere with trade to Europe. That was the monopoly of the Company. The locals welcomed this trade as it helped with business. For example the trade could involve sending salt up-river, and saltpetre, used in the manufacture of gunpowder, back down. Personal profits were taken home in the form of diamonds. This was known as 'country' trade.

Junior factors were called 'writers' and they certainly wrote a great deal. In the corporate empire of the EIC paperwork was everything. It has been said that, being merchants by profession, the Company's men *lived by the ledger and ruled with the quill*.[4]

To protect themselves, the three presidencies built forts: Fort William in Calcutta, Fort St George in Madras, and Bombay Castle. The land at Madras was purchased by Francis Day in 1639. It was said he had a mistress at the nearby Portuguese colony at San Thomé. [5] Madras was an unusual place to set up a major trade centre as it had no natural harbour. Ships had to stand off in the Madras 'runs' while unloading their cargo, which then had to be transported to the shore through huge breakers. This was known as 'crossing the bar.' There were frequent storms necessitating the quick withdrawal of ships before they were blown ashore. The climate on the Coromandel Coast was better and a lot of money had gone into the construction of Fort St George (£3000). That, and the availability of British sea power, enabled the colony to survive through many troubles and wars in future years.

The EIC was one of the first share-based companies. Investors expected their dividend, or profit, as they do in the present day. In good times the return on investments was in the region of six to eight per cent per annum. However investors wanting a fast return did not hold total power and it was the second 'Court of Committees' that controlled the day to day running of the Company. In the main this committee was run by merchants who sensibly took a more long-term view. The EIC was very much a halfway stage in company evolution, from a medieval guild to one of today's Public Limited Companies (PLCs).

6. The Honourable East India Company

By the beginning of the eighteenth century the EIC was purely a trading organisation with no interest in territorial rights. So how and why did the Company transform itself into a political power and territorial ruler over the next 100 years?

There were many reasons this change happened, and one of them was because of the need for security. Trade is highly sensitive to uncertainty and conflict. As already mentioned, consequent to the decline of the Mughal Empire, India had become a much more unsettled place. Rival contenders for power were willing to seek outside help. Another major reason was because of rivalry with other European powers, particularly the French, who wanted to acquire territory themselves. Finally, because of the slow communication with Europe, more entrepreneurial Company leaders had the freedom to take their own path. As it took up to a year to communicate with the Company directors at Leadenhall Street they needed to take their own initiative when necessary. The most significant of these entrepreneurs was Robert Clive (1725 to 1774).

In 1743 Clive was appointed as a writer at an annual salary of five pounds per annum. Like Solomon he set sail for India at the age of seventeen. But he found the work of a writer, and life in Madras, extremely tedious and as a result became depressed. But everything changed when war broke out with France in 1746. Initially the French had the upper hand and they succeeded in taking Madras. The British retreated to Fort Saint David, their last remaining factory in the Coromandel. The French were led by a commander perhaps even more entrepreneurial than Clive. His name was Joseph-Francois Dupleix.

It was clear to Dupleix that central authority in India had disintegrated. His plan was to achieve power by supporting an Indian leader, Chanda Sahib.

However the English had support from the Royal Navy and also, very significantly, from an effective army commander, Major Stringer Lawrence. Stringer Lawrence re-organised the army and set up proper training and employment for the sepoys (Indian soldiers) who had previously been used on a very ad hoc and disorganized basis.

In 1749, when the European war ended, Madras was returned to the English. The colony remained at risk and the English needed to develop local military alliances. In other words they had to *follow suit or leave the*

6. The Honourable East India Company

table.[6] In direct opposition to the French they supported another contender for power, Mohammad Ali Khan, a rival of Chanda Sahib.[7]

In an extremely bold and risky move Clive marched out of Madras at the head of a small force of 700 troops in support of Mohammad Ali Khan. When he reached Arcot he came up against a 15,000 strong Mughal army, supported by the French. Against all odds his small force triumphed against the combined Muslim and French forces. Company presence on the Coromandel Coast was secured. Clive returned to England in 1753 as a hero.

But over 1000 miles north in Bengal things were not going so well for the English. In 1756 the Nawab of Bengal, Alivardi Khan, had been succeeded by his grandson, Siraj-ud-Daula. The Nawab was technically under the control of the Mughal Emperor in Delhi but in practice external control was very limited. At around the same time Clive was on his way back to Madras, having been appointed as the new president there. He was still in his twenties. On route he became involved in an attack on the Maratha 'pirate' strongholds at Suvanardurg and Gheria in the Konkan, just south of Bombay. With his supply of loot from defeating the pirates, the Commodore, William James, built Severndroog Castle, at Shooter's Hill in London.

Back in Bengal, Fort William was in a poor state of repair. Siraj-ud-Daula had become incensed by abuses of the 1717 *farman* (an agreement for free trade given to the EIC by a previous Emperor) and he objected to the erection of fortifications around Calcutta. One of these was the so-called 'Maratha Ditch'. He sent his ambassador to negotiate but Narayan Singh was humiliated and expelled by the insightless Company council. Apparently Narayan Singh reported back saying, *what honour is left for us men when a few traders, who have not yet leant to wash their bottoms, reply to a ruler's orders by throwing out his messenger?*[8] The final straw came when the Council at Calcutta gave sanctuary to a hated rival, Krishna Das.

The story of the brief siege and capture of Fort William by Siraj-ud-Daula has been fully described elsewhere.[9] The cowardly council leaders, under the leadership of Roger Drake, escaped on ships leaving the garrison to its fate. Even then things might have been all right, but apparently some of the soldiers got drunk and attacked their captors. They were therefore put in the nearest prison with the rest of the garrison, about 100 to 200 souls. This happened to be a tiny room built into the walls of Fort William.

By the next morning over half had died. This prison became known as the Black Hole of Calcutta.

A few months later Clive and Admiral Watson's relief force arrived at the mouth of the Hoogli River. Further up river a curious event took place when a drunken English sailor (Strahan) attacked the fort of Budge Budge, on his own. He had apparently *made too free with the grog* and took it upon himself to swim the moat and scale a breach that had been made in the wall the day before by Admiral Watson's ships. He claimed the fort, which then necessitated an early attack by the Company army, much to the annoyance of Clive and Watson. The sailor was summoned before Watson for indiscipline and was threatened with a flogging. He apparently replied, *if I am flogged for this here action, I will never take another fort for as long as I live, by God.*[10] Some years later, in 1774, Solomon Earle was put in command of the fort at Budge Budge.

After Clive had retaken Calcutta he could have stopped there and made terms. But being the entrepreneur that he was he made the decision to march on up river. This was an unprecedented move and set the pattern for all that was to follow.

To start with the English attacked and took Chandernagore, the French settlement, with the aid of Watson's ships. War with France had just restarted and Clive took a pre-emptive strike. After a number of failed negotiations with Siraj-ud-Daula, he then marched on upriver to a place called Plassey, just south of the Nawab's capital at Murshidabad. Various excuses were made for this aggressive move against a local ruler, including the excuse that the Nawab had broken the terms of an agreement made after Calcutta had been retaken. There were also concerns that Calcutta would always be at risk, particularly if the Nawab allied with the French.

On the 13th June 1757, 3000 Company troops faced 50,000 opponents. But Clive had made a secret treaty with a rival contender to the Nawab's throne, Mir Jafar. This reduced the odds and, further to Clive's advantage, a sudden storm helped to immobilize some of the opposing cannon by drenching their gunpowder. The Nawab's army were routed and Siraj-ud-Daula retreated to his capital. There is an interesting eyewitness description of the battle in Major John Corneille's account of his service in India. Corneille was a member of the regular army, the 39th Division, the first complete Royal regiment to be posted to India.[11]

6. The Honourable East India Company

What happened next had terrible consequences for Bengal. After taking Murshidabad Clive simply emptied its treasury. He sent all this loot back to Calcutta on several barges. Corneille described how the spoils were distributed and the jealousies that erupted as a result. The ready cash also had a detrimental effect on the 39th as a fighting force. *The excesses which their prize money furnished them with the means of gratifying, the badness of the climate at that time of year, as well as the very inactive state they were allowed to remain in, all joined to sweep them off by dozens a day.* The regimental strength reduced from 270 to 120.[12]

The Nawab was captured and murdered by Mir Jafar's men. Clive was awarded a £30,000 annual *jagir* for life after he assisted Mir Jafar to retake Patna. This *jagir* came back to haunt Clive at a later date when he had to answer for his actions to the British parliament. The looting of its treasury was a terrible thing for a country already impoverished by war. There were no reserves left to cope with recession and famine. Not only that, Bengal lost a relatively stable system of revenue collection and government.

Clive sailed back to England in 1760 a very rich man.

Meanwhile Mir Jafir could not govern Bengal. His treasury had been denuded and the demand of the Company in tax was excessive. The amount of revenue thought to be available had been grossly exaggerated. Native agents, known as *banyans,* were reported to be terrorising the countryside with the approval of their English principals.[13] There was no proper government or control. Mir Jafar's successor, Mir Kasim, ended up declaring war against the English. Various major battles were fought until in 1764, the English gained the upper hand at the bloody battle of Buxar.

In 1764 Clive was sent back to Bengal as Governor. He was expected to sort out the mess and get the country back to safe and effective government. What he actually did was obtain a mandate to govern Bengal from the Mughal Emperor, Shah Alam II, in return for an annual tribute of £325,000.[14] This was the famous *Diwani* that was signed at Allahabad and depicted in the painting by Benjamin West, now on display at Powis Castle. The *Diwani* gave the Company the right to collect taxes and therefore to rule the country.

But to his credit Clive did bring in a number of reforms and took on the money-grabbing Calcutta Council. In doing so he made many enemies. A society of trade was set up and the first salaried civil service. Attempts were made to restrict presents and bribes – you could say that Clive had become poacher turned gamekeeper. He developed the so-called *Dual System* with the local Muslim rulers staying in charge of administration and the collection of taxes, but with the Company in overall control.

He returned to England in 1767 for the last time. In the same year Solomon Earle set off for London to seek his fortune.

But poor Bengal was not to be relieved of its miseries. In 1769 the monsoon failed. This resulted in a terrible famine that lasted throughout 1770. Miseries were exacerbated by inflexible taxation and the lack of food reserves and organisation. The famine ended up wiping out huge numbers, estimated to be up to one third of the population of Bengal. Reports from the resident at Mushidabad at the time recorded that *the living were feeding on the dead and the streets were choked with corpses*.[15] The results of the famine are eloquently described in the classic novel Anandamath, written after the 1857 rebellion.[16]

In addition to the misery in Bengal this famine was to spell the beginning of the end for the independence of the EIC.

The amount of revenue available from Bengal had been highly exaggerated. A bubble developed with shareholders buying up Company shares in London at inflated rates. Stocks doubled in value over eight months. The government became greedy too and upped the financial payments from the EIC to £400,000 per year. As the famine took hold, the gravy train abruptly ended and dividends were stopped. Share values plummeted. The Company asked the government for a one million pound loan. Something similar happened in recent history with the crash of the banks in 2008. Because the government relied heavily on the EIC, they agreed to pay. But there were conditions, notably increased government control.

The first move was Lord North's Regulating Act of 1773, followed by Pitt's India Act of 1784. The British Government did not want to take over the administration or responsibility for governing British dominions in India, but they did want to dictate what happened. In some ways this is understandable given what was happening in the rest of the world at the time; the revolutionary war in America. The British had surrendered at York Town in 1781 and the American Colonies were finally lost in 1783. But the consequences for both the Company and Bengal would cause endless misery. In effect the EIC became quasi civil servants acting for the Crown.

6. The Honourable East India Company

Three new governors were sent to India in 1769 on the frigate *Aurora*. After they called in at the Cape, the frigate was never seen again. In 1774 Warren Hastings was appointed as the first Governor-General of Bengal. We will hear a lot more about him later.

Meanwhile in London, Robert Clive was in deep trouble. He had antagonised too many powerful people and his enemies were intent on revenge. He was called before the House of Commons to explain his actions, including how he got his *jagir*. He eventually became unwell and, in 1774, died at his house at 45 Berkeley Square. The exact cause of his death is uncertain but one report stated that he cut his throat with a penknife. He was buried at dusk in an unmarked grave inside St. Mary's Church, Moreton Say, Shropshire, many miles away from London. A small plaque was put up at a later date bearing the words, *Primus in Indis*.

In 1768 when Solomon embarked on the *Salisbury* things were about to change. It is doubtful that Solomon knew much about all this. He was going to India to seek his fortune, presumably with the intention of returning home with enough capital to set up a home and possibly start a family.

Below is the extent of Company Territory around the time of Solomon's arrival in India. Things stayed much the same until the next set of expansion at the end of the Second Anglo-Mysore war in 1792.

6. The Honourable East India Company

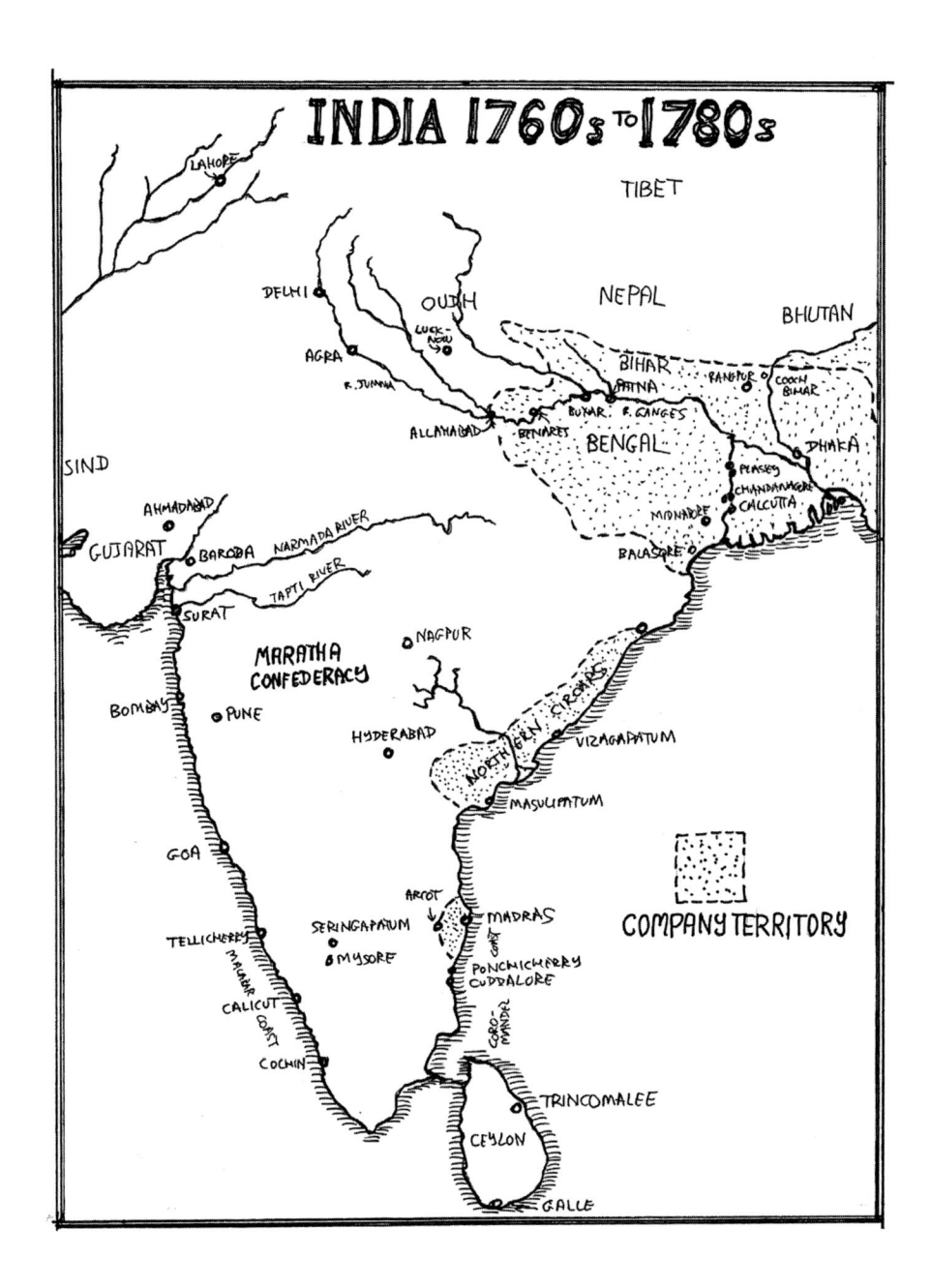

7. The Rise of the Gaekwads and the start of the Anglo-Maratha War

Like all history, in looking at the rise of the Gaekwads and how they managed to carve out their kingdom of Baroda (Vadodara), the outcome could easily have been different but for the ability and ambition of certain leaders. A contemporary publication, 'Baroda, Know Your Roots,' described the rise of the Gaekwads from farmers to rulers as *one of the most remarkable episodes in Indian history.*[1] It is also significant as the dispute between the Gaekwad family and the Maratha Politic enabled the EIC to increase its influence over the west side of India and ultimately take over all the territory.

The Gaekwads are still very much in resident to this day in Baroda although they no longer rule. The current Maharajah is Samarjitsinh Gaekwad.

The Gaekwad family were originally called *Matre*, or *Mantri* and were ranked amongst the *Kshystrya,* or warrior class.[2] They came from the village of Bhare, near Pune. The word Gaekwad means *cow-protector.* This does not mean that the Gaekwads herded cows but the term is a mark of respect, as cows are sacred to Hindus and to save a cow was, and still is, a meritorious act. There are several explanations as to how the Gaekwads got their name; whether they saved a cow from a tiger, or the title was a gesture of defiance against the ruling Muslims. Whatever the case, the name change came about in the late seventeenth century.

Soon after this the grandson of the first Gaekwad set out to seek his fortune. Twenty years later Damaji Gaekwad had risen to the position of deputy commander of the Maratha army.[3] Soon after rising to this position he was killed in battle but had apprenticed his nephew Pilaji to take over – it was common at the time to adopt heirs if male offspring were not forthcoming. By 1718 Pilaji Gaekwad was in command of 300 horsemen and had been successful in a 'revenue-collecting' expedition into Gujarat.

7. The Rise of the Gaekwads and the start of the Anglo-Maratha War

He then set off with his force to take the fort of Songarh, just inside the borders of Gujarat, beating back a force sent by the Mughals to dislodge him. Songarh (now known as Songadh) then became the capital of the Gaekwads for the next fifty years. The fort is still there, situated 367 feet up on a hill, fifty miles east of Surat, just south of the Tapti River. It was an ideal base for raids into Gujarat.

The Marathas sent troops into Gujarat on a regular basis to collect taxes, known as *chauth*. This tax amounted to a fourth part of the annual income derived from the sale of produce from the land. This was the Mughal way of collecting taxes. As previously mentioned land was not owned, but the right to collect taxes could be passed on. But no less than four separate Maratha groups thought they had the right to collect this tribute. Understandably there was trouble, as nobody likes his or her livelihood being taken. However Pilagi was more acceptable as a ruler as he tried to govern the district and give something back, rather than just extract taxes from it. This led him into conflict with the other Maratha commanders who resented him taking on ruling powers.

The Mughal leader tried to hang onto power in Gujarat by making deals with the Marathas. He sent his envoy, Hamid Khan, into the province with the result that deals were struck with two of the Maratha leaders, Pilagi Gaekwad and Kadam Bande. Pilagi was to have the exclusive right to collect taxes from the area south of the Mahi River. But this upset the two other Maratha groups, including the leaders of the Politic.

However the situation was more complex than this as the leaders of the Politic were also in conflict with each other. The field commanders in Gujarat were forced to take sides. Pilagi sided with the Senapati, Dabhade. This led him into dispute with the Peshwa. The dispute was passed on to the next generation and eventually resulted in the Gaekwads making an alliance with the British against the Peshwa. It has been argued that this dispute provided the excuse that set in motion the Company's war against the Peshwa which eventually lead to the ruin of the Maratha Confederacy itself.[4]

In 1725 Pilagi captured Baroda. There is a story that Pilagi was actually invited to take over the city after the locals were incensed by an incident when corrupt Mughal officials abducted and ravished some local maidens.[5] More likely the rule of Pilagi was probably thought to be much more tolerable than that of the Mughals. The chiefs of the Bhil and Koli tribes, who inhabited the area, had cooperated with Pilaji for some years. Baroda

7. The Rise of the Gaekwads and the start of the Anglo-Maratha War

was, and still is, a prosperous city just south of the river Mahe, surrounded by fertile farmland.

Meanwhile, further into Gujarat, the Mughals were fighting each other. The Mughal Emperor sent an army under Abhaysingh to chastise the local governor, based in Ahmedabad, and take him in chains back to Delhi.

On the Maratha front, the Peshwa sent an army into Gujarat to subdue the Senapati and his ally Pilagi. The two armies met at Dabhoi, near Baroda, in 1731. Senapati Dabhade was killed and Pilagi was wounded. However the end result was favourable for the Gaekwads as the Peshwa then appointed Pilagi to act as his agent in Gujarat.

Abhaysingh was unable to subdue Pilagi and, in 1732, invited him to a parley. An unanswered question is why Pilagi agreed to this. Abhaysingh had murdered his own father and had a reputation for deception. Pilagi entered into the trap and was duly murdered. Abhaysingh took Baroda back and the Gaekwads were forced to retreat back to Songhar.

Enter another Gaekwad legend, another Damaji, the son of Pilagi. Damaji II retook Baroda in 1734 and, for good measure, pushed Abhaysingh out of Gujarat and back to where he came from, Jodphur. But the enmity with the new Peshwa, Balajirao, continued and, in 1751, Balajirao demanded a half share of all the gains Damaji had made in Gujarat. Damaji rejected these demands and ended up sending an army of 15,000 men to Satara. The Peshwa was ready for him and made a surprise attack. In consequence of this treachery it is said that Damaji ever after refused to salute the Peshwa except with his left hand.[6] Damaji was taken prisoner and brought back to Pune where he remained for the next two years.

But Balajirao was unable to hold Gujarat by himself so he released Damaji, under the condition that he had to share any future gains with the Peshwa, as well as pay a heavy revenue contribution. Damaji joined Balajirao's brother, Raghunathrao, and between them they took Ahmedabad in 1755, an action that finally ended Mughal rule in Gujarat. But then, in 1761, when it looked as if no one could defeat the Marathas, came the aforementioned defeat and slaughter at Panipat. Damaji Gaekwad was lucky to escape with his life and troops intact.

Balajirao died in 1761 and was succeeded by his son Madhavrao. Initially uncle Raghunathrao supported him. But Raghunathrao's wife, Anandibai, and Madhavrao's mother, fanned the flames of rivalry.[7] In 1768 Raghunathrao marched on Pune. Damaji agreed to send a column under

7. The Rise of the Gaekwads and the start of the Anglo-Maratha War

his son, Gavindrao, to support the rebel army. Why had he done this? Resentment had been building up over the tribute he had to pay to the Peshwa (a half share of all his gains) and he had fought beside Raghunathrao on many previous occasions against the Mughals.

Raghunathrao's army was defeated at Dhodap and both he and Gavindrao were taken prisoner.

Normally this would not have created a major problem as the Gaekwads were strong in Gujarat and terms of release could have been negotiated. But then Damaji picked the wrong time to die. His death was in effect a tragedy as it resulted in a succession dispute amongst Damaji's sons, one of whom was Fatesingh, our future Maharajah.

Damaji had six sons. The eldest, Sayajirao, was described as *feeble-minded* or, by Grant Duff, as *an idiot*. Presumably Sayajirao suffered from a learning or intellectual disability. Govindrao, currently a prisoner of the Peshwa, was next in line to take over. It was then that Fatesingh made his bid. The future leader of the Gaekwads has been described as *more resourceful and energetic* than the others.[8] Initially the Peshwa supported Govindrao but Fatesingh, back in Baroda, made himself the champion of Sayajirao. He went to the Peshwa's court and managed to persuade the Peshwa to change his mind. In one account he was described as directing his *remarkable talents and energy* to win over the courtiers with *judicious bribes and tempting promises*.[9] At this time Madhavrao was terminally ill and may not have shown much interest. In 1771 Sayajirao was appointed as Damaji's successor, with Fatesingh as his agent.

Unfortunately for the Gaekwads the terms imposed by Pune remained harsh. In fact the amount of tribute that had to be sent to Pune was unsustainable.

The British had actually arrived in Gujarat long before the Gaekwads. As mentioned the Company set up a factory in Surat in 1612. But the EIC only had trading posts at Surat and Bombay Island and they did not have control of any of the hinterland. There had been no Clive in western India and no take-over of territory, as in Bengal and Madras. The Bombay Presidency had its eye on securing its base on Bombay Island by taking over the neighbouring island of Salsette (Salsette is now part of the suburbs of Mumbai). In addition they wanted to take control of the fortress of Bassein, just up the coast. But the strength of the Marathas and their refusal

7. The Rise of the Gaekwads and the start of the Anglo-Maratha War

MAHRATTAS.—From Forbes, Oriental Memoirs; and Burnouf, L'Inde Française.

Maratha Horseman. Print from Beveridge History of India. 1862

to concede territory made this impossible. But this did not stop them from keeping an eye out for the main chance.

This became possible in the 1770s with the split between Raghunathrao and the Peshwa and developed into what later became known as the First Anglo-Maratha War (1774 to 1783).

When Fatesingh returned to Gujarat in 1772 he had no intention of following the terms of the treaty with Pune.[10] This would have been financial suicide. But his brother Govindrao was not prepared to step aside and let him rule on behalf of his older brother, Sayajirao. Fatesingh decided to move his capital from Songhar to Baroda and appealed to the British in Surat for help. The British wanted to help but they did not want to antagonise the Peshwa. They did however agree to attack Broach (Bharouch) and continue to pay the tribute from that district to Fatesingh. This was the first land-grabbing action by the British in western India. Broach is a strategic town on the mouth of the river Narmada, just south of Baroda.

7. The Rise of the Gaekwads and the start of the Anglo-Maratha War

In November 1772 the Peshwa, Madhavrao, died at the age of twenty-eight and was succeeded by his younger brother Narayanrao. Raghunathrao was to be his mentor and actual rule was to be shared. Madhavrao's widow, Rumna Bye, immolated herself on his funeral pyre.[11] Duff described the death of Madhavrao as a tragedy. *The plains of Panipat were not more fatal to the Mahratta Empire than the early end of this excellent prince.*[12]

Eight months later Narayanrao, aged eighteen, was murdered, supposedly on Raghunathrao's orders. Raghunathrao admitted that he had planned to seize Narayanrao, but not murder him. He admitted to writing an order to *seize* the young Peshwa, but the gossip was that his wife had altered the order from seize (*dhurawè*) to kill (*marawè*).[13] At the time the murder took place Raghunathrao was being held in protective custody in Pune. Contemporary accounts describe Narayanrao running to Raghunathrao and clinging onto him for protection. The attackers then threatened Raghunathrao so he released Narayanrao who was dragged away by his feet and dispatched with a sword stroke.[14]

But Raghunathrao did not last long as Peshwa. Because of the mode of his ascent to power, and his general manner and distrust of others, he had made many enemies. And Gangabai, Naranyanrao's widow, was found to be pregnant. When Raghunathrao was away campaigning in the Deccan, Ramshastri, the chief judge, pronounced him guilty of the plot to murder Narayanrao.[15] The Brahmins in Pune, led by Nana Fadnavis and Haripant Phadnis, plotted to subvert Raghunathrao. Gangabai's son was born on 18th March 1774 and pronounced as the new Peshwa with Nana Fadnavis and his ministers as regents.

So Raghunathrao was out in the cold again. He sought help from Mahadji Scindia and Tukoji Holkar without success and ended up being taken prisoner by them. He escaped and fled to Gujarat, allying with the displaced Govindrao Gaekwad. He then asked the British for help. The Bombay Council agreed to help and the Treaty of Surat was signed in 1775. In return for 2500 Company troops, Raghunathrao agreed to cede Salsette and Bassein in perpetuity to the British, should the campaign prove successful.[16] The need to take over Salsette and Bassein was becoming increasingly important to the British as the Portuguese were threatening to invade.[17]

In February 1774 the Company army advanced from Bombay across the island of Salsette to the fort of Thana, supported by navy ships. The fort had been originally built by the Portuguese and was situated to the north end of Salsette, just across from the mainland. The final assault did not take place until the following December.[18]

The war around Surat did not go so well for the combined forces of the EIC and Raghunathrao. They were poorly commanded by Colonel Keating and had insufficient resources to attack Pune. In May 1775 they were defeated at Adas by the Peshwa's forces supported by Fatesingh, who was familiar with the territory. Although both sides claimed victory it was clear that the battle had been a shambles on the part of the Company. Apparently orders were misinterpreted and a *face to the right*, became a *right about face*, in other words a retreat. Up to 400 Company troops, including eighty-six Europeans and eleven officers, were killed. The survivors of the Bombay army camped at Dabhoi, near Baroda, when the rains set in. The Marathas retreated to Songar.

There is an interesting account in Duff's 1826 history of a meeting between the Company and Peshwa's forces just prior to the Battle of Adas. Colonel Keating made an *unauthorised attempt* to ally with Fatesingh in a move to detach him from the Pune army. Fatesingh pretended to accept the overtures. Colonel Keating's agent, a certain Lieutenant George Lovibard, was sent to the Maratha camp. When he got to the camp he was shown to a tent where he was made to wait for a whole day in the company of *inferiors*. But *Mr Lovibard, by not bursting into a passion, which would be expected in a European, probably disappointed them of half their mirth.*[19]

But Fatesingh did eventually decide to join the British after Colonel Keating was persuaded by Govindrao to reduce Baroda. This plot backfired on Govindrao as, to stop this happening, Fatesingh agreed join the British and supply 3000 horse. His brother was sent to exile in the Deccan.

While all this was going on the British parliament had become increasingly concerned with events in India. In 1773 a decision had been made to reduce the power of the EIC. This will be looked at in further detail in a later chapter. The 'Regulating Act', passed by parliament that year, gave the Bengal Presidency overall power over the other Presidencies in relation to war. Furthermore a decision was made to run the Bengal Council as a committee where the majority of members would be appointed by parliament. Although Warren Hastings was appointed as Governor-General, he had no casting vote over the other members of the

Council. Not surprisingly this led to many difficulties and ultimately to a duel that took place between Warren Hastings and Phillip Francis, the council member who most opposed him.

The Council was set up when the so-called *new gentlemen* arrived at Calcutta in October 1774. The opinion of the Supreme Council was that the war with the Marathas should be stopped. This ruling is best summarised by transcribing the letter that was sent to the Bombay Council on the 31st May 1775:

Our duty imposed upon us the painful necessity that we totally condemn the measures which you have adopted; that we hold the treaty which you have entered into with Ragoba invalid; and the war which you have undertaken against the Maratha State impolitic, dangerous, unauthorised, and unjust. Both are expressly contrary to the late Act of Parliament. You have imposed on yourselves the charge of conquering the whole Maratha Empire, for a man who appears incapable of affording you any effectual assistance in it. The plan which you have formed, instead of aiming at a decisive conquest, portends an indefinite scene of troubles, without an adequate force, without money or certain resources to extricate you from them; nor have you the plea either of injury sustained from the party which you have made your enemy, or of any obligation to defend the man whose cause you have espoused. We solemnly require you to withdraw all the Company's forces to your garrisons in whatsoever state your affairs may be, unless their safety may be endangered by an instant retreat.[20]

The Bengal Council also announced plans to negotiate with Pune and send an envoy, Lieutenant Colonel Upton, to Pune, to apologise and make a new treaty. Understandably the Bombay Council was not happy with this plan. One wonders what Fatesingh and Raghunathrao would have thought about all this too. Is this how the British conduct their affairs?

Lieutenant Colonel Upton travelled the arduous 948 miles overland from Kalpi to Pune and arrived there in December 1775. The end result was the Treaty of Purandhar, which was eventually signed by all parties in April 1776. The terms of this treaty was that Salsette was to be returned and Raghunathrao was to be handed over.

However the Bombay Council were not in full agreement with the treaty and thought it best to continue to offer Raghunathrao protection

7. The Rise of the Gaekwads and the start of the Anglo-Maratha War

in Bombay. Bizarrely the Court of Directors in England then supported Bombay by advising that the terms of the Treaty of Surat should be honoured. Who was in charge here? The decision to give overall control to Bengal was hard to operate in practice as the journey time between the two Presidencies could be several months. And it took a year to communicate with London.

Then the French got involved.

On the 16th March 1777 a French ship, *Le Sartine,* arrived at Chaul, just down the coast from Bombay. The ship carried a military cargo and a French envoy, Monsieur le Chevalier de Saint-Lubin, who proceeded to the Maratha Court at Pune. On the world stage, the British were at war with the Americans colonists. In 1776 they were forced to evacuate Boston. At the time the French were allied to the Americans but had not as yet declared war against the British.

The problem for the British was that Nana Fadnavis, the regent in Pune, appeared to be accepting the overtures of Monsieur Lubin. In a letter to Hastings, Thomas Mostyn, the new envoy in Pune, wrote that *this diabolical scheme had opened a door the most destructive to our interests that could have been thought of.*[22] Furthermore a letter had been intercepted by the English in which Lubin had written to the Portuguese in Goa asking for free passage for French regiments. At the time no such regiments existed.[22] The opinion of the British was that, if the Marathas allied to the French, this could mean the end of the EIC in India.

Clearly this was a very volatile situation. With the new Peshwa still an infant, Pune was ruled by a regency and the British were unsure who really had overall power. And the French were hovering in the wings, about to declare war.

Meanwhile Fatesingh, in Baroda, was in a difficult position. His alliance with the EIC was now void and the Treaty of Purandhar had put him back under the control of Pune who were now demanding their arrears in tax.[23] He had no option but to pay up. As a result, in February 1778, he was officially appointed by Pune as ruler of the Gaekwads.

We will now leave the complexities of the Anglo-Maratha War and travel back in time to 1768 and return to Solomon Earle. You will remember from Chapter Four, a Passage to India, that he had just arrived in Calcutta.

PART THREE : EARLY YEARS IN INDIA

8. Bengal and the Company Army : 1768 to 1772

This chapter will cover the four-year period from Solomon's arrival in India in August 1768, to Jan 1772, when he was posted to Lucknow. During this time he was learning his new career as an officer in the Bengal army. As mentioned in Chapter Four, when he arrived in Bengal, Solomon only spent a few days in Calcutta before being sent up river.

June to September is monsoon time in Calcutta, so August would have been one of the most humid and unpleasant months of the year in which to arrive. In 1768 Calcutta was still in the process of being rebuilt following the ravages of the 1756 war. Fort William, originally in the centre of the city, was in the process of being rebuilt at a more suitable site. The old fort had become a centre for the civil rather than military establishment. No doubt the 'black hole,' the prison in its outer wall, was still there and Solomon was likely to have visited it.

When I went to Calcutta in 2016, I tried to find in vain to find the location of the black hole. The site is now occupied by the Post Office Buildings. A plaque that used to mark the spot has been removed and the memorial is now in the grounds of St. John's Church.

The inhabitants of the native village situated between Chowringhee and the river got notice to quit to enable the new Fort William to be constructed.[1] Trees and buildings were cleared to make the new fort defensible, opening up clear lines of fire for artillery. In practice the defences of the new fort, now garrisoned by the Indian army, were never put to use. The old fort had been particularly vulnerable because warehouses had been built right up to its walls and other buildings overlooked it.

The area around the new fort is now a large wide-open space called the Maidan. At weekends it is packed with men and boys playing cricket. In Solomon's time it was the place where the British went for their evening rides. The remains of the old St. John's church, the Governor's House, the original Writer's Building and numerous Company offices and warehouses would have occupied the centre of the city. The church was rebuilt

8. Bengal and the Company Army : 1768 to 1722

from 1784 to 1787. The churchyard still contains the mausoleum of Job Charnock, founder of the city.

St. John's Church, Calcutta, Photo 2016

When Charnock first came to the bend in the Hoogli River to found his factory there were just two small villages on the mud-flats, Sutanuti and Kalikata. Kalikata consisted of a few dwellings gathered around a temple dedicated to the goddess Kali. The temple is still there.

James Macintosh, quoted in Newman and Co.'s Handbook to Calcutta, described the city in 1780:

> *It is a truth that from the Western extremity of California to the Eastern Coast of Japan, there is not a spot where judgement, taste, decency, and convenience are so grossly insulted, as in that scattered and confused chaos of houses, huts, streets, lanes, alleys, windings, gutters, sinks and tanks, which, jumbled into an undistinguished mass of filth and corruption, equally offensive to human sense and health, compose the capital of the English Company's Government in India.*[2]

In other words Calcutta was similar to London at the time. The *tank* was an area just east of the old fort where water was once stored. It is now a large square.

Out on the river Hoogly there would have been a profusion of boats and ships of all shapes and sizes. The Hoogly was navigable by larger ships, but only at high tide. Beyond the town there would have been mudflats, swamps and jungle. Malaria was rife and other diseases such as cholera were common. In those days doctors believed that cholera was spread by *miasma* in the air, rather than by contaminated water. The South Park Cemetery, just south of the city, was opened in 1767, but closed in 1790 as it had filled up. It is now a fascinating place to visit, packed with mausoleums and shrines of East India Company officers and merchants, most of who rarely lived to old age.

As mentioned, when Solomon arrived in Calcutta, he wrote that he received some sad news. He learnt that his uncle, Captain Mills, and his cousin, Captain Adams of the Engineers, had both died just a few months previously. It is likely Captain Mills was the brother of his mother, as her maiden name was Mills. I have been unable to trace his cousin, but Adams was a common name in Ashburton, so it is likely that he came from there too.

Solomon wrote that, although these were *heavy losses,* he soon recovered his spirits in the *new success* around him, and on receiving *great kindness from several gentlemen in the civil and military service,* to which he had letters from Mr Sullivan and Sir Robert Palk.

Perhaps Solomon was invited to a few of the larger houses for dinner or tea. In some ways it was probably good for him that he did not stay too long in Calcutta. Apart from the risk of infectious disease there were also other temptations including the consumption of prodigious amounts of alcohol, over-eating and gambling. The locals in Calcutta tried to reproduce life in England and wore western dress, including wigs and coats, despite the oppressive heat.

Soon after arrival Solomon left for *Moaghip* where he was appointed as ensign. Moaghip is likely to be Monghyr Fort, now known as Munger, in the state of Bihar. Monghyr Fort was the final refuge for Mir Kasim, the last Moslem ruler of Bengal, when he was deposed by the British after the Battle of Buxar in 1764. The British had considered attacking Monghyr

8. Bengal and the Company Army : 1768 to 1722

Fort in 1757, after Plassey. After the battle Colonel Eyre Coote pursued Jean Law, the French Governor, to the fort, but it was considered too risky to attack it at that time as it was well defended. In 1766 the fort became the site of one of the so-called 'white mutinies' when British officers mutinied after it had been decided to reduce their *batta* (extra pay when away from base). Robert Clive personally travelled to Monghyr to suppress the mutiny. The main instigator, Colonel Robert Fletcher, was court-marshalled and cashiered. But he still returned to England a rich man, before joining the ranks of Clive's enemies.

THE FORT OF MONGHIR.—From Bacon's Oriental Portfolio.

Monghyr Fort. Print from Beveridge. 1860s

Monghyr Fort was built in 1330 by Emperor Tughluq of Delhi. However there are signs of Hindu habitation from centuries before. It remains an imposing structure on the banks of the Ganges. There are various tombs inside the fort, including one of a Sufi saint.

Samuel Taylor Coleridge's older brother John, who was know to Solomon, wrote a letter home from Monghyr in 1774. It is thought that some of the wording in this letter may have inspired John's younger brother when he wrote the poem, Kubla Khan in 1797. John wrote:

8. Bengal and the Company Army : 1768 to 1722

You have no doubt heard of Monghyr famous for its wild romantic situation, and especially for its being the Mountpelier [3] of the East. About 2 miles from the garrison there is a Hotwell in which the water continually boils. The Natives esteem it sacred and flock thither from all parts of the Country to receive a holy sprinkling, as they imagine it has the Virtue of cleansing them of their sins. [4]

During his time at Monghyr garrison Solomon would have received some basic training. In 1769 he was posted to the 17th Battalion of Sepoys, commanded by Captain Briscoe.

At this juncture it would be of benefit to outline the organisation of the EIC army, essentially a private army set up to guard the Company's interests in India. The EIC army should be distinguished from the regular army, or King's Army, which was administered by the Crown.

There has never been a private army as large as that of the EIC. By 1803 the Company army employed 260,000 men. [5] In 1780 there were around 1000 officers commissioned, but only fifty-two of the rank of major and above. [6] Because of this, promotion above the rank of lieutenant was hard to come by. Before 1775 commissions could not be purchased, as they were in the regular army at the time. [7] This meant that the social composition of Company officers was different from the regular army as appointment was not dependent on money and influence. The result of this was that some officers in the regular army looked down on their counterparts in the Company army as they were deemed to come from a lower social order. As we have seen with Solomon, in order to enter as a cadet in the Company army, a candidate needed a recommendation from a person of good standing, local to the cadet's place of birth or long-term residence, together with a sponsor from a member of the Court of Directors in London.[8]

During Solomon's time in India there were few British troops employed in the Company army. Company officers commanded Indian battalions manned by sepoys (Indian soldiers). In addition to the soldiers there were hoards of support staff, not to mention the dependents of the soldiers. It is an incredible fact, when looked at from the modern day, that each soldier had between five to ten camp followers, including wives and servants. [9]

To be successful, officers had to earn the respect of their men. Many of the sepoys were high cast Brahmins and others were Moslems. They

8. Bengal and the Company Army : 1768 to 1722

had a reputation for fighting hard, but only if well led. In the eighteenth century there was much more social interaction between the soldiers and their officers. In those days many Europeans took Indian wives, who were known as *bibis*. But by the end of the eighteenth century inter-racial liaisons were discouraged and racial and religious discrimination became more prevalent.

Sepoys in the Bengal and Bombay armies.
Prints from Beveridge, History of India. 1862

As previously described, the origins of the Company army go back to the war in the Carnatic in the 1740s when the French, under Dupleix, took Madras. Major Stringer Lawrence organised the defence forces into battalions with native officers and non commissioned Officers (NCOs) commanded by British officers. Holmes argued that these forces were particularly successful, not necessarily due to superior weaponry, but due to better organisation and discipline.[10] Hence Company troops were able to triumph against far superior odds. Navarane explores this in more detail in the conclusion to his account of the battles of the EIC.[11] Company officers were trained to drill troops and instil confidence in their ability to succeed against the odds.

8. Bengal and the Company Army : 1768 to 1722

The Maratha armies deployed highly effective cavalry soldiers armed with razor sharp cutlasses known as *tulwars,* which were kept in leather scabbards. These weapons were far superior to army officers' swords that were blunted by their metal scabbards. The Marathas also had field artillery and rockets at their disposal. Generally the British were more successful when they adopted quick and organised offensive action, rather than defence or retreat. When forces retreated, disasters were more likely to happen, as we shall see later at Wadgaon in 1779.

The pay of Company officers at the time barely covered their expenses and expenses on campaign could be huge as officers had to purchase their own equipment. An example of an equipment list at the time included: a tent, camp bed, camp table, a good horse (expensive in India), bullocks, two servants, baskets of provisions, cheroots, telescope, rifle and ammunition. In some cases, for those who could afford it, a palanquin and bearers were employed.[12] To fund these expenses junior officers borrowed money, with a plan to pay off their debts when they got promotion. As we shall see later, when we look at the letters of John Coleridge, junior officers could build up large debts. Extra funds could come from three sources: (1) 'detached' commands, (2) *batta,* and (3) prize money, or loot.

An example of a detached command is a secondment to another force. In 1772 Solomon was posted to Lucknow. At the time members of the Company army had been sent to support the Vizier of Oudh, funded by that state. They were effectively a mercenary army. The reasoning behind supporting Oudh in this way was in order to create a buffer zone to protect the western borders of Bengal.

Batta or *country batta* was the extra pay awarded to troops serving away from their base. This was paid during campaigns. *Batta* could amount to a four-fold increase in pay. Officers got used to this extra pay and mutinied on three occasions between 1766 and 1809 when there were threats to abolish or reduce these payments.

Prize money was a legal form of loot paid out from the distribution of the enemy's public property after they had been defeated in battle. Prize money was distributed by a strict code where more senior officers were allocated a great deal more. The word loot comes from the Hindustani *lut,* which means robbery or plunder.[13] Attempts were made to stop uncontrolled looting, sometimes unsuccessfully, after towns had been taken by storm. Later in our account Solomon wrote, with some satisfaction, that he was able to control his troops after the storming of Ahmedabad in 1780.

8. Bengal and the Company Army : 1768 to 1722

But this was not the case when Seringapatum was finally taken in 1799. Some of the loot from Seringapatum can be viewed at the Victoria and Albert Museum in London. In practice it was quite normal in those days for armies to profit in this way following a victory.

The basic weapon of the Company army at the time was the 'Brown Bess' musket. This was a muzzle-loading, smoothbore musket that was standard issue in the British army from 1722 until 1838. It is unclear where the name came from. Part of the weapon was brown in colour, the stock being made from walnut wood. The name Bess could have come from the word arquebuss or blunderbuss. The 'India' pattern Brown Bess was eventually adopted for the regular army in the Napoleonic wars when up to three million were manufactured.

The Brown Bess musket was only effective up to 175 yards, being most effective when fired en mass at fifty yards. The musket fired a ball made smaller for ease of loading. Cartridges were made up with a measured amount of black powder (gun powder) wrapped in paper. The soldier bit off the end of the paper and poured a small amount of black powder into the pan. The rest was rammed down the barrel, followed by the ball and its paper wrapping. Trained and disciplined soldiers could fire three rounds per minute. A triangular shaped bayonet was attached to the end of the barrel when the soldier engaged in hand-to-hand combat.

The Brown Bess was replaced after 1838 by percussion cap muskets that were more reliable. These were in turn replaced in 1857 by the Enfield rifle. The Enfield rifle was accurate to a much greater range due to its rifled barrel. However the introduction of the Enfield rifle caused major unrest amongst the sepoys in India. This was because the cartridge came pre-manufactured and ready-greased. It was never clear where the grease came from, but rumours spread that it was made from beef or pork fat. This understandably upset both Hindus and Muslims alike and became one of the triggers for the 1857 rebellion.

It is likely that, in addition to drill, Solomon would have been trained in the use of artillery. In Chapter Four we saw that the *Salisbury* carried different types of artillery and shot to India. This included nine and twelve-pounder canon, many brass cannon and one mortar. Field guns could fire both round shot and canister.[14] Canister shot consisted of a container filled with metal balls. The canister exploded on exit from the canon ejecting the shot forward with devastating effect. Round shot from a twelve-pounder

8. Bengal and the Company Army : 1768 to 1722

would hit the ground initially at 1063 yards (the 'first graze'). Mortars fired explosive bombs used in siege warfare.

We know Solomon stayed at Monghyr for about eighteen months. On the 11th June 1770 he was promoted to the rank of lieutenant. Soon after this he saw his first action when he was ordered on an expedition to attack *Burrareah, a strong mud fort about forty miles to the northward of Chuprah.* Chuprah was a major centre for the refining of saltpetre, used in the manufacture of gunpowder. Saltpetre was shipped down the Ganges and, together with salt, became a large part of the *country* trade. There is no trace of *Burrareah* fort on the map now. His commander at the time was Lieutenant Colonel Goddard. We will come across Thomas Goddard later in this account. He was a favourite of Warren Hastings and they exchanged numerous letters, many of which can be seen at the British Library.

Solomon wrote that this action was, *the first, and had nearly been the last time I had seen service.* As duty officer at night, near the fort, he heard a noise and thought that the *Killadar* of the fort might be trying to make his escape by boat. He described creeping on his hands and knees to the edge of the ditch and spotting a canoe. But at that moment the guards of the fort raised the alarm. He could see blue lights of the matchlocks of about twenty to thirty of the enemy just near him. Luckily they did not fire and he was able to make his escape, *at a tolerably quick pace,* the moment their lights were extinguished.

A breach was then made in the walls of the fort and his battalion got ready to storm. But before they could attack, the Killadar surrendered. Solomon wrote that nothing of value was found in the fort. They then *adjusted matters* with the Killadar and returned to Dinapore. Dinapore is now a satellite town of Patna situated on the south bank of the Ganges. It is famous as a shelter and hatchery for migrating Siberian Cranes who land there during the monsoon season.

Unfortunately no information is available, apart from the above, about this action, or who the Killadar was. At the time, the Company army was kept busy defending the frontiers of the State of Bengal that were often subject to raids from the north. It could have been a punishment raid to secure tax payments.

In the autumn of 1770 Solomon and his battalion were ordered to Buxar where they stayed for eighteen months. At the time Buxar was a small, fortified town. In 1764 Buxar had been the location of the decisive

8. Bengal and the Company Army : 1768 to 1722

battle, previously mentioned, between the Company army and an alliance consisting of Mir Kasim, the Nawab of Oudh and the Mughal Emperor, Shah Alam II. The alliance fell apart at the time of the battle and a smaller force of 7 to 10,000 Company troops were able to defeat the combined opposition of 40,000 men. The EIC commander at Buxar was Lieutenant Colonel Hector Munro, a gentleman we will come across in a later chapter.

Throughout his account Solomon does not record anything about the famine of 1770. He must have been aware what was happening in the countryside at this time, but the effects of the famine may not have affected Bihar as much as Bengal. As previously mentioned the great famine of Bengal had its origins in the failure of the monsoon in 1769. The worst effects on the population of Bengal took place the following year when the food ran out. Some attempts were made to provide food from Calcutta but this could only be a drop in the ocean. Millions died across the State of Bengal. At the same time the full effects of the EIC policy of leaving the running of the country to the corrupt older administration had taken their toll and this had resulted in an almost complete collapse of government.[15] As a result of Clive's *Dual System* attempts to rule by the Nawab's government had let loose a horde of minor officials to prey on the peasants.[16] This state of affairs was made worse by the *banyans,* who attached themselves to minor Company administrators who in turn encouraged this as they needed to make money to supplement their meagre pay. There was limited regulation from Calcutta where the pressure to make money to send back to England became paramount.

Nick Robins described the Bengal Famine as, *perhaps one of the worst examples of corporate mismanagement in history.*[17] Proper government of a country included the responsibility to put aside some of the tax revenues to provide for the population during bad times. There is evidence that attempts were made to provide for the population during future famines. For example, in 1784, Warren Hastings commissioned the construction of a huge grain store, the Golah, at Bankipur, near Patna. This immense structure was finally completed in 1786 and still stands, towering nearly 100 feet over the Ganges.

8. Bengal and the Company Army : 1768 to 1722

The Grain Golah at Bankipur.
Photograph by permission of the British in India Museum, Nelson, Lancashire, UK

In January 1772 Solomon was ordered to Benares (Varanasi). At Benares he joined the *first brigade of a large body of troops belonging to the Vizier Sugah ul Dowlah, commanded by the Nabob in person.* This was one of the first batch of troops to be sent to Oudh (Awadh) to help the Nawab defend his kingdom. At the time there was a risk of invasion from the Marathas situated to the south and west. Benares, on the banks of the Ganges, is the holiest of the seven sacred cities of the Hindu and Jain religions.

9. Warren Hastings

Warren Hastings. From Beveridge History of India 1862

It is impossible to follow the history of the British in India in the 1770s and 80s without coming across the EIC's first Governor-General, Warren Hastings. On the one hand he comes across as a man who did his best to correct some of the problems of Bengal. But from the very beginning his task as Governor-General was to keep the EIC solvent. Because of this it was inevitable that some of his actions would be controversial. In fact, after he returned to England in 1785, Hastings became the subject of a great trial, or impeachment, which lasted for seven years. The trial was held in Westminster Hall, London and was attended by all the important

9. Warren Hastings

people of the day, including royalty. In subsequent years some of his more positive contributions to the development of modern India have been acknowledged and several favourable biographies have been published about his life.

The most notable of these is the biography by Mervyn Davies, entitled *Strange Destiny, A Biography of Warren Hastings*.[1] This book was published in 1935, a time when the British still ruled India, and is gushing with praise for Hastings. The next significant biography was by written by Keith Feiling in 1954.[2] This account of Hasting's life is more comprehensive, but written in a rather off-putting, verbose style. Bernstein's biography appeared in 2001.[3] Two more recent historians, Hardy[4] and Robins,[5] are less positive about Hastings' contribution, but they were concentrating more on Clive and the EIC respectively, rather than the man himself. The three aforementioned biographies start with the premise that Hastings was a great man who was sadly misunderstood, then badly treated and used as a scapegoat by the British establishment.

Hastings himself did not publish any autobiographical memoirs, but he wrote copious letters and reports as part of his job. He also wrote many letters to his friends and family and was obliged to minute all his actions as Governor-General. Bernstein described this paper trail as filling some three hundred volumes.[6] Much of this correspondence is stored in the British Library. One advantage of conducting a study of the EIC is that there is plenty of documentation. But it is also daunting due to the sheer volume of material, and the fact that the majority of it is hand-written and can be hard to decipher.

There is no doubt that Hastings had some faults. He would have been the first to accept that he had some *dark spots in his fame*, as put by Macauley.[7] But it is also clear he was a man who strived hard to be fair in an unprejudiced way and it is hard to claim he lacked personal integrity. The problem was that he had to restore the Company to profitability and security after the crash and he made a number of dubious decisions when it became necessary to raise money to fund the Maratha and Carnatic wars.

Hastings was born in 1732. He never saw his parents as his mother died in childbirth and his father took off, leaving Warren and his sister Anne in the care of others. In the past the Hastings family had owned Daylesford Manor in the Cotswolds. But the family had fallen on hard times. It was Hastings' ambition to buy back the family seat. He finally succeeded in

9. Warren Hastings

1788, but at great financial cost. Despite this he was never accepted by the British aristocracy.

After years of neglect young Warren had a stroke of luck when his uncle decided to pay for his education at Westminster School, in London. His education ended when his uncle died a few years later and Hastings enrolled as a writer in the EIC. He sailed for India in 1750 at the age of eighteen. Two years later he was sent up river from Calcutta to Kasimbazar, where the Company had a trading post.

The young man was studious and keen to learn the local languages, including Urdu, Bengali and Persian, the language of the Mughal government. He avoided the excessive drinking and gambling culture that was prevalent at the time. When Calcutta was sacked by Siraj-ud-Daula in 1756, Hastings had risen to a senior position. He was initially taken prisoner in Kasimbazar but was then helped by his Dutch and Indian friends and allowed a certain amount of freedom.

As previously described there were then several years of anarchy and misrule in Bengal following Clive's victory at Plassey. Mir Kasim replaced Mir Jafar and in 1761 Hastings was promoted to a seat on the Calcutta Council.[8] But this promotion proved to be a poisoned chalice as he then became part of the dysfunctional establishment and, in trying to make changes, he made enemies. The Company were part of the problem in Bengal at the time as their huge demands for payments from Mir Kasim were unsustainable and inevitably resulted in war. Mir Kasim retreated to his fortress at Monghyr. A foolish attempt was made by the EIC, under Ellis, to seize Patna. This resulted in a massacre of the British mission. Many battles followed and, as mentioned, the Company army eventually triumphed at Buxar in 1764.

Hastings waited until the end of the war before sailing for home. He felt that he could no longer work for the Council because of his criticism of their actions and their failure to seek working compromises with the Mughal government. But he was not to remain in England for long. In 1768, he was appointed as 'second' to the new Governor of Madras, Josias Du Pre.

During the outward voyage Hastings became a close friend of the woman that he was later to marry, Maria Imhoff. At the time she was married to Baron Imhoff who had enrolled as a cadet in the Company army. Despite this Hastings remained on close terms with Maria's husband and supported them both financially.

9. Warren Hastings

To put things in context, Solomon sailed for Calcutta in March 1768, while Hastings sailed in March 1769. In the same year the *Aurora* sailed for Calcutta bringing three new governors to Bengal. They had been appointed by the Court of Directors in London in an attempt to resolve the problems there. As previously mentioned, this ship disappeared without trace. Then the monsoon failed in Bengal precipitating the great famine. Back in London the Company increased share dividends to 12.5% in an attempt to raise money to pay their debts. The bubble was about to burst.

On his arrival in Madras Hastings found that the commercial department was so grossly mismanaged that it was a comparatively simple matter to devise improvements.[9] He tried to find ways of improving the lot of the Indian weavers who depended on trade with Madras for their livelihood. Just to the west of Madras, Hydar Ali had taken over as ruler of Mysore and periodically sent armies to lay waste to the countryside around Madras.[10]

During his short time in Madras Hastings developed a reputation for able and just administration. There were no objections when he was appointed as Governor of Bengal in 1771. He sailed for Calcutta in February the following year.

The period from 1772 until October 1774 was the time of Hasting's greatest achievements. After this the 'new gentlemen', the appointed representatives of HM Government, arrived in Bengal and opposed his every move. At first he had a considerable amount of leeway in his role as governor to make necessary changes. So that was what he did. Mervyn Davies described the Bengal of 1772 as having *no organised government, that was functioning regularly and properly through all its branches; there was no systematic administration of law and order, no security for person or property, no system of taxation. There was only anarchy, universal and unlimited.*[11] In practice Bengal was approaching bankruptcy.

The reforms made by Hastings can best be divided into those relating to the civil government and those reforms necessary for the security of the province:

In relation to civil government, Hastings put forward proposals to institute law and order by developing and building on Indian law. At the time Indian justice could be described as being less barbaric than the English version.[12] In England you could be hung for petty theft and flogged for lesser crimes. As a result of the great famine and the breakdown of law and order, the countryside of Bengal was awash with bandits, vagrants and dacoits. Hastings went on tour to see the results of the famine for himself. Villages had been left empty and deserted and were gradually returning to the jungle. One of Hastings' first acts was to arrest the Mughal governor, the corrupt Mohamed Reza Khan. The *Dual System* set by Clive was abolished and Hastings made plans to set up a civil service where officials would be properly paid for their work and would be banned from dabbling in *country* trade. These officials were to be called district collectors and they were to be part administrator, part magistrate and part developmental officer.[13]

He cancelled the tribute to the Mughal emperor (the price for the *Diwani*) and enforced a ban on private trade. He also decided to establish corporate rather than private monopolies over opium, salt and saltpetre as a way of increasing revenues.[14] In relation to opium it could be argued that this planted the seed for the eventual state-supported exportation of opium to China, resulting in the so-called opium wars of 1839 and 1856.

Hastings instituted a system of land reform and tried to reform tax collection to protect the ryots and help the country recover from the famine. Three parties: the State, the *Zemindar* (the collector for the State) and the cultivator of the soil (the ryot), all had a share in the revenue from the land.[15] The problem was how to secure a just share of the revenue and protect against encroachments by either of the others. It was a system very different from that in Europe where land was owned. Hastings created a postal service and backed James Rennell's completion of his geographical survey. His end plan was that Indian civilisation, *will by degrees assimilate with ours, and breed a kind of new relation and attachment to us.*[16]

In a sense it is possible to see where Hastings was trying to go. The problem was how to get there in a just and fair way. In practice his aims were never realised.

In relation to security there was much to do. As you will see from the map, the rich lands of Bengal were surrounded by many potential enemies. The Marathas had made a remarkable recovery from Panipat and had returned to invading northern India. They reoccupied Delhi in 1771 and renewed their demands on Bengal for *chauth*. They started to encroach on Rohilkhand, the area north of Oudh, and boasted that Oudh and Bengal would be next.[17]

Rohilkhand had been invaded in the 1730s by Pathans, Sunni Muslims from Afghanistan. They were known as the Rohillas. They ruled the local ryots (mainly Hindus) collecting taxes rather like the Mughals did. The

9. Warren Hastings

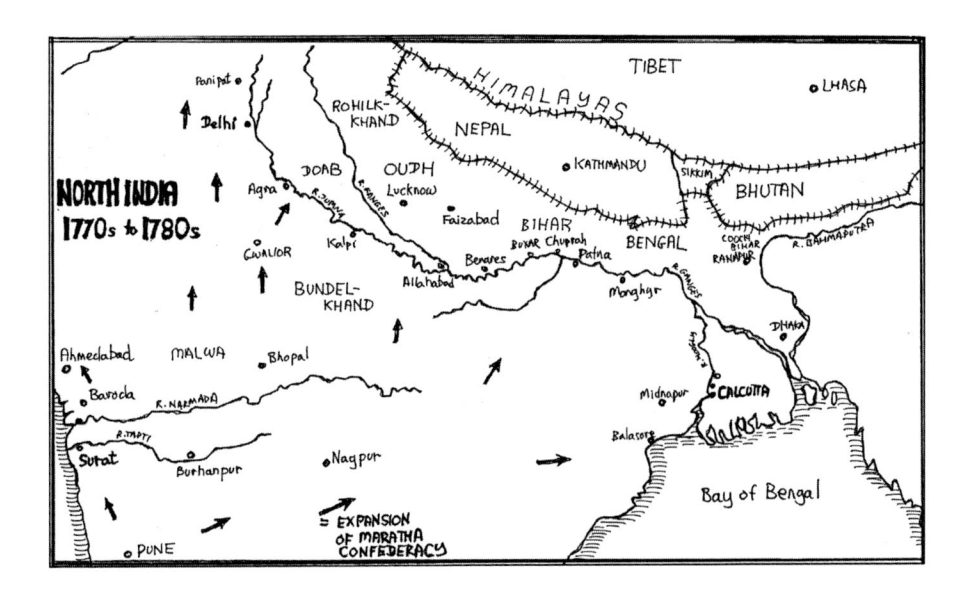

[Map: North India 1770s to 1780s, showing Tibet, Himalayas, Nepal, Bhutan, Delhi, Panipat, Rohilkhand, Doab, Oudh, Lucknow, Faizabad, Kathmandu, Sikkim, Agra, Gwalior, Kalpi, Bundelkhand, Allahabad, Benares, Buxar, Chupra, Patna, Bihar, Bengal, Cooch Bihar, Rangpur, R. Brahmaputra, Dhaka, Monghyr, Ahmedabad, Baroda, R. Narmada, Malwa, Bhopal, Surat, R. Tapti, Burhanpur, Nagpur, Midnapur, Calcutta, Balasore, Pune, Bay of Bengal, Lhasa; arrows indicate expansion of Maratha Confederacy]

Marathas, Rohillas, and the Vizier of Oudh, all had their eyes on the rich plains of the Doab, the area between the Ganges and the Jumna.[18]

Hastings was understandably concerned that Oudh might ally with the Marathas. In view of this he decided to forge an alliance with Shuja-ud-Daula, the Vizier of Oudh (a Shia Muslim). The two met at Benares in August 1773. According to Feiling, *so began a fortnight of strenuous oriental haggling.*[19] The Vizier wanted help from the British to rid him of his enemies, the Rohillas. The end result of this meeting was that Hastings agreed to cede the city of Allahabad, for cash, and in return provide a brigade to protect Oudh, paid for by the Vizier. This part of the agreement was fine, being financially advantageous to Bengal as the Vizier had to finance his own protection. But, at the same time, a verbal agreement was made to help the Vizier invade Rohilkhand should he decide to do so. This was later acknowledged to have been a step too far as the Vizier did indeed invade Oudh a year later (in 1774) and Hastings effectively supplied mercenary troops to attack a state which had not threatened Bengal.

Colonel Alexander Champion, commanding officer of the Company army, took part in this successful campaign. As with any campaign at the time a certain amount of looting took place, mainly on the part of the Vizier's troops. However Champion later exaggerated the extent of this in order to discredit Hastings. We will hear more about Solomon's impression of Colonel Champion in the next chapter, when we look at an account of a crossing of the Ganges.

9. Warren Hastings

In 1772 Hastings sent a force of sepoys into Cooch Behar on the Bhutanese border, the northernmost border state of India, to assist the local ruler against raids by the Bhutanese. [20] After peace was eventually established Hastings had in mind encouraging trade with Bhutan and Tibet. In 1774 he sent George Bogle to trace the course of the Brahmaputra River to the north, to Tibet. Bogle got as far as Shigatse in Tibet, but did not get to Lhasa, the capital. An account of his journey was published in 1876. [21]

By 1774 Hastings was beginning to solve the problems of Bengal. But storm clouds were gathering. A year earlier, unbeknown to Hastings, the British Parliament had passed the Regulating Act. This Act was the price the government had imposed for the payment of the one million pound loan to the EIC. There was a strong argument that the Company needed regulating, particularly as it had taken over the running of a province as large as the Great Britain and, as outlined, there was evidence of many abuses. But the organisation of the governing council was to cause major problems. The new Governor-General, Warren Hastings, would have no casting vote in any decisions. And the new Council, based in Calcutta, was to have overall responsibility for all three of the Presidencies. This all sounds reasonable. The difficulty lay in the choice of the 'three gentlemen' appointed to serve on the Council and assist Hastings run the province.

The most vindictive and destructive of these men was a certain individual called Philip Francis (then aged thirty four). Why Francis had been chosen to take up this high office was, and remains, unclear. He had no track record in government and no experience of India. But he did have powerful friends. For some years an anonymous pamphlet writer, with the pseudonym *Junius,* had been amusing Londoners with cynical and cutting descriptions of those in power. It is highly likely that Francis was this *Junius*. One theory is that he may have been sent to India as a way of getting him out of the country. [22] Francis was a vastly ambitious and narcissistic man who had designs to take over the governorship, despite his lack of experience. By the time Francis reached India he had the other two Governors, John Clavering (51) and George Monson (53) well under his control. It was to be three against two as Hastings had the support of the other Council member, Richard Barwell, a local man.

The three gentlemen arrived at Calcutta in October 1774. Trouble started as soon as they arrived as Hastings had only organised a seventeen-gun salute when Clavering had expected twenty-one. And Hastings was not there to great them.

What happened afterwards is described in many other accounts. Basically the three new members of the council opposed all of Hasting's plans to improve government and security. When the Vizier of Oudh died in 1775, the Council voted to increase the tribute from his son, an action that eventually had the effect of bankrupting the state of Oudh. English law was to be introduced into Bengal by the three law lords who accompanied the gentlemen. This effectively ended Hastings' plans to adapt Indian law. The previously corrupt Mughal and Hindu officials were brought back into power.

Why all this happened can be partly explained by ignorance and a failure to understand the ways and culture of the country. But there was also a feeling of ambivalence in England at the time about the right to govern Bengal. Further conquests were not part of the plan, and guidance about what Britain really wanted to do with India was unclear.

There is evidence that Francis sent a flow of correspondence back to his powerful friends in England, including the Prime Minister Lord North. This correspondence misrepresented the situation, spread rumours and decried Hastings as a monster.

The three gentlemen backed accusations of corruption against Hastings brought by an Indian factotum called Nandakumar (Nuncomar). Hastings counter-attacked by bringing charges against Nandakumar of forgery. As a result of the establishment of English Law, Nandakumar was tried, found guilty, and executed, all within the space of two months. As Nandakumar had been found guilty of the charges, British law had to follow to its inevitable conclusion. The court was presided over by the new chief justice, Elijah Impey. At his impeachment in 1788 Hastings was accused of judicial murder. Notably the three gentlemen did not come to Nandakumar's aid, despite encouraging him to bring the charges against Hastings in the first place.

By 1775 Francis was falling out with Clavering and Monson was sick, but the damage had been done. But now Hastings had the casting vote.

Mervyn Davies was scathing about the character of Philip Francis.[23] His opinion was that Francis was driven by hatred and that he used others, such as Clavering, Monson and Champion, to lead from behind. Francis' correspondence with London was effective as there was strong consideration to ask for Hastings' resignation. Unfortunately the then Prime Minister, Lord North, was in the throws of trying to contain the American rebellion and he sat on the fence regarding India.

9. Warren Hastings

By 1776 a decision was made to recall Hastings. Hastings refused to resign. Anticipating Hastings' resignation, Clavering actually staged a sort of coup d'état and tried to take over the Council and arrest Hastings. Hastings referred the matter to the Calcutta judges and they decided in his favour. By the 20th June 1776 Clavering was dead.

While all of this was going on in Bengal, the Presidencies at Bombay and Madras, *seemed to be possessed of an infinite capacity for folly.* [24] Due to poor diplomacy the Madras Presidency had failed to make peace with Hydar Ali in Mysore. In fact they had managed to instigate a bitter hatred of the English that was then passed down a generation to Hydar's son, Tipu Sultan. This had longstanding consequences.

As we saw in Chapter Seven, the Bombay Council had decided that they needed a piece of the action. They had their eyes on the adjoining island of Salsette and the fortress of Bassein, just up the coast. As part of the Regulating Act, the Governor-General in Bengal was supposed to have overall control of the three Presidencies. In practice this took some years to take effect and Bombay wanted to achieve their aims before Calcutta took over. As previously described they decided to support Raghunathrao in his bid for the Maratha Peshwaship. The end result was the commencement of what later became known as the First Anglo-Maratha War.

We will now return to Oudh to catch up with what Solomon had been up to since we left him in 1772.

10. India 1772 to 1778

A wide interminable forest. Most of the trees are sals[1], but other kinds are not wanting. Treetops mingling with treetop, foliage melting into foliage, the interminable lines progress; without crevice, without gap, without even a way for the light to enter, league after league and again league after league the boundless ocean of leaves advances, tossing wave upon wave in the wind. Underneath, thick darkness; even at midday the light is dim and uncertain; a seat of terrific gloom. There the foot of man never treads; there except the illimitable rustle of the leaves and the cry of wild beasts and birds, no sound is heard.[2]

This is a quote from the Prologue to the 1882 novel, Anandamath, by Bankim Chandra Chatterji. The novel covers the Sannayasi revolt that started in the early 1770s. After the Bengal famine, large parts of the countryside became depopulated and the forests gradually returned. Some of the dispossessed locals formed robber bands known as dacoits, a result of the general lawlessness after the famine and the breakdown of government. A group particularly affected were holy men, as they were no longer able to survive without alms donations. Some of them formed themselves into armed groups known as Sannayasis. They took refuge in hilly, forested areas like Midnapore, where Solomon was sent in 1774.

We left Solomon at Buxar. In January 1772 he was *ordered to Benares to join a large body of troops belonging to the Vizier Sugah ul Dowlah*. The Vizier was the third Nawab of Oudh, a semi-independent state. The state of Oudh had been founded in 1724 by Sa'adat Khan, a Shia Muslim from Persia, following the breakup of the Mughal Empire. The province is now known as Awadh. The capital was originally based at Faizabad, eighty miles east of Lucknow, and the state included the cities of Benares (Varanasi) and Allahabad. The capital was moved to Lucknow in 1775 by the fourth Nawab.

10. India 1772 to 1778

Benares is one of the world's oldest continually inhabited cities and remains a major centre of pilgrimage for Hindus.[3] It is situated along the south bank of the Ganges, above a series of ghats. At the time Benares was governed by the Rajah Chait Singh, who paid a tribute to the Nawab.

Solomon remained at Benares *but a few days only,* before, *proceeding to Lucknow and then into Rohilcund country, in pursuit of the Mahrattas.*

As part of the research for this book I followed the route of the Company army across the peninsular of India from Lucknow to Surat. Instead of walking, or riding a horse, I travelled by train. The first part of my journey involved taking the overnight express from Calcutta to Lucknow. In 1772 most of the incredible buildings of Lucknow were still to be constructed. When the fourth Nawab, Asaf-ud-Daula, moved the capital to Lucknow, he began a building programme. One of the most impressive of his structures is the Bara Imambara. This building was completed in 1791 and at the time was the largest hall in Asia to be erected without supporting beams. Not only that, the building also contains a labyrinth, the Bhulbhulaiya, situated in the roof space. It remains in a good state of preservation.

Lucknow is also significant in history because of the siege of the British Residency during the sepoy rebellion of 1857. The siege lasted 147 days and claimed many thousands of lives, both British and Indian. The Residency buildings have been preserved as they were after the siege and now form part of a memorial garden.

In *Rohilcund country* Solomon wrote that the Company army *obliged* the Marathas to cross the Ganges at *Rhamgaut,* where the river was fordable. An assumption can be made that the Marathas were *obliged* to cross the Ganges to the south, into the Doab region, although this is by no means clear as Rhamgaut cannot be found on the map and probably relates to some ghats on the riverbank. But it was at this place that Solomon described *one of the most ridiculous manoeuvres I have ever witnessed.* And the commander of this escapade was none other than the aforementioned Colonel Alexander Champion.

Solomon wrote that during the engagement he caught his foot under the wheels of one of the gun carriages. Luckily he escaped severe injury as the ground was sandy, although he mentioned that he was *lame* for some weeks afterwards. Colonel Champion ordered four battalions of grenadiers to cross the river, followed by the rest of the army. They arrived on the opposite bank, soaking wet and in a very vulnerable state. Their

10. India 1772 to 1778

The Residency, Lucknow. Pre 1857 Print from Montgomery Martin

The Residency, Lucknow. 2016

10. India 1772 to 1778

cannon had been totally submerged and the troops had been *obliged to carry their firelocks and cartouch boxes on their heads*. In Solomon's opinion, if the Marathas had counter-attacked at that time, the Company army would have been cut to pieces.

There must have been much discussion about this manoeuvre amongst the officers. Solomon wrote; *what induced the Commander in Chief to have followed the enemy at such a disadvantage was the astonishment of all who were capable of judging properly on the occasion, but for myself I thought the Colonel a second Alexander crossing the Granicus*. Perhaps Solomon was being ironic. At the battle of Granicus, in 334BC, Alexander took the Persians by surprise when he attacked them straight across the river.

After waiting on the opposite bank for a Maratha attack that never came, Colonel Champion then ordered the troops to re-cross the river. During the return crossing some were drowned and others wounded by random shots. Colonel Champion was later promoted to Commander-in-Chief of EIC forces in Bengal and, as mentioned, led the army during the Rohilla campaign of 1774. There is a memorial to him in Bath Abbey.

Solomon was then appointed as adjutant to six battalions of sepoys. The army continued to *Anopshuria* before returning to *Suttanpore*. At Suttanpore he was appointed adjutant and quartermaster. As far as it is possible to work out, Suttanpore is in the vicinity of Benares, near Chunar. They built temporary cantonments and waited until the rains subsided before travelling back to Bengal, arriving at *Chillipore*, within a few miles of Calcutta, in November 1773.

The reason Solomon was sent to Oudh from 1772 to the end of 1773 was presumably part of the plan to send troops to Oudh to support the Nawab and prevent Maratha encroachment into Bengal. The plan was to defend the 'line of the Ganges'. What is unclear was why Solomon was sent to support the Nawab in January 1772. The meeting between Warren Hastings and the Nawab, when the treaty was drawn up, did not actually take place until August 1773. Clearly there must have been a plan to support the Nawab with troops before Hastings took over as governor.

In January 1774 Solomon was put in command of the *forts at Budge Badgee*. There was only one fort at Budge Budge. This was situated just south of Calcutta in a strategic location on the left bank of the Hoogly River. As described in Chapter Five, Admiral Watson and Robert Clive captured the fort on their return to Calcutta in 1756. After a breach had

10. India 1772 to 1778

been made in its walls, the troops were kept on hold for the assault later the same day. As previously described, a drunken sailor, a certain Mr Strahan, walked up the breech and managed to enter the fort. This effectively required Clive and Watson to storm the fort several hours earlier than they had intended.

Budge Budge is now part of the southwestern suburbs of Calcutta. It became a major centre for jute manufacture until Partition and is now occupied by oil terminals. There is no sign of the fort now. It was closed in 1793 and all its munitions were taken to Calcutta.

In 1774 relations with the French were uneasy. As previously mentioned there was a small French colony at Chandernagore, twenty-two miles upriver from Calcutta. This meant that the French had to navigate their ships through Calcutta. War did eventually break out with the French in 1778, when they decided to support the American revolutionaries. But prior to this relations were volatile. The Seven Years War had ended in 1763 with a French defeat but they remained major rivals to the British in India.

In January 1774, three French ships of war with a pilot sloop had anchored opposite the forts. In Solomon's words; *as a war with that country was daily expected, I sent a note to the Commodore to desire that he would immediately weigh, and proceed either up the river, or to drop further down, as it was contrary to my instructions to permit ships of any foreign nation to anchor within reach of the fort guns.* But he received a reply from the Commodore that he would not move until the tide was favourable to go up-river. Clearly a decision had to be made. Solomon recorded that he *immediately ordered every gun to be loaded, and made as formidable appearance as possible.* Solomon then *dispatched a note by my sergeant, declaring, if he did not weigh anchor and drop down (as he could not proceed) and place his squadron out of reach of my guns, I would instantly do my utmost to destroy it.*

It cannot have been easy waiting for the reply. If the French did not agree to move, Solomon might have been responsible for starting the war with the French four years earlier.

Luckily they did move and Solomon wrote that his note had *the desired effect* and the ships dropped down river for about two miles. He then informed the Governor-General (Warren Hastings) and the officer commanding Fort William and *was honoured with a very flattering reply.* On the return of the tide the French squadron continued up river but the garrison at Fort William was kept under arms in case of attack. Solomon

10. India 1772 to 1778

wrote that it was *a very unusual thing for so many ships of war belonging to any foreign nation to be seen in the Hughley River.*

Later in 1774 Solomon's battalion was ordered to Midnapore where they stayed for several months. They had been sent there to *subdue a chief, residing in the hills, who had rebelled against the Company.* Midnapore (Medinipur) is a town eighty miles west of Calcutta, surrounded by hills and forests. In the eighteenth century the area had suffered from Maratha raids and also from the 1770 famine. As a result whole areas had become lawless.

Mir Kasim ceded the Midnapore district to the Company in 1760. The region would later have a reputation for rebellion. The Chuar tribe (1799) and later the Santhals (1850s) rebelled against British rule. In the 1850s they were brutally repressed. The Santhals lived in villages in the hills and supported themselves by farming and hunter gathering. They used poisoned arrows, but not apparently against humans.

It is unclear which tribal chief Solomon was referring too. Presumably his battalion had been sent to the area to re-assert law and order and the payment of taxes and, at the same time, discourage the Marathas from conducting any more raids.

Clearly Solomon and his troops had a job to do, but it is also clear that they were a modern army moving into a primitive tribal area to suppress a population who's main misdemeanour had been their lawlessness, and a failure to pay taxes. But Solomon's troops had a very hard time of it. In fact he stated that this was *the most unpleasant service I was engaged in.* Not to mention the constant risk of attack, there was also the risk of illness. By the end of the tour of duty Solomon was evacuated to the coast for several months in order to recover his health.

As they entered the forests up to one third of his battalion were killed or wounded. He wrote that anyone who was captured was sure to *suffer a cruel death.* The jungles were so thick that they could not see the enemy until they felt the effects of their *arrows or matchlocks.* Solomon was in charge of the rear guard that consisted of forty sepoys and three Indian officers. Their job was to protect the baggage train. In a few minutes, twenty-seven sepoys had been killed or badly wounded. The *Subedar*[4] and one of the two *Jamidars*[5] were among the casualties. That left just thirteen troops and they were about to be overwhelmed. But fortunately for them, reinforcements arrived and they were saved, together with the supplies.

10. India 1772 to 1778

The Company troops then carried on marching around the forests pursuing the enemy *to very little purpose* and losing *many brave men* until the commanding officer devised a plan that was more effective. Basically he sent out parties every night, consisting of 80 to 100 men, under a lieutenant and an ensign, who were instructed to arrive at a *certain point* by daybreak. They then located the enemy by the smoke of their village fires, or from temporary huts in the jungle. He relates that this method *brought in many prisoners and quantities of cattle.*

Solomon was put in charge of the last of these expeditions and described being *fortunate enough to surround* a *large party of the enemy. As their position being desperate and having considerable property at stake, they made a stout resistance and suffered considerably before they would surrender.* He described capturing more prisoners than he had soldiers to guard, together with *800 head of cattle, 4000 goats and other plunder of little value to the captors, but of infinite importance to the enemy.* This had the result that the Chief sent his *vakeel* to beg for a truce, followed soon after by a peace treaty. One condition of the peace treaty was that the chief had to pay all his arrears due to the Company and give a promise of future good conduct.

Solomon does not record whether all the livestock were returned. Presumably a proportion of them were kept back for tax arrears. As previously described, the ruler of the country had the right to collect taxes, a proportion of the produce of the land. This was paid either directly or through various *zamindars*. With the *Diwani,* the Company had taken over this right from the Mughals. Warren Hastings needed to collect the tax to fund the provision of law and order and defence throughout Bengal, as well as bolster the Company profits.

Solomon's account gives a vivid picture of what it must have been like for red-coated troops to fight in sweltering and dangerous forests, presumably against enemies using guerrilla tactics. Not only was there the risk of death from disease or wild animals, there was also the constant risk of death from arrows or muskets balls, or an even more terrible death if captured. Solomon wrote that no one escaped severe illness and they lost two excellent officers (Lieutenants Blair and Smith) as well as NCOs. He was unwell himself from April to November 1776 and was sent to Ballasore with three other officers for the benefit of the sea air.

Ballasore (Baleshwar) is a town on the coast just below the mouth of the Hoogly, where the Company had established a factory in 1633. When Calcutta took over prominence, Ballasore found a new role as a base

10. India 1772 to 1778

providing river services for craft travelling up-river. The Maratha chieftain, Mudhoje Bhonsle of Nagpur, had taken the town from the Mughals.

Solomon described being *confined* there for seven months. But by the time of his return to Midnapore he was *little better and too weak and emaciated to stand.* He had to be transported in a palanquin. During the journey a body of Marathas attacked his escort. The bearers fled and he was left at their mercy. The Maratha chief apparently threw back the curtains of Solomon's palanquin and flourished a *tulwar* over his head. But Solomon was very lucky as, seeing the condition he was in, the Maratha chief took pity on him and sent his men off to bring back the bearers. Solomon thanked his *generous enemy*.

Later that same year (1776) Solomon was promoted from third to senior lieutenant in the Second Battalion which, at that time, was stationed in *Coos Behar*. As mentioned, Cooch Behar is a district in the far north of Bengal, just south of Bhutan in the Himalayas. Warren Hastings had sent troops to Cooch Behar in 1772 to secure the northern borders of Bengal. It is over 450 miles from Midnapore to Cooch Behar and Solomon must have recovered enough to undertake the journey.

Solomon wrote that his *friend and shipmate*, Colonel Leslie, had *removed* him from his previous posting to serve in a battalion commanded by Captain Popham, stationed at *Sub Gunge* near Cooch Behar. We will hear more about these two officers later, but for very different reasons. Captain Popham was to become one of the heroes of the attack on the Hill Fort of Gwalior in 1780. Colonel Leslie was criticised for his alleged ineptitude as a result of the ponderous advance of the Bengal army during the crossing of India in 1778. In fact Leslie was decried so much that Gleig, in his 'History of the British in India' (1835) wrote; *happily he died, and left the command to Colonel Goddard, an officer formed from a very different school.*[6]

We will now leave Solomon in Cooch Behar while we return to the politics of the British in India and look into the reasons why two years later Warren Hastings decided to take the very risky step of sending an army right across India into hostile territory. In Solomon's words, *in 1778, the 1st, 2nd, 4th, 5th, 6th and 7th Battalions of sepoys, two troops of native cavalry, 500 Candahar horse and a good park of artillery, the whole commanded by Colonel Leslie, and not exceeding 7000 fighting men, were ordered to cross the Peninsular of India, and forming a junction with a detachment of the Bombay Army, attack Poonah, the Capital of the Maharatta Empire.*

PART FOUR : CROSSING THE PENINSULAR : 1778 – 1780

11. The Crossing I : Antecedents

In April 1778 a large Company army assembled in Oudh and made ready to cross the Jumna (Yamuna) River into potentially hostile territory. *Passports* had supposedly been obtained from the Maratha chiefs, Holkar and Scindia, but Nana Fadnavis, the Regent in Pune, had been less enthusiastic about allowing a foreign army to cross Maratha-held land unopposed. The Bundelkhand, a region governed by a number of Rajput chieftains under the overall control of the Marathas, had to be crossed first. The region was technically unexplored, and certainly unmapped, by Europeans. Beveridge wrote; *this place* (Calpee) *is nearly equidistant in a direct line from Calcutta and Bombay, being about 600 miles WNW of the one, and 680 miles NNE of the other. In the latter direction, the distance by any practicable route cannot be less than 1000 miles.*[1]

It was therefore an enterprise fraught with danger that, if it went wrong, could end in disaster. It was also an expedition that, in the words of Mervyn Davies, *only success could justify.*[2]

The force consisted of six battalions of sepoys, appropriate artillery and a corps of cavalry. It mustered *in all 103 European officers and 6234 native troops, with a cumbersome mass of followers estimated at not less than 30,000.*[3] It is almost inconceivable nowadays to imagine such an undertaking, without the aid of motorised transport. The figures roughly equate to four to five camp followers per fighting man. Solomon would have been accompanied by his servants, and possibly an Indian consort.

As mentioned previously, it was common practice in the eighteenth century for European men in India to take a 'native' wife, or *bibi*. Family history research has uncovered christening records from the Anglican church at Stokenham in Devon.[4] Two of Solomon's daughters were baptised by his wife's father, the Vicar of Stokenham, on the 7th October 1788. Solomon was married in August 1787. One daughter, Elfrida, is recorded as having been born on the 13th May 1788. However the second

11. The Crossing I : Antecedents

daughter, Sophia, is recorded as being the daughter of Solomon, rather than Solomon and Rose, his wife. Sophia was born on the 4th July 1780 while Solomon was in India. There is no information about her mother.

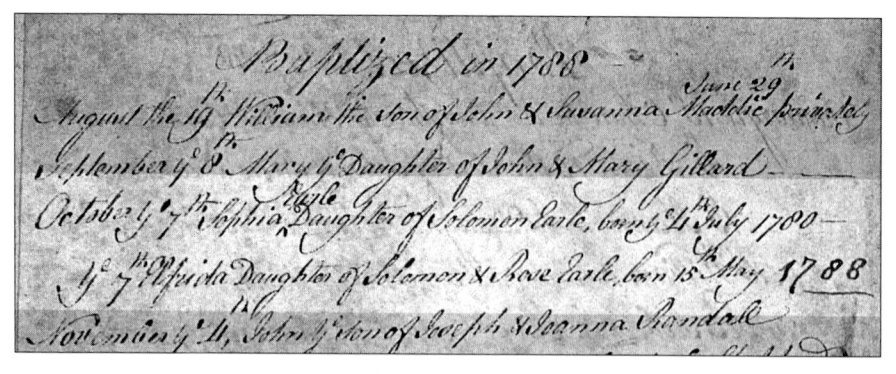

Baptism records, Stokenham, Devon, 1788

This puts Sophia's conception as the month of October 1779. In October 1779 Solomon was in the region of Surat, after crossing India. What we do not know is when he met Sophia's mother, who she was and whether he travelled with her from Bengal, met her on route, or after he arrived at Surat. We do not know whether she died, whether they separated, or whether Solomon just left her behind on his return to England in 1785. On his return he was presumably accompanied by his then five-year-old daughter. It was not uncommon for Europeans to leave their Indian wives in India, often well provided for, as evidenced from financial records.

Returning to the decision to send troops across India, a question worthy of consideration is why this whole enterprise was undertaken in the first place. The transfer of Bengal troops to Bombay was strongly opposed by Philip Francis who argued that this would leave Bengal vulnerable at a crucial time. He had a point. He was also of the view that the whole expedition was likely to go horribly wrong and result in an end of the British presence in India. But Philip Francis was opposed to almost everything Warren Hastings tried to achieve. The two members of the Bengal Council who supported Francis, Monson and Clavering, had both died in 1776 and Hastings now had the casting vote, despite the recent appointment of Edward Wheler.

The reasons behind the decision to send the army can be divided into a number of areas:

11. The Crossing I : Antecedents

1. There was understandable concern in Bengal that the Bombay Presidency did not have the ability and funding to support an army strong enough to take on the Marathas. For example, at the start of the Maratha war, they had been under the impression that an army of only 1500 men could take on the whole Maratha Empire. The fiasco at the Battle of Adas (1775) was evidence that the commanders of the Bombay army lacked competence. It was also felt that the Bombay Council could, by their own impetuousness, get themselves into grave difficulties, putting the foothold of the EIC on the whole west coast at risk.

2. There were major concerns that Company interests on the west coast were under threat from the French and, to a lesser extent, the Portuguese. Monsieur Lubin had arrived at Pune and the Maratha leader, Nana Fadnavis, appeared to be taking him seriously. At the time the French had a staging post from which to strike at Bombay, the Island of Mauritius, and they already had a firm alliance with Hydar Ali in Mysore. Apparently Lubin had even provided uniforms for a French army, but they had been supplied without buttons! From the mid 1770s the French had designs on war with the British. They were watching closely what was happening in America and had been covertly supporting the American colonist's rebellion. The American Declaration of Independence was made on the 4th July 1776. France formally declared war on Britain in March 1778.

3. The Portuguese had threatened to invade the Island of Salsette. This was one of the excuses made by the Bombay Council, in 1774, to invade the island and take Salsette from Maratha control.

4. The volatility of the Maratha Politic. As previously mentioned, a number of Maratha clans had formed semi-independent states. But although they were still under the overall control of the Peshwa in Pune, there was scope for jealousies and internal war. With the murder of the previous Peshwa, Narayanrao in 1773, the Politic was ruled by a regency with Nana Fadnavis in overall control, ruling on behalf of the infant Peshwa, Narayanrao's son. At the time Ragunathrao was under the protection of Bombay and had designs on invading Pune. An 'imposter' to the Peshwa had raised a rebellion, but that had been unsuccessful and he had been caught and executed.

11. The Crossing I : Antecedents

5. The Company were concerned that the Marathas might ally with the Nizam of Hyderabad and/or Hydar Ali of Mysore and attempt to drive the English out of India altogether.

6. Warren Hastings wanted to form an alliance with Mudhoji Bhonsle of Nagpur. The Bhonsle lands were co-terminus with Bengal and Hastings thought that Mudhoji might be persuaded to ally with the British. Hastings was also under the impression that Mudhoji might want to make a bid to take over as Peshwa.

So we have the Bombay Council supporting Raghunathrao's bid, while Bengal wanted to support Mudhoji Bhonsle. The situation was complex and evolving all the time.

Another question that could be asked was why had Hastings decided to send the army overland, rather than by sea?

Hastings may have been attracted by the grandeur of the whole enterprise.[5] The very threat of a powerful army could persuade the relevant parties to make peace and form alliances of value to the Company. And a powerful army on the ground, to the northeast of Pune, was necessary if Mudhoji Bhonsle could be persuaded to help. However the over-riding reason may have been simply that the sepoys, particularly the Brahmins, would not agree to travel by sea.[6]

The plan was to advance as soon as possible so as to cross the Nerbudda (Narmada) River before the rains set in.[7] However, as you will see in the next chapter, this did not happen.

Before we leave the antecedents, it would be of value to summarise the situation in the state of Mysore, that part of India south of Maratha country and west of Madras. The Chief Minister of Mysore, Hydar Ali, had staged a coup in 1761 and had displaced Khande Rao to become sultan. Despite being illiterate, Hydar Ali was a clever and able administrator and military commander. He had pioneered the successful use of rockets in warfare. In the Carnatic wars (1760s) he had allied with the French against the British in Madras. Hydar Ali was frequently in conflict with the Marathas and the Nizam of Hyderabad, just to the north. In 1772 he had the titular leader of Mysore, Nanjaraja Wadeyar, murdered when he had been informed that Nanjaraja had been making secret negotiations with the Marathas.

11. The Crossing I : Antecedents

Around 1776 Hydar Ali was in the process of negotiating an alliance with the Marathas and the Nizam against the British. He hated the British because the Madras Presidency had snubbed him on more than one occasion and he wanted to drive them out of Madras altogether. He also had links with the Catholics on the Coromandel Coast, as he preferred to ally with the French.

The situation in 1778 was now more than a melting pot. It was like a cauldron slowly coming to the boil.

In April 1778 the army began to assemble at Corah, *about twenty coss from Culpee.*[8] A *coss* is an intriguing Indian measurement that varies from between 1.5 and 2 miles. *Kos* is Hindi for 'to call or shout,' so the distance is literally the extent a man's shout can be heard. Part of the army had marched from Allahabad, which stands at the confluence of the Jumna where it joins the River Ganges. By May 19th the army had arrived at Kalpi and started to cross the river in boats. The crossing was supported by artillery consisting of two 12 pounders and two howitzers placed on the heights on the left bank of the river. It took over a week to get everyone across.

12. The Crossing II : Kalpi to the Narmada

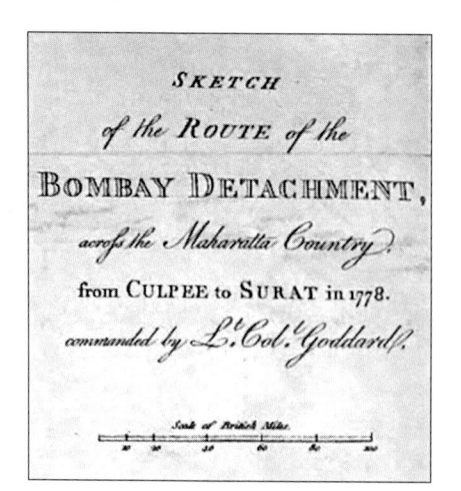

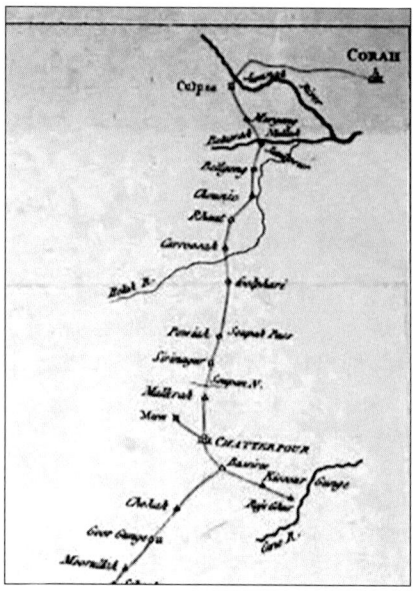

Extracts from a sketch map of the route of the 'Bombay Detachment'

To supplement Solomon's account of the crossing of the peninsular another source, authorship unknown, was published in 1779.[1] This account includes a sketch map of the route.

Both accounts tell of the terrible privations that the soldiers and camp followers had to endure during the first few weeks of the march. In addition to regular attacks and raids on provisions, the weather was unbearably hot and there was insufficient water. The terrain was particularly difficult too, especially for heavy artillery and supplies. The difficulty of moving 30,000 people and many thousands of horses and bullocks through hostile territory is scarcely imaginable. The Marathas had learnt their trade attacking ponderous Mughal armies and they were therefore formidable opponents. They avoided direct confrontation, where they would be at a disadvantage, and instead attacked the baggage train making hit and run raids.

12. The Crossing II : Kalpi to the Narmada

The attacks began as the army made its slow crossing of the Jumna River commencing on the 19th May 1778. 2000 Maratha horsemen were waiting on the far bank. But fire from British twelve pounders persuaded them to retreat into the surrounding ravines. Major Fullarton then advanced with four grenadier companies to *drive them out of a hollow way they occupied*. The Marathas counter-attacked and tried to surround the Company soldiers, but without success. The fort and town of Kalpi, now empty of inhabitants, was then taken.

At 2am on the 3rd June 1778, the 1st, 4th, 6th and 7th Battalions began the long march into the interior of the Bundelkhand. Solomon described the first day as disastrous. The heat was intense and the road was so bad that the carriage bullocks could not proceed. *Most singular, hillocks of naked concker attracted surprise, in the most irregular forms, and as far as the eye could reach not a tuft of verdure was to be seen, which the scorching heat seemed to have totally excluded.*[2] A concker presumably means a rocky outcrop.

By 7am they came across a well (*a pukka one*) only to find it had been stopped so not a drop of water could be drawn. Solomon wrote, *at the end of five hours we reached the only well that had been seen on the road, this renewed our spirits, and those who were ready to perish, thought their troubles were at an end when the dismal announcement was made that the well was dry.*

They then had to cover another eight coss to get to the first town, Murgong, but found its wells had been stopped up too. Solomon wrote that some of them had been poisoned by *throwing into them large quantities of the prickly pear, a shrub which abounds in most parts of India*.

This is how the author of the Journal described the march:

The scorching hot winds, with the intense heat of the sun, on a dry extensive plain, from eight o'clock to a quarter past eleven, exposed us to sufferings of the superlative degree; about twenty sepoys dropped down quite exhausted for want of water; several dogs and other animals gasped their last; not less than fifteen or twenty of our followers shared their like fate, and twenty officers were taken sick merely from the bad effects of this ridiculous march; for without the shadow of an enemy to obstruct us, or the badness of the road (which no more than fifty bildars would have levelled in four hours) we might have suffered annihilation.

A popular officer, Captain James Crawford, lost his life and was, *justly and feelingly lamented by the most unthinking of us*. Solomon wrote that

12. The Crossing II : Kalpi to the Narmada

Captain Crawford *died raving mad* and five others died in a similar way a few days after. He recorded that fifty sepoys and camp followers perished, simply for want of water.

They had to cover another nine miles to get to the River Butawah Nullah before finding water. Solomon wrote that *the thermometer at this time was from 140 to 200 degrees in our tent, though they had thick linings and a large fly some feet above them*. Either Solomon's thermometer was malfunctioning or this was a misprint as ambient temperatures above 131 degrees Fahrenheit (55 degrees Celsius) are unlikely to be compatible with life.

The author of the Journal berated the planning of the expedition. He wrote that the road should have been properly explored during the fourteen days the army spent crossing the Jumna and precautions should have been made to supply adequate water. However the Betawah Nullah River was *delightfully clear, and exceedingly wholesome*. He recorded the deaths of various officers including *Lieutenant Arichard* (died of gout), *Ensign Dariquunknave* and *Mr. Walter Gold, Commissary of Musters*.

The distance travelled by the army was measured by a perambulator, a surveyor's wheel. The author of the journal recorded that he regularly made thermometer readings between 88 and 107 degrees. He stated that others recorded 114 to 117 degrees. At night hot winds blew and kept the temperature high. During the day they were kept cool by pouring water (presumably when available) onto blinds made of grass. When things improved they passed through *fine and well cultivated lands* and provisions became more plentiful. They were then averaging between eight and fourteen miles per day. The Journal author arrived at Chhatarpur on the 3rd July.

Solomon wrote that the fatiguing marches continued until they arrived at *Chatterpore, the capital of the Bundelkund, where the rains set in and detained us from the 3rd July to the 12th of October*. Chhatarpur is about eighty miles from Kalpi and they still had over 900 miles to go. Bombay needed their help. What on earth was going on?

Part of the answer may well be that they were detained by the rains, which made transport impossible. But there were other reasons. Colonel Leslie had got them involved with an internal war between the chieftains of the Bundelkhand.

The Bundelkhand is a barren, hilly region situated at the northern end of the Deccan plain. Northeastward of this region the land gradually descends

12. The Crossing II : Kalpi to the Narmada

into the Yamuna and Ganges plains. It is a remote region with poor transport links due to mountain ranges and ravines, or *nullahs*. Principle towns include Jhansi, Kalpi, Mauranipur (*Mau*), Chhatarpur (*Chatterpore*) and Khajuraho, home of wonderfully preserved Jain and Hindu temples. The region was dominated by the Chandelas from the 10th Century until invasion by the Bundelar Rajputs. The Rajputs were followed by Muslim invaders, culminating with the Mughals, from the 16th to the 18th century. With the decline of Mughal power, the area had been taken back by the Bundela Chieftains, assisted by the Marathas. By the 1770s the local chieftains held power, but under tribute to the Marathas.

In 1778 there was an internal battle going on between the chieftains. The Rajah, Anrodh Singh, had usurped the leadership from his elder brother, Sarnet Singh. Sarnet Singh was fighting back with the support of family members. He had an army, of *about 5000 match-lock-men and cavalry*.[3]

Anrodh Singh offered to supply provisions to Leslie's army, provided they took a route that avoided Chhatarpur. Colonel Leslie replied that there was no other route through. When the army got to Chhatarpur they found the place abandoned. Leslie received word that Anrodh Singh planned to oppose his passage. Troops were massing at Mauranipur, six miles to the west. At Rhajgar, fourteen miles to the east, another body of cavalry and infantry, most likely to be Marathas, were amassing between the town and the River Caine (Kan). Sarnet Singh sent his agents to Leslie offering to make an alliance and promising grain if the army supported him. For better or worse Leslie agreed to an alliance with Sarnet Singh to help him regain his throne.

Attempts were made by Anrodh Singh's soldiers to cut off communications with Kalpi. For example a detachment of *twenty-four sepoys and three hundred cooleys*, together with Captain Munro, an army chaplain, on route from Kalpi, were attacked by 200 cavalry. *These banditti surrounded him and fired. He repeatedly called out to them to take everything they chose but to spare his life. Deaf to his entreaties, they continued firing, wounded him in two or three places, then closed on his party, cut him down with their broad swords, and many others.*[4] Munro was then left for dead but, *although dangerously wounded*, was able to send off a man for help. Two companies were instantly dispatched to his aid. A boy, Munro's servant, met them and gave them the bad news. His master had initially been taken care of by a Brahmin and carried into a small fort. But then *a few of the banditti returned, took him out of the fort into a neighbouring jungle, and in cool blood butchered him, and cut his head off.* Captain

12. The Crossing II : Kalpi to the Narmada

Alexander Munro was in his mid twenties and was a nephew of Sir Hector Munro who had commanded the Company forces at Buxar.[5]

Supplies, including cattle, were also taken. Colonel Leslie decided to extricate himself from these difficulties by an attack on Mau.[6]

On the 10th July Lieutenant Colonel Goddard led a successful attack on the town and fort of Mau with three battalions and a body of horse, with little loss of life. The author of the Journal wrote that *the sepoys on this severe service behaved with great spirit and resolution. The irregularity entirely proceeded from too great an eagerness to engage, which a little practice must annihilate.*

But although the success at Mau resulted in some supplies of grain, Anrodh Singh proved elusive, crossing the river Caine and encamping with his troops opposite Rajgarh.

Solomon wrote that the army (together with Sarnet Singh's troops) then *marched to Raji Ghur, within a mile of the Cane, a rapid river full of rocks.* Anrodh Singh's army, consisting of *6000 Cavalry and infantry, had taken possession of the opposite side of the river.* The author of the journal noted that *six or seven pieces of cannon played away very smartly at us the whole day.* On the 1st September Solomon wrote that Captain Popham *marched with the 2nd Battalion and 500 Candahar horse, with a view to intercept a body of about 2000 of Amaroods Sing's cavalry* (Solomon actually records 20,000), which *had crossed the Cane in the hope of cutting off our supplies. We fell in with them next morning at daybreak, and although they had taken a strong post, soon put them to rout, with considerable loss to the enemy.*

The fort of *Goor Gunge,* described in the Journal as, *a small pukka fort on the side of a hill,* was taken, and put under Solomon's charge.

While all this was going on there was considerable concern at the Bengal Council due to the slow progress of the march. Philip Francis wrote that *on the 25th of July Colonel Leslie was still at Chatterpore. At the rate he proceeds he may not probably reach Bombay in the course of the present century.*[7] Hastings supported Leslie, wondering if Leslie was attempting to make peace with Anrodh Singh and, if this was not the case, and instead it was his intention to dispossess the Raja and raise his brother instead, then he had *disobeyed the positive orders of the Board and proved himself unworthy of the confidence which they had reposed in him.*[8]

Leslie wrote to the board outlining that he had avoided interfering with the Bundela chiefs, *except in the instance of Sarnet Singh.* He also complained about the incessant rains that were preventing all possibility of marching.

12. The Crossing II : Kalpi to the Narmada

By then Hastings was getting increasingly concerned. With Francis urging that Leslie's conduct should be looked into, Hastings finally agreed, remarking on the slow advance of 120 miles in the space of three months. Both Francis and Wheler advised recalling the whole army, referring to the enormous dangers, difficulties, disappointments and enormous expense of continuing.

There was also some evidence that Leslie's conduct towards his subordinates was proving to be a problem. At one point Goddard, the second-in-command, had demanded a court martial in consequence of some aspersions thrown upon him by Leslie in the course of a dispute about command.[9] Hastings was still convinced that an alliance could be made with Mudhoji Bhonsle at Nagpur and wanted the army to get on with it. A decision was therefore made to remove Leslie's command and replace him with Goddard. But Leslie never received his order of recall. He died of a *bilious fever* on the 3rd October 1778.

Throughout the march from this time Goddard communicated directly with Warren Hastings by letter. These letters are available at the British Library and provide a useful record of the progress of the detachment.[10] The first of these letters is transcribed below in full:

My Dear Sir,

It is with sincere sorrow, I am about to communicate a piece of intelligence which I am persuaded will be productive to you of much concern and anxiety, the circumstances I allude to are the death of Colonel Leslie who demised this evening at 6 'clock after a few days illness ... I lose no time in informing you of this event and of assuring you at the same time of my absolute and entire devotion to your interests, which I shall hold dear to me as my own ...

I have done myself the honour of addressing the Board on this occasion, and have acquainted them, that I shall immediately proceed to inform myself fully of the instructions they may have transmitted to my predecessor, which I shall endeavour to execute with the most attentive obedience.

I need not assure you of my firm resolve to prosecute the instructions of this detachment with the utmost vigour and dispatch, because I am persuaded you will confide in the sentiments of attachment, I have experienced to your service in particular, and to the interest and honour of your administration, which shall ever be my duty to promote ...

12. The Crossing II : Kalpi to the Narmada

I am at present in the dark respecting the terms entered into with the Rajah of this Country, but as Colonel Leslie on the day he was first attacked with his indisposition, issued an order for the troops to prepare for proceeding on their march, I am led to deliver hopes, that every impediment to the prosecution of this Expedition is effectively removed ... I shall however immediately inform myself of every circumstance relative to this Business, and transmit you an exact account of it, as will as of every thing else connected with the present service.

I offer once only more to assure you further that the approaching fair season ... which I shall not neglect.

I have the honour to be your ...

Goddard

Camp at Rage Ghur
3rd Oct 1778

After Colonel Goddard took over command any indecision regarding progress dissipated and the army set off again on its long march across the sub-continent.

Solomon wrote*: On the 16th of October we joined the army from Raji Ghur and proceeded towards the Narbuddah. During the whole of this march (285 miles) we were much harassed by the enemy who cut off straggling parties and carried away our cattle &c., we also suffered much by the rockets they threw into our camp at night, which did great execution wherever they fell.*

The Journal recorded that the army averaged between six and twelve miles per day. On October 17th *three hundred Pindaries drove off two elephants and ten or twelve camels.* The animals were recovered using a detachment of *grenadiers and Condaharians* (Kandahar cavalry).

As they continued the Marathas made an attempt to carry off the baggage by attacking to the rear and both right and left flanks in three different bodies. But this did not check Goddard's progress and he was able to reach the comparative safety of Bhopal where he was supplied with *rations and other sundries* by its Nawab, Hyat Khan.[11]

According to the journal, on November 20th the army arrived at *Bopaul Tol* (Bhopal). The walls of the city were described as being *nine miles in*

12. The Crossing II : Kalpi to the Narmada

circumference, situated on the side of a hill, the lower part of the town is close on a lake of nine or ten miles in extent. The town is built of stone, the houses good, and the wall of the fort of hewn stone, mostly pukka work. It is reported that they (the Nawab's army) *have several guns, with a number of the Company's firelocks, and is said to have six or seven hundred fighting men under him.* The Journal also recorded that many of the people were *very white and in general well clothed and are seemingly under a flourishing government.*

At the time Bhopal was a small Muslim-ruled state originally founded by Dost Mohammad Khan, an Afghan in the service of Aurangzeb. After the decline of the Mughal Empire, Dost Mohammed assumed the title of Nawab and ran a successful government with the support of *an able Hindu minister, Bejee Ram, and a lady of remarkable ability, who for more than half a century greatly influenced, if she did not control, the councils of the principality, under the name of Mahjee Sahiba, the 'lady mother'.* [12] In the 1770s the power behind the Bhopal state was a lady called Mamola Bai (1715-1795), a forerunner to the legendary Begums of Bhopal, [13] of the following century. The Muslim rulers of the state of Bhopal were threatened from all sides by the encroaching power of the Marathas and they are likely to have welcomed a potential alliance with the British. The British generally remembered who had helped them during difficult times as, in the later years of British rule, Bhopal was allowed to govern itself as a princely state.

The Company army stayed in Bhopal for seven days. Beveridge wrote that the *Nabob of Bhopaul*, in contrast to other chiefs, gave the army *every assistance in his power, and greatly facilitated its progress.*[14] Goddard wrote to Hastings commending Hyat Khan's behaviour to the English especially at a time when he was threatened by Balaji and the Marathas. [15]

After Bhopal the march continued, according to Solomon, along *an exceedingly bad road, the whole way a jungle and pass. We crossed three or four deep stony nullahs.* Luckily they were unopposed as *a very few people, with resolution, might have defended them against thousands, but not an enemy did we see or any fort.*[16] The army reached the Narmada River on the 30th November having marched forty-six miles since leaving Bhopal. Solomon wrote that they passed many towns, including *Bopoltle* (Bhopal) and numbers of *delightful villages,* and reached the *Narbuddah River at Husnabad where they stayed until the 6th of January 1779, waiting for orders from Calcutta.*

12. The Crossing II : Kalpi to the Narmada

In 2016, following a similar route to the Bombay Army, I took a train from Lucknow to Allahabad. I then had to wait several hours for the Khajuraho connection, which did not seem to exist. It turned out that Khajuraho was at the end of a branch line. Some young men tried to help us, telling us that the Khajuraho train did not exist. We eventually found some carriages at the rear of another train that were apparently going there.

We arrived at the deserted station of Khajuraho the next morning, deserted apart from a battalion of Indian army soldiers mustering at the far end of the platform. It was cold before the sun came up. As our auto-rickshaw took us to the town, a few miles away, we passed a huge and brand new international airport. The Indian government presumably have plans to open up Khajuraho to mass tourism. We stayed at the 'Hotel Harmony and Zorba the Buddha Restaurant' in the old town.

The temples of Khajuraho escaped destruction by Moslem invaders as they were so remote and had become covered in jungle. The Chandelas built them during a hundred year period at the end of the first millennium. It is thought that they then had to abandon them for more secure mountain fortresses when the Moslem conquest got underway. They were 're-discovered' by Captain T.S. Burt in 1838. Although shocked by them, he recognized their significance and date of construction from a Sanskrit panel found at the site.

It is difficult to describe the feelings you experience walking around these wonderful temples and it is impossible to understand what motivated the Chandelas to spend so much time creating them. They built a total of eighty-five temples of which only twenty-five still remain. What were they for? Some historians argue that they were designed to portray the union of Vishnu and Shiva. Others have described them as a sort of wedding party to entertain and placate the gods. Some argue that they were created to act as a 'Kama Sutra,' a sort of love manual for the population. War and hunting are portrayed as well as the erotic themes. But we will never know for sure as the Chandelas barely mention the place in their surviving texts.[17]

The temples of Khajuraho are situated just a few miles away from where the Bengal army had their skirmish with Anrodh Singh's troops at Rajgarh, next to the Kan River. Except, of course, nobody knew they were there at the time.

After leaving Khajuraho we took the train to Jhansi. We passed through an area of cultivated land interspersed by huge outcrops of rock, rather like

12. The Crossing II : Kalpi to the Narmada

Detail from carvings at Khajuraho

the tors of Dartmoor in the UK, but on a much larger scale. These types of rocky outcrops must have been the conckers mentioned by Solomon and the author of the Journal. We passed through Mau Ranipur, described as *Mow* by Solomon, and the scene of Colonel Goddard's successful attack. We then took a second train from Jhansi to Bhopal.

Sadly Bhopal is better known in the present day as being the site of the Union Carbide poison gas disaster of December 1984. However it is well worth visiting the city for other reasons. It has vibrant streets and markets, picturesque upper and lower lakes and mosques, the majority of which were constructed in the nineteenth century by Bhopal's female rulers, the Begums of Bhopal. The derelict pesticide factory remained a malevolent presence, dominating the north part of the town and still contaminated by the poisons it produced. We visited the Sambhavna Trust Clinic and witnessed the work that is still needed to support the victims, estimated to be more than 20,000 people.

We then took a train to Burhanpur. En route we passed through the mountain pass described in the Journal. We crossed the Narmada River at Hoshangabad, were we left Solomon, encamped for Christmas 1778.

13. The Crossing III : The Battle of Wadgaon : January 1779

We will now take a break from the arduous march of the Bengal Army across India and will leave them safely camped on the south bank of the Narmada River at Hoshangabad, approximately 500 miles northeast of the Maratha capital, Pune. Bombay is about 80 miles west of Pune. To understand how events evolved over the course of the next few months we need to take a look at what was about to take place in that part of the country. Of course Goddard, waiting for orders at Hoshangabad, was not aware of any of this.

In 1778 the Bombay Council made a decision to support Raghunathrao's bid to retake power and furthermore, they decided not to wait for the arrival of the Bengal army. They had in effect decided to jump the gun and achieve their ends without help from Bengal. The Bengal Council had not disapproved of the resolution per se to support Raghunathrao, provided it did not interfere with Hastings' plan to form an alliance with Mudhoji Bhonsle. Philip Francis pointed out, sensibly, that the policy of supporting two separate contenders for power at the same time was ludicrous.

In Bombay the Council were strongly influenced by Thomas Mostyn in the light of his experience as Company agent in Pune. Mostyn argued forcibly that the Bombay Council needed to act now, before the opportunity was lost. He made the point that, if there were any further delays, the French would increase their influence at the Maratha court.[1] Mostyn also argued that there would be little serious opposition to re-instating Raghunathrao at Pune.

How wrong he turned out to be.

The resolution to support Raghunathrao's bid for power was passed at the Bombay Council on the 12th July 1778 but no further action was taken until October.

The Bombay Council had not thought it through. With the benefit of hindsight it is easy to see that the re-instatement of a hated contender for

13. The Crossing III : The Battle of Wadgaon : Jamuary 1779

the Peshwaship, an ex-Peshwa who had already been deposed, was not going to go down well with the Marathas, a proud warlike race. And to support such a bid with an invading army of ferengis could make matters worse. Such an invading force could even act as a catalyst to bring many disparate groups together in opposition. This is exactly what happened.

In October 1778 the Bombay Council started to make the necessary arrangements. A committee was set up consisting of Colonel Egerton, John Carnac and Thomas Mostyn, to lead the force. Colonel Egerton was described by Duff as *extremely weak and totally unacquainted with India, its natives, its warfare*. Even more damning he described Egerton as, *typical of a group of officers of rank coming to India only to make their fortunes by any means*.[2] Before the expedition departed Colonel Egerton protested that, as commander-in-chief, it was not right to share command with two civilians.

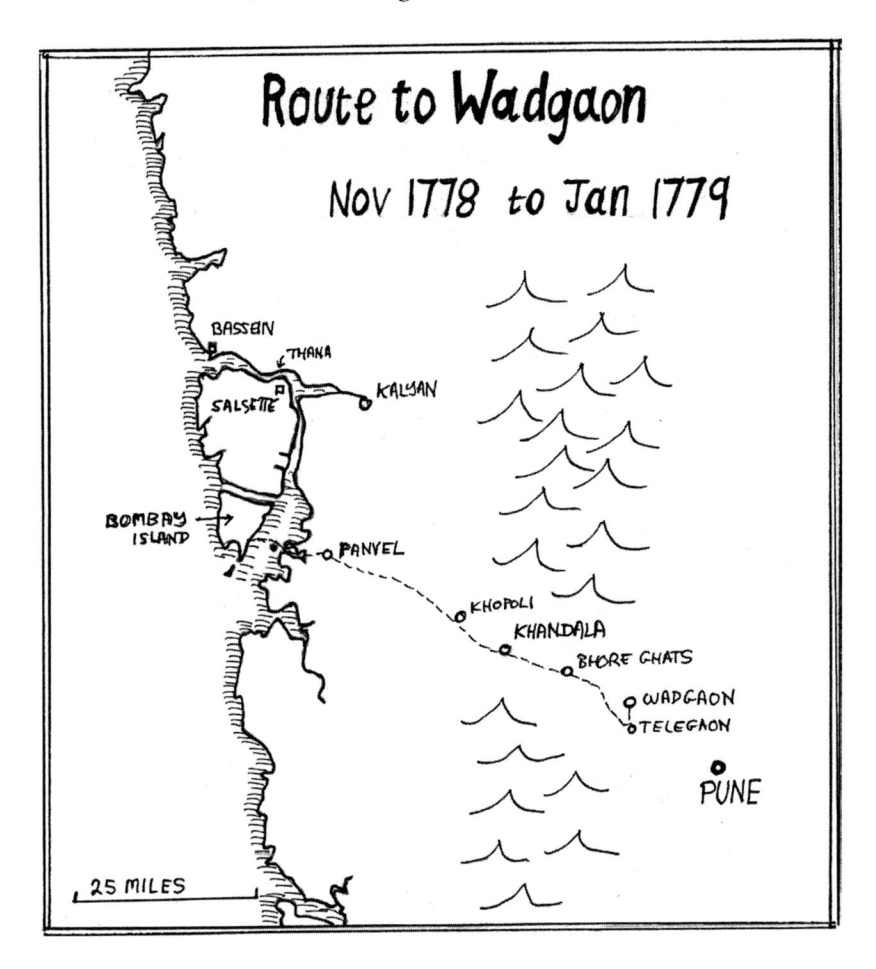

Route to Wadgaon Nov 1778 to Jan 1779

13. The Crossing III : The Battle of Wadgaon : Jamuary 1779

In practice John Carnac had had considerable experience as a military commander under Robert Clive. Carnac had returned to England in 1767 but then lost all his money in a failed business venture to develop Portsmouth into a fashionable town. In an attempt to revive his fortunes he returned to India in 1773 as a member of the Bombay Council. He should have stayed in England.

An advance party of 600 sepoys under Captain Stewart was sent to take possession of the Bhore Ghats, the top of the pass. They advanced without opposition, camping at the village of Khandala on the 25th November. The rest of the army followed.

Grant Duff described the preparations for the invasion as *dilatory*. The whole force consisted of 591 Europeans, 2278 native infantry and 500 gun lascars – 3,900 men in total. The force also included artillery and no less than 19,000 bullocks to drag the artillery train and supplies through the mountainous terrain. Presumably there was also the usual contingent of camp followers. On route Colonel Egerton apparently managed to upset the locals in one of the villages when he occupied a Brahmin's house, thus defiling it.[3] Raghunathrao's small army joined them on the 12th December. Progress was no more than one to two miles per day. Mostyn became unwell and had to return to Bombay where he died. This reduced the leadership to a committee of two.

The Marathas had plenty of time to organise their opposition and lost no opportunity to harass the army all the way up the Ghats. As usual they deployed mobile horsemen familiar with the territory. When the army reached Khopoli on the 15th December, intelligence was received that a Maratha force consisting of 10,000 horse and fifteen pieces of cannon had gathered to oppose them. Another 5000 horse were waiting at Pune.[4]

The army finally reached the summit of the Ghats on the 23rd December and, around New Year's Day, commenced a forward march formation towards Pune, proceeding six furlongs (6/8ths of a mile) per day. This left plenty of opportunity for the Marathas to harass them. They fired rockets and cannon at them all the way, refusing to engage. In addition to this the Marathas carried out a scorched earth policy, destroying all crops and shelter in the vicinity. They also attacked baggage trains and provisions, cutting off communication. They even evacuated Pune itself. Captain Stewart was killed by a cannon shot.

But if this was not enough, none of the Marathas joined Raghunathrao's bid to retake Pune. Nana Fadnavis had been active on the political front

13. The Crossing III : The Battle of Wadgaon : January 1779

and had persuaded Mahadji Scindia and Tukoji Holkar to join him. This meant he now had 40,000 cavalry and 16,000 infantry available.[5] Mahadji Scindia was to take charge of the defence of Pune.

The Bombay army continued its slow advance and by the 9th January 1779 had reached Talegaon, just sixteen miles from Pune. Egerton had been taken ill and command of the army had passed to Lieutenant Colonel Cockburn with Egerton continuing to issue orders from his sickbed. By the 11th January it was felt too dangerous to continue as supplies were running low. The army started to retreat. Captain James Hartley, with a select body of grenadiers, supplied the rear-guard, and in doing so was repeatedly attacked.

Cockburn could see that Hartley's troops were in trouble and sent orders for them to join the main body. But Hartley *returned an answer that, if he once turned his back to the enemy, it might be destruction to the whole.* [6] Reinforcements were sent instead and they managed to keep the Marathas at bay with grape shot, in the process losing 124 men. They retreated to the village of Wadgaon. The Marathas continued to attack and were repulsed. 350 more Company troops fell.

For the next three days discussions took place as to what to do next. The army had limited provisions and had no means of acquiring more and they were completely surrounded by a superior Maratha force. On the other hand they had disciplined troops and the Marathas were not prepared to meet them in the open field. Cockburn had earlier argued that they should have continued to Pune, but in doing so would have been cut off. Cockburn was now arguing that they should seek terms as he was of the opinion that, to retreat the forty-five miles back down the Ghats to Panvel, would be suicidal. In fact he refused to organise such a retreat, even if ordered to. Egerton supported him. Carnac and Hartley favoured a fighting retreat. In the end, terms were sought.

In some sense it is difficult to understand why the Marathas agreed terms. They clearly had the upper hand and could have carried on their siege of Wadgaon and destroyed the Bombay troops. But they must have known that Goddard's army was only a few weeks march away and they had the chance to make considerable gains quickly.

In the end terms were agreed:
1. Bombay would give up all its recent acquisitions.
2. Raghunathrao would be handed over.

13. The Crossing III : The Battle of Wadgaon : Jamuary 1779

3. Broach would be ceded to Scindia
4. There would be a considerable cash settlement
5. Hostages would be taken to insure compliance.
6. Goddard's troops would be ordered to return to Bengal.

What was left of the Bombay army then marched back to Panvel under a Maratha escort and took ship to Bombay. Raghunathrao was delivered to the custody of Scindia. Mr Farmer and Ensign Stewart were delivered to Scindia as hostages.[7]

Back in Bombay the recriminations started.

If Cockburn and Carnac had continued to Pune, they would have had to hold the city, pending the arrival of Goddard's army. But they were concerned about the lack of provisions as a result of the Maratha policy of denying supplies by attacks on baggage and destroying crops. Hastings later wrote to Sullivan in London stating that, *the terms of the treaty made me sink with shame while I read them.*[8]

Formal charges were brought against Egerton and Cockburn for refusing to conduct the retreat of the army from Wadgaon. Carnac initially stayed on the Council, but was then dismissed by the Court of Directors in London. He later died in Bangalore in 1800.

Captain James Hartley was acknowledged as having been the saviour of the army due to his rear-guard action at Wadgaon. He was promoted to Lieutenant Colonel.[9] He went on to serve in Goddard's forces in Gujarat (see Chapter 15). But his promotion was not without incident as there were objections from other senior officers – promotion in the Company army was usually through order of seniority, rather than by heroic deed. Much to his dismay the Court of Directors in London later decreed that his promotion had been invalid. In 1781 he returned to London to put his case before the Court of Directors in person. They refused to concede. He then appealed to King George III who gave him a Lieutenant Colonelcy in the regular army. He went on to serve in the British forces fighting against Tipu Sultan at Seringapatum.

Wadgaon was a significant victory for the Marathas and demonstrated that the Company armies were not invincible. Hasting's strategy in the west of India was now in total disarray due to this precipitous and ill-timed action by the Bombay Council.

13. The Crossing III : The Battle of Wadgaon : Jamuary 1779

In the village of Wadgaon (Vadegaon) a recently erected pillar and plaque commemorates the Maratha victory. Here are some quotes from the plaque:

THE INDIANS ARE SECOND TO NONE

Here at Wadgaon Maval, the forces of the Maratha Confederacy, led by General Mahadji Shinde, imposed a crushing defeat on the invading forces of the East India Company on January 14th 1779, thus establishing the superiority of the Indians over the colonials. However the British had deliberately obscured this golden page of our history…

The plaque goes on to describe the battle and its antecedents, adding that the British dumped their heavy artillery in the tank at Telegaon. It then makes the point…

Had the magnanimous Indian victors ruthlessly exploited their success by uprooting the stronghold of the East India Company at Mumbai, while keeping all the captive English in their custody, they could have changed the course of Indian history.

Maybe.

The Bombay army could have marched the final few miles to Pune, occupied the deserted town, and waited for assistance. By mid January Goddard's army were on their way to Burhanpur. Burhanpur is 283 miles from Pune and Goddard's army arrived there at the end of January. At a fast average rate of ten miles per day, the earliest they could have got to Pune was the end of February. However it is highly unlikely the Marathas would have let them march unopposed.

Strangely, the grave of Captain James Stewart is still honoured to this day, after nearly 240 years, with an annual ceremony. He is known as *Ishtur Phakre,* Stewart the Brave. His grave is hidden behind the police station at Vadegaon and in 2011 was still lit by candles.[10]

14. The Crossing IV : Hoshangabad to Surat

Meanwhile at Hoshangabad, on the banks of the Narmada River, the new Commander-in-chief, Colonel Goddard, was waiting for orders. It was December 1778.

On the 2nd of December the army started to cross the river. The Journal author gives the following description: *The stream gently glides along; the bottom is sand, intermixed with rocks. The hills are very high, on the north side they are within one mile and a half of the river, on the south side they appear about three coss distance… The tumbrils passed at the ford, as did most of the battalions. The water was about three foot deep.* The area was described as, *very jungly*.[1] They the waited on the south bank for about two weeks.

Meanwhile Colonel Goddard had sent Lieutenant Watherstone to Nagpur, about 270 miles away, to negotiate with Mudhoji Bhonsle. However Lieutenant James Anderson, already in Nagpur, had failed to make any progress with the plan to establish an alliance with the Bhonsles. On the 2nd December Anderson had written a secret report to Hastings stating that the Bhonsles, *will on no account whatever assist the English* because an *apprehension of immediate ruin to themselves from the threat of the Ministerial party operates at present more strongly on their minds.*[2] In other words they were afraid of reprisals from Pune. It was no different when Watherstone arrived at court on the 19th December. The threat of *numberless opposition* against them was likely if they agreed to support the British.

If we look at what was happening over at Bombay and Pune then this decision is hardly surprising. Goddard had not received any useful communications from Bombay about the plan to send an army to Pune and, by the 25th November, Captain Stewart's detachment had already reached the top of the Ghats. The fact that the English were supporting Raghunathrao's bid for power could hardly have inspired confidence with Mudhoji Bhonsle, even if he had had any prior aspirations of throwing in his lot with the English.

14. The Crossing IV : Hoshangabad to Surat

The army recommenced their march on the 16th January 1779. News from Bombay was still unclear and Goddard presumably wanted to press on for the time being. Duff implied that he made this decision himself rather than wait for orders.[3] They made good progress, covering between eleven and eighteen miles per day, passing through what was described as very fertile country. *A fine plain country covered with grain, principally wheat, the ears of which were just formed.*[4] Two of the officers became unwell. Captain Wray had to return to Calcutta, but Lieutenant Colonel John Fortman developed an *extreme illness* and died the next day of the same *tedious* illness.

The countryside became *more jungly*. On the 29th January they reached *Ichanabad*, just five miles from *Boorhampore* (Burhanpur), where they halted for seven days. Solomon stated that they reached *Burhampore*, after a march of 153 miles. He described passing, *a few miles to our right*, a fort that he considered to be *the strongest fort in India*. The author of the Journal described it as *one of the most impregnable fortresses in the world*. This place had clearly struck a chord with the English officers. What on earth was it?

They called it *Ashere Gurr*, or *Assurghur*. It is actually the fortress of Asirgarh. It was built in the early fifteenth century by Asa Ahir and later taken by the Mughal Emperor Akbar in 1601. When the Company army passed it was occupied by the Marathas. It must have been an impressive site, rising over 800 feet above a rocky plain. Described as the 'Gateway to the Deccan' it commanded a pass between the Narmada and Tapti valleys.

Both Solomon and the Journal author described Asirgarh as resembling Table Mountain, at the Cape of Good Hope. The Journal author wrote:

> *the mountain is of conker and stony rock, the walls of pucha stone work, with round towers, or cavaliers, at convenient distances; it seems not less than an English mile in diameter, and is in triangular form. The neighbouring country for several coss all around Ashere Gurr, is exceedingly broken, with various hills of conker, so that the approach to it, is only by a narrow lane or hollow way, that a single bullock loaded can pass at a time. It is said there is a large lake at the Summit, and a canal, which runs the whole length of the fort, although they grow corn sufficient for the garrison, consisting of 1500 men. If all this is true, with every circumstance, I could confirm, it is one of the strongest places that history can record.*

He is clearly seeing it through the eye of a potential attacker. Solomon was also very impressed describing Asirgarh as being situated at the top of an *inaccessible mountain* and able to hold, *perhaps 2000 men*. He was of

14. The Crossing IV : Hoshangabad to Surat

NORTH VIEW OF THE FORT OF ASEERGHUR.—From Journals of the Sieges of the Madras Armies, 1817-1819.

Asirgarh, from the North. Print from Beveridge History of India. 1862.
The two towers on the left are the minarets of the mosque.

the opinion that the only way the fort could be taken would be *through treachery, or the cowardice of the Killadar.*

What also impressed them about Asirgarh was that the gardens on its summit were able to produce, and sell them, an abundance of delicious grapes and oranges, in January.

After all those superlative accounts of this place, it was imperative that I visited. Yes, it does hold a lake, but not just one, three huge and deep cisterns, still full of clear water to this day. It also boasts an impressive mosque with two solid minarets and an eighteenth century Hindu temple dedicated to Shiva. The dedication of the temple links to a story in the Mahabharata where Ashwatthama is said to offer flowers to Shiva every morning.

The fort was not totally impregnable. The British did eventually take it during the Second Anglo-Maratha War in 1803. They attacked the *pettah*, the town nearby, and erected a battery within range of the fort. The garrison surrendered. In 1819 the British had to take the fort again, but this time after a twenty-day siege. And, in another coincidence of history, one of Solomon's sons, John Lucas Earle, the father of Harriet Tytler, was appointed as adjutant to the fort in 1819.

Asirgarh is now uninhabited and in a ruinous state, but the Hindu temple is still used for worship. The ruins of the British barracks still stand including the derelict shell of a prison, used to intern opponents of the Raj. Just up the hill, near the entrance gates are the remains of a British cemetery. It is a sad and lonely place.

The Journal author was also impressed by the nearby city of Burhanpur. He described as follows:

It is very large, equal in size to Patna, surrounded by an indifferent pucha stonewall. It is the capital of the rich province Candish, now totally under the dominion of the Poonah ministry. The inhabitants continued in their habitations, and with great hospitality supplied us with everything for the ready cash; here we got very excellent grapes, and some indifferent oranges, at this season of the year, it appears extraordinary the former should be ripe, and the mangoes only in blossom; but we were told the grapes all come from Ashere Gurr.

I was equally impressed with the city. Burhanpur has changed little over the last two centuries. It is still surrounded by an *indifferent* stonewall and the locals are still very friendly. It is also the site of a magnificent crumbling Mughal palace, once inhabited by Shah Jahan's favourite wife, Mumtaz

The King's Fort at Burhanpur. Print from Montgomery Martin, 1850

14. The Crossing IV : Hoshangabad to Surat

Burhanpur Palace in 2016

Mahal. We were told that she died there, in childbirth, although others said she died at Asirgarh. As mentioned previously the Taj Mahal was built as her mausoleum.

I spent a most interesting two days at Burhanpur. We stayed at the idiosyncratic *Hotel and Holiday Resort Ambar*, run by an eccentric Zoroastrian. We took a car to visit Asirgarh. They do not get many tourists in Burhanpur and we felt like celebrities. We saw plenty of *flying foxes,* huge fruit bats that hang upside down from trees in the town. We then took the overnight train to Baroda, via Surat, spending many hours waiting for a connection at Bhusaval junction. Incidentally, Burhanpur railway station was where Saroo Brierly, the hero of the film and book *Lion,* lost his brother at the age of five.[5] He got on a train and ended up in Calcutta – my journey in reverse.

According to Solomon, it was while at Burhanpur that Colonel Goddard received the disastrous news of the *total defeat of their troops by the Maharattas on the top of the Gauts*. Goddard, on his own initiative, made the decision to march to Surat as soon as possible. There had been some intelligence coming through about the defeat, but it had been rather *dubious*.[6] When

14. The Crossing IV : Hoshangabad to Surat

Goddard made the decision to proceed at full speed to Surat, he considered that it was necessary, *not only to be the means of restoring the affairs of the Bombay Presidency, but to save it from utter ruin.*[7] Orders from Bombay or Calcutta would have taken weeks to arrive and by then it might have been too late. His decision to march probably changed the course of history.

Apparently a force of 20,000 Maratha horse was on its way from Pune to intercept the Company army. Solomon mentioned a force of over 100,000 men. It is likely Goddard would have gathered his senior officers together, including Solomon, to confirm the disastrous news about the surrender at Wadgaon and the plan to march post haste.

The race was on.

The Bengal Army left Burhanpur on the 6th February 1779 and proceeded at a fast pace in a westerly direction, the shortest route to Surat. Solomon wrote that they passed through *a delightful country, well cultivated and populous, with numbers of small rivers and nullahs, the villages surrounded with pucka and mud walls.* The Journal author described passing along narrow lanes and through deep ravines. The roads were good – just as well as they were making between twelve and fourteen miles per day. Imagine an army of over 6000 men, with a train of artillery pulled by thousands of bullocks, and over 20,000 camp followers with their carts, bullocks and horses, travelling at that pace. The Journal noted all the villages they passed each day.

On the 16th February they reached Nandurbar, the first substantial town. Solomon wrote, *the city of Noondabar is also defended by strong walls and towers, this last is said to be the Capital of Tuckoagee, the Hulcar's country.* At the time Tukoji Holkar's capital was situated at Maheshwar, on the banks of the Narmada, to the north. The Holkar capital moved to Indore in 1818, when Indore became a princely state under the British.

The journal author described Nandurbar as *a very large city, surrounded with a stonewall, and round towers on a lonely height. This is said to be Tuckoagee Hulcan's country. To the westward of the town is a very large tank, with plenty of duck and teal, and the greatest quantity of batts, or flying foxes; the hills appeared all round the country dry and parched up.* They were allowed one rest day before resuming the march.

There is little of note about the remaining eight days of the march except to say that the army made fourteen miles each day until they reached the safety of Surat on the 25th February. The Journal author described the

14. The Crossing IV : Hoshangabad to Surat

terrain on the 20th February as being *exceedingly jungly. Near this is a very high hill, with a pucha fort on its Summit, it is in the shape of a sugar loaf. This is Scampore.* This fort could well have been Songadh, the stronghold of the Gaekwads. Songadh was also made of stone and shaped like a sugar loaf. As mentioned Pilagi Gaekwad took Songadh in the 1720s and it remained the main base of the Gaikwads until Fatesinghrao moved the capital to Baroda in 1772.

The short time taken to march from Burhanpur to Surat was a momentous achievement when you consider the size of the army, the hilly nature of the terrain and the lack of any previous survey of the route. They had covered the 223 miles from Burhanpur to Surat in a total of just nineteen days.

Solomon wrote: *while the Bengal army lay on the banks of the Narbudda; Captain Popham was appointed paymaster, and soon the command devolved on me as senior lieutenant, and very soon after our arrival at Surat, Captain Popham quitted the army and returned to Bengal by sea; he was soon after appointed Major; when I was promoted to the rank of Captain; and succeeded him in the command of the 2*[nd] *Battalion.* This was a significant advance for Solomon, given the slow rate of promotion in the Company army.

News of the debacle at Wadgaon reached Hastings on the 25th February 1779.[8] It must have been a relief, soon after receiving that news, to learn of the safe arrival of the Bengal army at Surat. Hastings warmly testified to Goddard's *activity and prudence.* Before they heard about Goddard's decision to march to Surat, the Supreme Council were in the process of ordering Goddard to march southeast to support Madras due to threats from Hydar Ali. There was much disagreement between Francis and Hastings and many debates about how to *retrieve the disgrace.* Prior to receiving the news about Goddard's safe arrival Francis had *continually circulated the wild tale to his friends that Goddard would meet with 'insurmountable difficulties' and would never reach Bombay.*[9] He had been proved wrong.

The next few months must have been a relief for Solomon. He had survived the long march and had been promoted to the rank of captain and was now in charge of a battalion. His future was secure.

He remained in the vicinity of Surat for nearly a year until the 1st January

14. The Crossing IV : Hoshangabad to Surat

1780. He also found time to conceive his first child, Sophia. As mentioned we have no information about the mother of his child, or what happened to her.

A prejudiced view on this matter, from the East India Military Calendar, published in 1824, made reference to the difficulties supporting children of mixed race liaisons:

What is to be done with this increasing race of Indo-British subjects, or Eurasians, as they recently termed themselves, is a question that forcibly offers itself to the mind of every man conversant with India. It is very clear the precincts of Calcutta, Madras and Bombay do not offer a field wide enough, or the counting houses of merchants any chance of adequate employ, for so increasing a body as the descendants of our countrymen will speedily become.

Of the British subjects composing the King's and Company's troops, probably not 3000 are married to their own countrywomen; a great proportion of the remainder living in a state of concubinage with Native, Portuguese, and Musselman females, and the result is, as may naturally be expected, a vast increase in illegitimate offspring, which induces too many old and infirm officers to remain in the service, to secure some sort of provision for the mother, and employment for the children of such improvident, not to say ignominious early connexions.[10]

What did he expect? Sending young men to India for years on end with no female company and no provision to marry local women. In Solomon's time there were virtually no English women in India. The views expressed above may appear strange to our modern opinions but Indians did not welcome mixed race offspring either. In Calcutta an orphanage was established in 1783. According to the writer of the East India Military Calendar this produced a large number of educated children who could not be employed. They were not allowed to serve in the army as officers, or enter the higher echelons of the civil service. Such bigoted attitudes and the resulting lack of integration cannot have supported the British policy to stay in India for the future.

PART FIVE : BARODA AND BENGAL : 1780 – 1785

15. Campaigning in Gujarat : 1780 to 1781

Lithograph by Philip Baldeus depicting Ahmedabad and the Sabarmati River in 1672. Public Domain.

During the year 1779, while Solomon was recovering from the march at Surat, a lot was happening on the national and world stage. After France declared war on Great Britain in 1778, Hastings acted quickly and took Pondicherry, Chandernagore and Mahé from the French. Hydar Ali in Mysore preferred to ally with the French and vowed to take vengeance, making threats to invade the Carnatic.[1]

The war in America was not going well for the British. Spain had entered the war on the side of France and Gibraltar was now under siege. The siege of Gibraltar went on for nearly four years and remains the longest siege in British history. Retaining Gibraltar secured British dominance over the Mediterranean, which came useful during the Napoleonic wars at the end of the eighteenth century.[2]

The Dutch were about to enter the war on the side of the French. In fact Britain was now virtually isolated on the world scene. This can be compared with the more favourable situation during the Seven Years

15. Campaigning in Gujarat : 1780 to 1781

War (1756 – 1763) when Britain had alliances with Hanover, Prussia and Portugal and there was no conflict with the American colonies.

In Calcutta and London it was thought imperative to secure peace in India as soon as possible by making a treaty with the Marathas. But the Marathas wanted none of it. They had soundly defeated the Bombay Army at Wadgaon and felt in a strong position. In Pune, Nana Fadnavis demanded that the English keep to the agreement made at Wadgaon. He wanted Salsette returned and he wanted Raghunathrao, who had escaped from his captors and taken sanctuary with the English at Surat, returned to Pune. Furthermore Nana Fadnavis was known to have been negotiating with the Dutch. Correspondence had been intercepted with the Dutch director at Surat about a plot to assist the Marathas to surprise Surat Castle.[3] Nana Furnavis had already been liaising with the French and there was understandable concern that he would join with Hydar Ali. If this happened the British could be under threat from four fronts: Madras from Hydar Ali, Bengal from Mudhoji Bhonsle, the Circars from the Nizam of Hyderabad and Bombay from Nana Fadnavis, allied with Holkar and Scindia. If the French and Dutch joined them the situation could become unsustainable. The only saving grace for the English was the presence of the Bengal Army in Surat.

With Goddard as his agent in Bombay, Hastings continued to sue for peace. But he had no success. It was therefore decided to follow the familiar policy of divide and rule and attempt to seek an alliance with Fatesinghrao Gaekwad in Baroda.[4] The English knew that Fatesingh was discontented with the vast tribute he had to pay to Pune. Fatesingh apparently *procrastinated* and refused to play ball.[5] Furthermore it was known he was strengthening his army in Baroda.[6]

Plan B was therefore put into operation.

On the 1st January 1780 the Bengal Army was mobilised and sent north across the Tapti River. They crossed the Narmada on the 15th January with the battering train and stores joining them from Bharuch.[7] They were entering joint Gaekwad and Peshwa territory.

The army arrived at Dabhoi on the 18th January. At the time Dabhoi was garrisoned by 2000 of the Peshwa's troops.[8] They made preparations to lay siege to the city positioning a battery of three 18 pounders within 200 yards of the walls of the fort. The garrison surrendered before a shot was fired.

15. Campaigning in Gujarat : 1780 to 1781

THE GATE OF DIAMONDS AT DUBHOY.—From Forbes' Oriental Memoirs.

Gate of Diamonds, Dabhoi. Print from Beveridge. 1860s

The surrender of Dabhoi understandably had an effect on the resolution of Fatesingh to resist the British. In Solomon's words:

As the General (Goddard) was resolved to carry on the war with the Maharattas, and in order to prevent having an enemy in the rear, he judged it best to endeavour first to subdue Futty Sing, the 'Rajah of Guzarat,' Broderah his capital; we took Dubay a large walled city after a trifling resistance, and the Rajah was soon glad to become an ally of the English, to save his capital and his whole territory from being laid waste.

On January 26th Goddard met with Fatesingh near the village of Candeela to draw up an alliance. The resulting treaty had twelve articles including a defensive alliance, an agreement to exclude the Poona government from sharing territory in Gujarat and a promise from the English to *support and defend* Fatesingh in possession of his share of Gujarat province. In return Fatesingh would support the English with 3000 horse.[9] This treaty was of momentous significance to the English. It secured them an ally against Pune and strengthened the northern border.

15. Campaigning in Gujarat : 1780 to 1781

As we have seen General Goddard was not a man to hang around. Within two weeks the Bengal Army, with the support of Fatesingh's cavalry, were outside the walls of Ahmedabad, eighty miles to the north. At the time Ahmedabad was garrisoned by 6000 Arab and Sindhi foot soldiers, together with 2000 horse.[10] These troops were mercenaries, employed by the Peshwa. The walls of Ahmedabad were *of immense extent, and, for so vast a city, were remarkably strong.*[11] Batteries were set up and negotiations commenced.

Ahmedabad was, and still is, a prosperous city, capital of the State of Gujarat. In the eighteenth century it was surrounded by a defensive wall and had at least fourteen gates. The city had reached its peak during the time of Mughal rule and, as mentioned, was finally taken by the Marathas, Damaji Gaekwad and Raghunathrao, in 1755. Ahmedabad was used to sieges. It had sustained a seven-month siege in 1733, when the Marathas surrounded the city and plundered the surrounding area.[12] In 1756 the city was again under siege for a year when Momin Khan took the city and the Marathas tried to get it back. There were many deaths from starvation and disease.[13] By 1780 the Peshwa had control of the city. More recently, in 1915, Ahmedabad became a centre for the Indian independence movement when Mahatma Ghandi settled there after travelling from South Africa. The Salt March of 1930 started in Ahmedabad, and ended on the coast at the village of Dandi, 240 miles away.

Solomon wrote:

Our new ally joined us with a large body of his troops, and proceeding north soon arrived before the city of Amedabad, the capital of the Guzarat, commanded by a chief in the interest of the Poonah Government. The city is situated on the Suparmattea, a beautiful little river which falls in to the sea at Cambay. We opened our batteries on the 10th of February.

In effect several days had been spent in fruitless negotiation with the Maratha governor before the batteries were opened.[14] The state of affairs inside the city was complex. The Peshwa administrators were virtually under house arrest as the mercenary armies defending the city had not been paid. It was in their interests to keep the Peshwa in power until their pay and arrears had been honoured.

After receiving an evasive reply from the defenders, Goddard opened the batteries. Firing continued until the evening of the next day. By then a

15. Campaigning in Gujarat : 1780 to 1781

serviceable breach had been made. The breach in the walls had been made at the Khan Jahan Gate, just south of the fort. Goddard then held off the attack for a further day to continue negotiations in an attempt to avoid loss of life. But the garrison refused to surrender. On the morning of the 15th February Goddard gave orders for the assault. The newly promoted Lieutenant Colonel James Hartley was put in charge of the attack.

Duff gives an interesting account of the assault:

The advance was composed of volunteers from the Bombay division. Two unfortunate individuals,* of those who had been dismissed for misbehaviour in the preceding campaign, came forward to General Goddard and earnestly solicited permission to accompany the forlorn hope,[15] which was humanely granted, and both survived, after proving themselves worthy of being restored to the service.

* Their names were Fraser and Clancey. Fraser was dismissed for abandoning his post at the Bhore Ghaut, on hearing of the defeat at Wurgaom. But the infamy was rendered particularly striking and ridiculous, as it was from him that the first intelligence was received in Bombay of the disaster; and, writing from recollection, his note is on the Bombay records, in these words: Dear Sir. – our army is cut to pieces; I can effect my retreat, but I scorn it, at the risk of my honour. This is the last you shall hear from, yours truly, W. Fraser. Fraser, however, lived not only to retrieve his honour, but to be much esteemed throughout the army.[16]

We will come across Fraser again in Chapter 23. Clancy also survived and was later promoted to ensign.

The command of the storming party was entrusted to Sergeant Fridge of the Bombay European Regiment, *a corps always celebrated for gallant volunteers on such occasions.*[17] The grenadiers of the Bombay division followed the forlorn hope with a strong reserve chosen from the rest of the army. Perhaps Goddard was giving the Bombay division a chance to make up for their defeat at Wadgaon.

On a preconcerted signal, the whole moved off at a brisk pace, rushed up the breach where the garrison stood ready to receive them, and for a short time made a very determined stand, until three hundred of them lay dead, when resistance ceased. The most honourable part of this gallant assault was the subsequent steadiness and good conduct of the troops. No excesses were

15. Campaigning in Gujarat : 1780 to 1781

committed, and two only of the inhabitants, not composing the garrison, lost their lives. Of the British troops one hundred and six were killed and wounded, among the latter were ten European officers and four gentlemen volunteers, three of whom died of their wounds.[18]

Solomon wrote that Captain Gough, *who commanded the storming party*, fell in the attack. Solomon was then *commanded* to take possession of the city with 500 of the Bombay troops.

Our cannon did much havoc in a short time, houses &c. were battered down, and hundreds of fighting men, besides the poor inhabitants lying dead and dying in all directions. The next morning I discovered some thousand barrels of gunpowder, and reported it to General Goddard. Our army was supplied with as much as it could carry, and the overplus was thrown into the river.

On the 28th February Fatesinghrao was given possession of the city. Goddard proposed setting up a Company factory in Ahmedabad and putting an English resident into Fatesingh's durbar. But William Hornby, Governor of Bombay, opposed such measures at this time.

After the successful storming of Ahmedabad there was no rest for the Bengal army. There were reports that Scindia and Holkar had forded the Narmada and were heading north with something in the region of 20,000 horse. Goddard set off in that direction after sending the heavy artillery and stores to Cambay. They met the Maratha army in the vicinity of Baroda.

There followed a period of stalemate with the two armies camped a few miles from each other. Mahadji Scindia appeared ready to negotiate a peace and announced that he would rather be allied to the English than to the Peshwa. At the time Raghunathrao was at Surat and Scindia was thought to be keen to get him back. The English had been re-enforced by Lieutenant Colonel Brown and a body of troops from Madras who had arrived by sea. As a gesture Scindia released Farmer and Stewart, who had been kept hostage since Wadgaon.[19]

But Goddard did not entirely trust these overtures of peace. It was thought that Scindia's aim was to keep the English occupied until the start of the monsoons. Goddard therefore gave him three days to come up with an acceptable peace plan. But a peace plan never transpired. Goddard's suspicions were confirmed when it was discovered that Scindia was in secret negotiations with Fatesinghrao's brother and rival, Govindrao.

15. Campaigning in Gujarat : 1780 to 1781

The negotiations were over. Goddard ordered the army to advance on Scindia's troops, but the more mobile Maratha troops simply moved back out of range. Their heavy baggage had been left some miles to the rear at the hill fort of Pavagadah.

On the 3rd April Goddard tried to make a surprise attack on Scindia's camp in an attempt to bring the Marathas into action. He set off at 2am with part of the army, leaving the remainder in camp under Hartley.[20] But as fast as he advanced the Marathas withdrew, and all he could achieve were a few skirmishes. To make matters worse, when the English took over land previously occupied by the Maratha army it was found to be devoid of any grass or sustenance for their cattle and horses. Foraging parties were attacked. It was a hopeless game of cat and mouse.

Solomon gave an account of a skirmish in the vicinity of Baroda. On the 17th March they *lost several officers &c, &c* (I assume he means other ranks). *Had the enemy made a stand both the slaughter would have been great on both sides. The principle mischief they did to us was by their rockets. As our army advanced the enemy retreated, and finally quitted the country, leaving a large party to harass and cut off our supplies.*

Solomon then described a series of manoeuvres as Colonel Brown's troops from the Madras detachment approached Baroda. Before the Madras troops could reach the Bengal army, a large force of Marathas (Solomon states 10,000) moved forward to cut off the relieving troops. Solomon was *detached, with the greatest secrecy and haste,* to reinforce them. He marched overnight and reached Colonel Brown's detachment by daybreak, finding them in a strong position near Baroda. He wrote that he then, *lost no time in representing to Colonel Brown the urgency of hastening back to join the General, as his situation was critical, having weakened his small army by detaching me with nearly on third of his force.*

But Colonel Brown objected to this plan claiming that Captain Earle's detachment would be too fatigued to march back straight away. The march was delayed until the evening, after dark, with Solomon's detachment of Bengal troops taking up the rear guard.

According to Solomon this proved to be a highly dangerous manoeuvre as no sooner had the march started the Madras troops went on ahead, shining bright lights. Colonel Brown then sent word through his ADC that he intended to proceed with his own 300 Madras troops, leaving the Bengal and Bombay troops behind. Solomon remonstrated, pointing out *the impossibility of four battalions of sepoys with their guns, tumbrils, bazars*

15. Campaigning in Gujarat : 1780 to 1781

&c. &c., keeping up with a few Europeans, who had no encumbrances whatever. He also pointed out the agreement made previously to keep lights to the minimum.

Things continued in this vein until the Madras troops were at least a mile in front. Solomon halted his own solders to allow the rear guard to catch up. The gap was by then two miles. He wrote: *it was a happy circumstance for us, the enemy took no advantage of this opportunity of cutting us to pieces.* Colonel Brown arrived safely with the main army about midnight and, according to Solomon, received a *justly severe censure for his conduct (*14th *April).*

Solomon himself arrived some hours later. He wrote that he *was honoured with the General's approbation in the presence of Colonel Brown.* Presumably the Colonel was fuming. After Colonel Brown retired, *the General declared, before the Adjutant General and several of his own staff, that had the enemy made an attack on our detachment (as he had every reason to expect) before I took command, the whole must have been inevitably destroyed, and he hoped ere long to have it in his power to show me and the whole army the high opinion he had of my conduct.*

This may have been somewhat embarrassing for Solomon because he adds; *those present looked on the compliments paid me, very differently from what I did myself, for I was conscious I had done no more than any other officer in the Bengal army would have done in my place, and perhaps the General overrated my conduct the more, to mark his disapproval of that of Colonel Brown.*

Clearly there were rivalries between the two armies and Solomon had been caught up in the middle.

A soldier from the Madras contingent, Samuel Hickson, kept a diary at the time. The diary gives a graphic account of conditions, describing the desertion of a number of English soldiers. One of them, a William Mattrass, was caught and hung from a mango tree and many others died from disease. His detachment was then sent to Bassein by ship.[20]

Solomon wrote that Scindia and Holkar's forces then returned, Here is Solomon's account as to what happened next:

For several days they threatened an attack, constantly advancing nearly within reach of our guns, but could not be brought to engage with us in earnest. On this the General ordered me to move out with my Battalion about half a mile in front as a decoy, and in the event of the enemy retreating, to remain there as an advanced picquet until I should find it necessary to fall back to my ground in the line. Here I continued for some weeks, in expectation of

15. Campaigning in Gujarat : 1780 to 1781

their bearing down on my little party. From daybreak when they made their appearance, until sunset when they invariably retired, they were often within reach of my two long brass pounders, as well of the two field pieces attached to my Battalion, so I had frequent opportunities of playing with them, and must have done great execution.

One day they came so near that the General sent me orders to fall back into the line, supposing I might be pursued and a general engagement be the result. But the manoeuvre did not succeed.

Being now convinced that the Maharattas only meant to harass as much as possible, we proceeded towards Surat, in order to get into cantonments before the rains set in.

But Solomon never got to Surat. In late May 1780, General Goddard decided to leave two battalions and a small park of artillery at *Sennora* (Sinor) *on the bank of the Narbudda,* in order to protect Baroda and some of the lands ceded to the English by Fatesingh. Scindia and Holkar had apparently left 30,000 horse within two days march of Baroda, near *Bawarree* (?Barwani). Solomon was put in charge of this contingent, the 2nd and 4th Battalions, amounting to about 2500 men and artillery. He set about erecting temporary cantonments between two deep ravines, with the Narmada to the rear. He was to stay there for nearly a year.

While Solomon was at Sinor, General Goddard was put under increasing pressure to send troops south to support the Bombay Government. The Company now effectively controlled the seacoast from Cambay to Damãn, but Bassein was still an obstacle on the way to Bombay and the Marathas showed no signs of *wearing out.* [21] Solomon and his two divisions had been left at Sinor to provide protection to Gujarat and Fatesingh, as agreed by the treaty. Other divisions were left at Ahmedabad and Surat, under the overall command of Major Forbes. Goddard left for Bombay on the 16th October.[22]

Further north, in order to draw Scindia away from Gujarat and Bombay, Hastings made a treaty with the Rana of Gohad and sent Captain Popham with a force of 2400 men into Scindia's territory. Like the Bombay army two years earlier, they crossed the Jumna at Kalpi (February 1780) then headed west for Gwalior. In a daring move, the supposedly impregnable

15. Campaigning in Gujarat : 1780 to 1781

Gwalior. Print from Montgomery Martin, 1860s

fortress of Gwalior was captured in a surprise attack (3rd August). The fortress is situated on the top of cliffs, 200 to 300 feet high. Intelligence had shown that robbers had managed to gain access up these cliffs. Popham's attack, using rope and wooden ladders, was a great success.

Meanwhile the Bombay army moved east from Salsette and took Kalyan, but the Marathas counter-attacked. Reinforcements from Surat, led by Hartley, arrived just in time (24th May). As soon as the monsoon ended, Goddard moved to attack Bassein. On the 24th November a powerful battery of twenty-four-pounders and several mortars opened up. The Marathas tried to raise the siege by sending 20,000 troops to attack Hartley's division, to the east of Bassein, without success. The fortress of Bassein finally surrendered on the 11th December 1780.[23]

While at Sinor, Solomon gave an account of a war of words he had with Scindia. He described receiving *several insolent and threatening letters*. An incident then occurred when they captured one of Scindia's spies who expected death. Instead Solomon gave him his liberty and sent him back with a message described as *a pressing invitation to his master, which in spite of his threats he had not the spirit to accept.*

15. Campaigning in Gujarat : 1780 to 1781

When the rains ended Solomon described making frequent excursions around the country:

In one of which I had occasion to chastise an insolent fellow who had taken possession of a (neat) walled town (Cheempaneer), near Pawagur, which he supposed to be very strong. I then proceeded against Khyseer Cown, a most notorious rebel of the Company, who had destroyed several villages, murdered many of the inhabitants, and had the audacity to fix several of their heads on the walls of Dubay, a city that belonged to the English. This fellow was the chief of the Grashees country, bordering on our newly ceded Purgannahs, and I was very desirous to secure the villain, so leaving 4th Battalion and Artillery under Captain Archdeacon's care, [24] *I by forced march and great good luck came up with him just at day break; having secured him I intimated the same to the Council of Broach.*

But Solomon was greatly disappointed when the Council, after praising him, advised him to release the prisoner with *only a small reprimand*. He added that he afterwards learnt the true cause of their lenity, but unfortunately does not explain what this *true cause* was.

East Bhadra Gate at Champaner. 2016

15. Campaigning in Gujarat : 1780 to 1781

The aforementioned *Cheempaneer* is the ancient walled capital of Gujarat, Champaner, situated next to the hill fort and sacred mountain, Pavagadh. Both now form a World Heritage Site.

Solomon then went on to describe an incident when he had to relieve Major Forbes who had sent a letter to Sinor informing Solomon that he was surrounded by at least 10,000 Maratha troops at *Soanghur,* 80 miles away.

> *With all possible expedition I immediately left my heavy artillery, sick, wounded, and everything that could impede my march at Rhan Ghur, a strong fort, under the charge of a Jemadar and 30 Sepoys. After a most fatiguing march with my tumbrils and light field pieces across a country without a vestige of road, or even foot path, I joined the Major in three days. The enemy had fallen back near to Nowapora, about sixteen miles distant, so it was resolved to make an attack on them the following night, and as the Major took charge of my detachment, I proceeded with the Grenadiers of my own Battalion and two six pounders, as the advanced guard. I fell in with their picquets just before daybreak, and on their giving the alarm, the enemy was clear of the ground in a few minutes, having their horses saddled all night; they made a stand on a hill about half a mile in their rear, but on bringing our guns to bear on them, made a rapid retreat; nor did they ever return to Guzerat during the campaign.*

It is probable that *Soanghur* is actually Songhad, the Gaekwad fortress that Solomon previously described as *Scampore* (see previous chapter), the Gaekwads first base in Gujarat. *Nowapora* is likely to be Navapur, just to the east of Songhad.

Solomon then returned to Sinor and wrote that, *after settling the ryots in peaceable possession of their villages, and clearing the country to the entire satisfaction of the Chief and Council of Broach, the Resident of our newly ceded Purgannahs, and our new ally, Futty Sing, my detachment returned to Surat.*

Solomon then received instructions from General Goddard to *proceed to the Court of Futty Sing to settle some misunderstanding which had arisen between the General and the Rajah.* Solomon does not explain what this 'misunderstanding' was, but wrote that, *after a stay of three months, I had the satisfaction of settling all differences.*

15. Campaigning in Gujarat : 1780 to 1781

This is the first mention of any direct contact between Solomon and the Rajah, Fatesinghrao. However he would have come across him during the Ahmedabad campaign. They must have got on reasonably well and this says something about Solomon's diplomatic abilities. General Goddard clearly picked up on this as well because, when it was finally decided to appoint a resident to Fatesinghrao's court, Captain Solomon Earle was the man chosen. It was unusual to appoint a military man as Resident.

In Solomon's words:

On my return I accompanied the General to Brodera (Baroda) *where he was met by the Rajah, Futty Sing, where I was honoured by the appointment of Resident at the court of Brodera, on the part of the English Government, and was presented to the Rajah by the General as his adopted son, which had a wonderful effect on his behaviour during my stay with him of upwards of two years. I did not quit his Durbar until the peace was finally concluded between the English and the Maharatta States, at the end of 1783, when I returned to Surat, and from thence by land to Bombay.*

I stayed at Baroda (see Chapter 17) in 2016, and from there visited the World Heritage Sites of Champaner and Pavagadh. Champaner was founded in pre-Mughal times. The city was largely preserved when the Mughals moved their capital to Ahmadebad. It contains several beautiful mosques surrounded by crumbling city walls and gates. The neighbouring volcanic hill (Pavagadh) is over 2500 feet high and towers over the plains around. Pavagadh has been fortified for over 1200 years. The Rajputs occupied the site for many years until the Mohammedans ousted them in the thirteenth century. This took several campaigns until eventually, after a twenty-month siege, the conquerors stormed the heights. The Rajputs could see that the end was in sight and they set fire to the town and killed themselves and their wives and children rather than be taken alive. The few who were captured were eventually put to the sword after refusing to change their faith. The King's surviving daughters had to join the Sultan's harem.

At the top of the hill is a temple dedicated to Kali. It is now a pilgrimage site. We ascended the hill by truck, cable car and then on foot, joining the throngs heading to the temple on the summit.

16. The Duel and the Thunderbolt of Mars

In the small hours of Thursday morning on the 17th August 1780, a group of Englishmen gathered on the Alipur Road near to Warren Hastings' residence at Belvedere House in Calcutta.[1] It was a fine and calm day. One of the Englishmen had been woken by his second at 0400am, but had asked to be left alone for another half hour. They met up with two other men, who were walking up and down the road in an agitated fashion. It was getting near the time when people would be up and about for their morning ride and they did not want to be seen. They set about looking for a secluded place. An avenue of trees was too dark and eventually they found a quiet lane.[2]

Neither of the two protagonists had had any experience of firing a pistol before. A distance of fourteen paces was measured out. One of the duellists was the Governor-General of India, Warren Hastings. The other was Philip Francis, member of the Bengal Council. Hastings' second was Colonel Pearse while Francis had Colonel Watson. Hastings resolved to hold his fire until Francis had taken his shot. He appeared calm but was embarrassed when an old native woman noticed what was happening and called others from a nearby village to see what the sahibs were up to.

Philip Francis raised his pistol, took aim and pulled the trigger. Nothing happened. Just a click. His gun was recharged and he raised it on two further occasions. On the third time he fired and Hastings fired too, almost simultaneously. One of the men fell, crying, 'I am dead.'

Three months earlier, when Solomon was settling in for the monsoon at Sinor, the dispute between Warren Hastings and Philip Francis had started to escalate. Further south, Hydar Ali was preparing to descend on Madras with a huge army, like a *thunderbolt of Mars*.[3] 1780 was going to be a year of major conflict in all three of the Presidencies.

On the world stage, France and Spain continued to besiege Gibraltar, the war in America was in full swing, and Britain had just declared war on Holland. In London the Gordon Riots were about to start.[4]

16. The Duel and the Thunderbolt of Mars

The increasing conflict between Hastings and Francis had been building up ever since Francis arrived in Calcutta in 1774 and basically opposed everything Hastings tried to do. The other two Council members, Clavering and Monson, had supported Francis, but were now both dead. Edward Whelan, an ex chairman of the Company, had been appointed to replace Monson. But he was a man who could waver. In Calcutta gossip circles he was known as *Ned Silent* or *Ned Wheelabout*.[5] In the main, Whelan was largely under the thumb of Francis. John Clavering had been replaced by Sir Eyre Coote. Eyre Coote had returned to India in 1779 and had taken command of the army. He was described as *quarrelsome, waywood, vain and irascible*.[6] But he was a good soldier and had the respect of the troops, despite not speaking word of Hindi or Urdu. He had previously led the Company army to victory against the French at Wandewash (Vandavasi) in 1760 and, although now in his fifties, was reputed to have the ability to stay in the saddle for up to thirty hours.[7]

As usual Francis had remained active in his communications with London. He was under the impression that he might be in with a chance to replace Hastings as Governor-General. Unfortunately for Hastings, Richard Barwell, his main supporter on the Council, was itching to go home. Hastings had managed to persuade Barwell to stay when the Maratha war started but Barwell still wanted to retire home as soon as he could.

Incidentally Richard Barwell had actually taken part in a duel with Clavering five years previously. Barwell had apparently had his eye on Clavering's daughter Maria and had told her his *expectations*. General Clavering charged him with *peculation*[8] and Barwell called Clavering a *scoundrel* in return. As this exchange happened during a Board meeting, honour required satisfaction.[9] The two met at dawn on the Budge Budge Road. Apparently Barwell asked the General, 'Which distance do you choose, Sir?' Clavering had replied, 'the nearer the better.' The General fired first and missed. Barwell then apologised and the matter was closed.

In 1776 Clavering, probably on the instigation of Francis, tried to stage a coup to eject Hastings. Clavering demanded the keys of the treasury and fort by noon, on the assumption that Hastings was to be recalled and he would take over as Governor-General. But Hastings took decisive action. He secured the support of the army, at the same time appealing to the judiciary to decide on the legality of Clavering's coup, announcing that he would abide by their decision. The judges decided in Hastings' favour. Clavering died soon after.

16. The Duel and the Thunderbolt of Mars

In 1778 Francis had been caught red-handed climbing into the bedroom of a certain Mrs Catherine Grand, the beautiful seventeen-year-old French wife of George Grand. Francis knew Mr Grand would be dining out with Barwell at the time. He climbed up to her room on a bamboo ladder. Mrs Grand's ayah, who had been instructed to keep an eye on her mistress by Mr Grand, found her mistress' bedroom door locked and roused the menservants. Francis made good his escape. Grand later challenged Francis to a duel, but Francis refused.[10] The case was then taken to the Supreme Court with a huge claim for damages of £160,000. In the end Mr Grand was described as a 'cuckold' and only £5000 was awarded against Francis. Mr Grand then divorced his young wife and she took up with Francis as his mistress. Catherine Grand later went on to marry Monsieur Charles de Talleyrand-Périgord, the French politician who later became the first Prime Minister of France under Napoleon.

Mrs Catherine Grand.

In his journal William Hickey described receiving a *strange reception* from Philip Francis when he presented him with a letter of introduction. Hickey called him a *pompous gentleman*.[11] But Hickey had chosen the wrong time to present his letter as Francis had just lost the above court case and the order for damages had understandably lowered his opinion of lawyers.

16. The Duel and the Thunderbolt of Mars

It is a wonder how any of the Council were able to concentrate on governing the country.

In 1780, perhaps mistakenly, Hastings decided to make a truce with Francis. Mistakenly as he was under the impression that Francis had mellowed. The truce was mediated by Sir John Day, the Attorney General. But nothing was put in writing and Hastings was under the impression that the word of a gentleman would suffice. As part of the truce Francis agreed not to further oppose the war and, in return, some of his cronies would be re-installed in office. In consequence of this Hastings felt able to sanction the desire for his only supporter on the Council, Richard Barlow, to return to England.

Incidentally Hastings still had two close friends he could trust in Bengal. They were David Anderson, who was about to be sent to Pune to mediate the peace treaty with the Marathas, and William Palmer. There is a wonderful painting of William Palmer and his Indian family, presently hung just outside the entrance to the Asian collections at the British Library. And of course Hastings always had the support of his wife, Marian.

As outlined in the previous chapter, Hastings had proposed that a diversion to the north of Maratha territory might reduce the pressure on Goddard to the west. Captain Popham had already been sent with a small force to take Gwalior. There were now plans to send Major Camac to join Popham with a larger force with the aim of advancing further into Scindia's territory. Francis was out of Council when the agreement to send troops was made.

But on his return, Francis and Whelan opposed the plan, stating it was too expensive and too risky. They argued that sending more troops would leave Bengal open to invasion. Apparently Hastings almost went on his knees, saying that Francis had sworn not to oppose his military strategy. He even offered to finance the force out of his own pocket. [12, 13] It was all to no avail.

This was the final straw for Warren Hastings. Years of opposition had finally taken their toll. After the Council meeting he calmly wrote down the fateful minute that was to be delivered to Francis. As it was a public document the wording of this minute made it impossible to ignore.

Here is an extract:

16. The Duel and the Thunderbolt of Mars

In truth, I do not trust to his promise of candour, convinced that he (Francis) is incapable of it, and that his sole purpose and wish are to embarrass and defeat every measure which I may undertake, or which may tend to promote the public interests, if my credit is connected with them…

I judge of his public conduct by my experience of his private, which I have found to be void of truth and honour. This is a severe charge, but temperately and deliberately made from the firm persuasion that I owe this justice to the public and to myself, as the only redress to both, for artifices of which I have been a victim, and which threaten to involve their interests, with disgrace and ruin. The only redress for a fraud for which the law had made no provisions is the exposure of it.[14]

Hastings knew what he was doing. His private secretary, William Markham, pointed out that his words left Francis no choice but to respond. In reply Hastings, somewhat sarcastically, praised his secretary's *extraordinary discernment*.[15]

At the Council meeting on the 15th August 1780, Francis asked to speak to Hastings in private. Formal satisfaction was demanded and accepted. The date of the duel was set for Thursday, August 17th.

Before the fateful day, both Hastings and Francis began to settle some of their affairs. Hastings prepared a new will and wrote a letter to be given to his wife should he not survive:

Calcutta 16 Aug 1780

My Beloved Marian,

My heart bleeds to think what your sufferings and feelings must be, if ever this letter shall be delivered into your hands. You will soon learn the occasion of it. On my part it has been unavoidable. I shall leave nothing which I regret to lose but you, nor in my last moments shall I feel any other affliction. Let it be a consolation to you to know that at this moment I have the most grateful sense of all your past kindness, and of the unremitted proofs which you have daily and hourly afforded me of your affection. For these may God reward you! I know not how. How much I have loved you. How much beyond all that Life can yield, I still love you, He only knows. Do not, my Marian, forget me; but cherish my remembrance to the latest hour of your life, as I should yours were it my lot, and my misery, to survive you. I cannot write all that I feel and that my heart is full of.

16. The Duel and the Thunderbolt of Mars

Adieu, my best wife, and most beloved of women. May the God of Heaven bless you and support you. My last thoughts will be employed on you. Remember and love me. Once more farewell.

Your

Warren Hastings[16]

The man who fell in the duel on the 17th August was Philip Francis. When Francis called out that he was dead, Hastings muttered in a shocked voice, 'Good God! I hope not.' Francis had been hit just below the right shoulder, but the wound was not life threatening. A palanquin was found to take him to Belvedere House and Hastings hastily arranged for his own doctor to visit. Within a month Francis was back in Council.

Five days later news came that Hydar Ali had invaded the Carnatic with a force of 90,000 men. Seven days later came better news. Captain Popham's force had taken Gwalior. But on the 20th September 1780 terrible news arrived. The Madras army had been annihilated at Pollilur and the French navy was on its way. Madras appeared doomed.

But there was some good news for Hastings. In October 1780, Philip Francis resigned from the Council.

Hydar Ali had been planning to invade the Carnatic for a long time. He now had the support of France, and French officers had helped train and support his forces. Most descriptions of his advance into the Carnatic describe it in vivid terms. His army *burst into the Carnatic* [17] and *spread like a torrent over the plains.* [18] When the news broke the Madras establishment were in the process of holding a grand masquerade ball to honour a group of young women who had just arrived from England. Hydar's army poured down the Ghats laying waste to everything in their path. Villages and forts were burnt and the population were massacred. When they got to the walls of Madras it was time to do something.

Sir Hector Munro, the hero of Buxar, had allowed a large detachment of his force, under Colonel Bailey, to be separated from the main body of troops at Pollilur. It was 4000 Company troops against 10,000 of the Mysore army. The Mysore troops were led by Hydar Ali's son, Tipu. The British formed a large square but failed to hold the line and their powder store exploded. By the end only 50 British officers and 200 men survived, including the wounded Colonel Bailey, who was taken prisoner. This was the second major defeat of British forces in a year.

16. The Duel and the Thunderbolt of Mars

The battle is strikingly depicted in a celebratory mural that Tipu Sultan commissioned for one of his palaces at Seringapatum, the Dariya Daulat. Thankfully this mural has been preserved:

Detail from the Mural of Battle of Pollilur at Seringapatum. Collection of Clare Arni

The survivors were taken back to Hydar's capital at Seringapatum. Some were forcibly circumcised and others were left chained in a windowless dungeon. To this day you can visit the prison, built into the city walls, where some of the soldiers were kept. Colonel Bailey died in 1782 while in captivity. The prison is still known as Colonel Bailey's dungeon.

After the defeat at Pollilur, Hector Munro dumped his baggage train and cannon and retreated back to the comparative safety of Madras.

If all this was not enough, Hastings had other problems. The reduction in trade and the need to keep the army on a war footing and support Bombay as well as Madras, had emptied the coffers. Because of the war in America there was nothing left for India apart from one regiment of regular troops and a small naval fleet under Admiral Hughes. Hastings resolved to do three things. He decided to put Eyre Coote in charge at Madras and send a relief force. It was imperative to make peace with the Marathas and appease the Nizam of Hyderabad as soon as possible. Finally he had to find a way of getting some money.

16. The Duel and the Thunderbolt of Mars

'Colonel Bailey's Dungeon,' Seringapatum, Mysore. 2017

Canon that fell through roof

The methods he employed to obtain finances were questionable. In short he resolved to squeeze two Indian rulers, Chait Singh in Benares and Asaf-ud-Daula, the new ruler in Oudh (Shuja-ud-Daula had died in 1775). How he did this is described in a later chapter (18). He also commissioned two ships, the *Betsy* and the *Nonsuch*, on a fruitless mission to smuggle unsold opium to China.[19]

Large sums of money were paid to Mudhoji Bhonsle, who was amassing cavalry on the southern borders of Bengal, to dissuade him from attacking the land force that was to be sent down the coast to Madras. This proved successful.

Eyre Coote set off by sea for Madras with 600 European troops while Colonel Pearse was sent overland with a force of sepoys. Coote arrived on November 5th and found the situation desperate. He finally set out in January 1781 to take on Hydar's forces. He had no cavalry and relied on hoards of bullocks to transport artillery and supplies. The lands around Madras had been utterly devastated. The Mysore forces were able to evade any major battles that would put them at risk of defeat. The French fleet, under Piere-André Suffren, for some unknown reason, decided to leave the area, leaving the way open for supplies to reach Madras. In 1782, probably due to the stress of marching up and down the Carnatic trying to engage the enemy, Coote had an *apoplectic stroke*.[20] He continued to direct operations from his palanquin.

Lord Macartney arrived in Madras in June 1781 as the new Governor. Being fresh from England he knew the trend of public opinion at home, which was for peace on all fronts, including America and India.[21]

In 1782 Suffren was back with twelve ships of the line and transports of French troops. Rear Admiral Edward Hughes could only muster nine ships. The two fleets clashed in April 1782 at the Battle of Sadras. Both suffered damage and there was no outright victor. They clashed again after the French captured Trincomalee from the British, who had recently taken the town from the Dutch. Trincomalee is situated on the northeast side of the island of Ceylon (Sri Lanka). The results were again inconclusive with both fleets suffering severe damage.

William Hickey, who seems to appear everywhere in this story, was sailing back to India with his new 'wife', Charlotte Barry. The couple ended up as prisoners of the French at Trincomalee. They had had a terrible voyage from Lisbon, having failed to get passage on a ship from England.

16. The Duel and the Thunderbolt of Mars

Their overloaded Portuguese ship had been caught in a tremendous storm off Ceylon during which the ship had lost all masts and sails and was drifting helplessly. The surviving crew managed to rig up a sail to the stump of the mizzenmast and head for the nearest land. This happened to be Trincomalee, recently taken by the French. Hickey wrote, of Suffren, that he looked *in appearance, much more like a little fat, vulgar English butcher than a Frenchman of consequence*. Hickey and his wife were later invited to dinner. Apparently Suffren *ate voraciously*. Mr and Mrs Hickey were eventually released and managed to get to Madras where Hickey had an audience with Lord Macartney. Macartney made many enquiries respecting the state of the French fleet.[22]

While in Madras, Hickey witnessed the arrival of a French ship. The ship commenced firing at English shipping. Fort St. George failed to fire back. When Hickey enquired afterwards why this had been the case, he was informed that *the keys of the store-rooms under the works, in which the ammunition was kept, had been mislaid and could nowhere be found for more than an hour.*[23]

When Coote sent an envoy to Hydar Ali to ask for peace terms, the message that came back was that Hydar had entered the war with the intention of *destroying and laying waste your country till never a lamp is left to burn there.*[24] Mervyn Davies described Hydar Ali as *the most formidable foe that the British had hitherto encountered in India*. But the Mysore leader died suddenly in December 1782. With Coote back in Bengal recuperating from his stroke, the war was at a stalemate.

Tipu Sultan, Hydar's successor, was not quite ready for peace. His father had placed a letter in his own turban, to be found after his death. The letter actually advised his son to sue for peace and Lord Macartney had started to make overtures in that direction. However Tipu took this as a sign of weakness and rejected any moves for peace.[25]

In March 1783 Coote had recovered so Hastings sent him back to the Carnatic to resume charge of the army. But he died just before reaching Madras, after a chase by French ships. William Hickey witnessed the arrival of Coote's ship. He wrote that everyone was delighted with the arrival of this distinguished commander. But they brought *the sad tidings that he was dying, if not already dead*. He was brought on shore, *in a state of determined apoplexy, in which unhappy state he remained quite insensible, until the following*

16. The Duel and the Thunderbolt of Mars

HYDER ALI.—From a drawing by J. Leister of Madras, 1776.

TIPPOO SULTAN.—From a portrait engraved in Beatson's View of the War with Tippoo Sultan.

Hydar Ali   *His son Tipu Sultan*
Prints from Beveridge, History of India 1861

morning, when he expired. [26] His funeral took place in the fort church which had, *during the famine, been entirely filled with bags of rice. It therefore became necessary to clear the principle isle, at the end of which near the pulpit the grave was dug.*[27] Coote's body was later transported back to London and laid to rest in Westminster Abbey.

Hickey then gave a rather poignant account of a visit to a certain Mrs Barclay's garden house, a few miles from Madras; disconcerting coming after Hickey's description of all that rice stored in the church:

> *In going to their house, a truly melancholic spectacle met our sight, at which my dearest Charlotte was beyond measure affected, the whole road being strewn on both sides with the skulls and bones of the innumerable poor creatures who had laid themselves down and miserably perished from want of food, being on their way from different parts of the country to Madras, in the hope of obtaining relief there – a relief it was not, from the thousands and tens of thousands that daily flocked towards the presidency.*

16. The Duel and the Thunderbolt of Mars

The French managed to land their troops, but when news came in June 1783 that peace had been concluded with Great Britain, all hostilities ceased. The war with Tipu Sultan dragged on for another year. Peace was finally concluded in March 1784 by the Treaty of Mangalore. The terms were favourable to Mysore leaving Tipu Sultan in a strong position, ready to fight again.

Philip Francis left Bengal in November 1780 but did not reach London until October 1781, after a particularly long voyage. He immediately set about laying the seeds for the destruction of his enemy, Warren Hastings. A powerful ally had joined the field, the philosopher and politician Edmund Burke. Contrary to opinion in London, Hastings had not in fact started either war in India. The Maratha war had been started by the Bombay Presidency, supported by the Court of Directors in London. And the Madras war had been started by Hydar Ali, inflamed by the behaviour of the Madras Presidency. It could be argued that, without Hastings' intervention, both Bombay and Madras would have been lost.

In other words Warren Hastings had actually saved India for the British. This is in contrast to the situation in America where, in October 1782, the British suffered a major defeat at Yorktown, with the eventual loss of the American colonies. And who had been in command there? Lord Cornwallis, who was soon to take over from Hastings as the new Governor-General of India.

Philip Francis was clearly a clever man. Back in England he became a politician and, for a time, a member of parliament. Biographies that support Warren Hastings are full of invective about Francis. It is certainly clear that Francis was an arrogant and vindictive man who had a high opinion of himself. He stuck to his principles and then applied them in a rigid manner. He was a man well versed in underhand tactics, sending copious anonymous letters, as evidenced by his earlier role as *Junius,* and later, in attacks on Hastings. He was highly manipulative in his control of other, less clever, members of the Bengal Council. He clearly wanted to become Governor-General of India and was disappointed when this wish was not realised. However he was no supporter of EIC expansion and rule in India, although it is unclear how he would have handled things had he gained power.

We will now return to the west side of India where Solomon was about to take up his new appointment as Resident to the Maharaja of Baroda.

17. Resident at Baroda : 1781 to 1783

Baroda (Vadodara) is the third largest city in the State of Gujarat after Ahmedabad and Surat.[1] Back in 1780 it was a walled city with four gates and a central pavilion, now known as the Mandvi Gate, which was originally the north gate of the Royal Enclosure. The walls were around two miles long.[2] Baroda was an equivalent size to the walled cities of Chester or York, in England. The River Vishwamitri runs past the city and is still crossed by a bridge built by the Mughals in the sixteenth century. A public park now lies just along the opposite bank of the river. The four city gates are still present, but little now remains of the city walls.

Baroda has changed its name on many occasions. The city was originally known as Atoka when there was a Jain settlement on the Vishwamitri River in the 5th and 6th Centuries. When the Rajputs conquered the city, they changed its name to Chandanavati, after the Rajput king Chandan. Banyan trees are common in Baroda and because of this it was also called Vatodar, after *Vat*, a Banyan Tree and *Aodh*, a canopy or tent.[3] This links more to its present name of Vadodara. It is possible to see how the name Baroda could have originated from the name Vatodar, or Wadodra, as both of these names were in use in the eighteenth century. Solomon used the name Brodera, a name used by the British at the time. The city was known as Baroda until 1974 when its name was changed to Vadodara. If you say Vadodara quickly it can sound almost like Baroda, or even Brodera.

The Sultans of Delhi took the city from the Rajputs, before the Mughals arrived. We have already seen how the Gaekwad dynasty first encroached on Mughal territory in a previous chapter. Pilagi Gaekwad first took the city in 1724 but the Mughals got it back after they murdered him. Damajirao Gaekwad retook the city in 1734. It then remained in Gaekwad hands until Independence in 1947. The era of Sayajirao Gaekwad III, from 1875 to 1939 has been described as Baroda's golden age. At this time Baroda was the capital of the Gaekwad Princely State[4] under overall British rule. This was the period when the amazing Laxmi Vilas Palace, just outside the city

17. Resident at Baroda : 1781 to 1783

Street Scenes from the Old City of Baroda 2016

17. Resident at Baroda : 1781 to 1783

walls, was constructed, as well as the public park, university and various museums and other public buildings. It is difficult now to envisage the original shape of the walled city. Some of the landmark buildings, notably the Nazarbaug Palace (dating from 1871) have been demolished.

In 1780 the Maharaja lived in a maze of older buildings linked to the Mandvi Gate. Weedon (1911) described these buildings as *long rambling galleries with steep, narrow staircases of painted wood.* [5] Exactly where Solomon was billeted is not recorded. Given that part of his role as Resident would have been to support the Maharaja against attack from Scindia and Holkar's forces, it is highly likely that he would have been supported by a number of Company troops. If so, then it is likely he stayed with his troops in a cantonment in the area where the public park is now situated. The Mughal rulers were great lovers of blood sports, a tradition continued by the Marathas. An arena called the Aggad was set aside for elephant and rhino fights. There were many hunting opportunities in the surrounding countryside, an area of rich farmland.

Solomon would have become familiar with the city and surrounding area during his time there. His daughter Sophia was born on the 4th July 1780. This period may have been a happy and stable time in his life, away from the rigours of campaigning, living with his family and retainers. And, as he held a respected and commanding position with the ruling powers, he would also have spent some time at the palace. As mentioned, he had been presented to Fatesinghrao as General Goddard's *adopted son*. F.A.H. Elliott wrote that Solomon's brief term of office was *not distinguished by any particular merit.*[6] But Fatesinghrao kept to his side of the agreement and there were no invasions by Marathas loyal to the Peshwa during this time.

It may also have been a more settled time for Fatesinghrao too. He no longer had to pay massive tributes to the Peshwa in Pune, had secured control of Ahmedabad and had finally wrestled power from his brother, Govindrao. Although he had to put up with Solomon keeping an eye on him, his kingdom was protected from attack by the presence of the Company troops.

In considering the court of Fatesinghrao in Baroda, it is unclear what had happened to the rightful heir, Sayajirao I. Given the mental disability of Sayajirao, the next in line to rule should have been Govindrao. However the situation was complex as their father had actually had three wives. According to Elliott the eldest son, Sayajirao, was the son of Damaji's

17. Resident at Baroda : 1781 to 1783

second wife, Kasibai. Govindrao was the son of his first wife, Manubai. One assumes Fatesinghrao was also a son of Kasibai, but this is by no means clear. Elliott described Govindrao as having a *weak vacillating mind*, no match for his younger half brother, Fatesinghrao. He further described Fatesinghrao as *a person of a remarkably ambitious turn of mind, a quick crafty, decided prince, who could carry out a campaign with as much ability as he could hold his own in a political contest.*[7] One assumes Solomon and Fatesinghrao would have held many debates, initially through interpreters.

In 1778 the Pune Court had finally recognised Fatesinghrao as overall ruler of the Gaekwads.[8] Interestingly, in some contemporary accounts, there is no mention of Fatesinghrao as being Maharaja at all.[9,10] He appears to have been written out of history, perhaps because he was ruling on behalf of his brother Sayajirao. After Fatesinghrao died in 1789, without a son and heir, he was succeeded by his younger brother, Manajirao. But Govindrao finally got to be Maharaja in 1793, after the demise of Manajirao. He then ruled until his death in 1800.

It can therefore be assumed that Fatesinghrao's court must have been a complex place to fully understand. There would have been various factions, including a mentally disabled brother, possibly three mothers, and a very disgruntled brother in exile, ready to attempt to seize the throne whenever he got the chance.

Away from the comparative peace of Baroda, just a few hundred miles south, the Anglo-Maratha War was still raging. As previously mentioned, Bassein had been taken by the British in December 1780 and the British now had control of the coast all the way from Bombay to Gujarat.

On the 9th October 1780, General Goddard received a letter from Warren Hastings announcing the intention to make peace with the Marathas.[11] The reasons for this have already been outlined in the last chapter. Hastings advised Goddard that the English should keep Bassein and that Fatesinghrao should keep Ahmedabad. But then news filtered through of Colonel Baillie's defeat at Pollilur. In consequence Nana Fadnavis felt in a much stronger position. Peace was not an option.

According to Duff, Goddard then committed an error by taking only *half measures* to advance up the Ghats towards Pune.[12] Goddard's troops were to follow a similar route to the Bombay army during the ill-fated Wadgaon campaign.[13]

17. Resident at Baroda : 1781 to 1783

Nana Fadnavis, boosted by Hydar Ali's success, resolved to fight back rather than sue for peace. In March 1781 a successful attack was made on an English detachment at Chauk. Two regiments, under Captain Mackay, were returning from Panvel with a convoy of stores, when they were set upon.[14] English losses were heavy. It was then felt too risky to keep a large force at the Ghats during the monsoon and a general retreat was ordered.

Later that month a formidable force of 25,000 Maratha horse attacked three battalions of sepoys bringing supplies to the Ghats. Fortunately for Colonel Brown, who was in command, a relief force was sent which saved them from complete annihilation. 106 men and five officers were killed or wounded. The supply routes to the Ghats lay through *a country full of thick jungles, broken ground and narrow defiles*.[15] By the time Goddard got back to Panvel there were many more deaths. The Company army finally left Panvel for their cantonments at Kalyan at the end of May 1781.

This left Nana Fadnavis in an even stronger position to make demands in any subsequent peace proposals. Goddard wanted to restart the campaign after the monsoon. He went north to negotiate with Fatesinghrao for more troops. *5000 good horse* were promised.[16] It is unclear exactly when Solomon started his Residency at Baroda, however he wrote he was there for *upwards of two years* until the end of 1783. It is possible that this negotiation for extra troops may have been the *misunderstanding* that had arisen between the General and Fatesinghrao that Solomon had managed to resolve by attending the court in Baroda prior to his appointment.

While all this was going on, Hastings' plan to put pressure on Scindia from the north was being out into operation. To start with things did not go well. After invading Malwa, Lieutenant Colonel Camac's troops were surrounded by Scindia's forces at Sironj and *the want of provisions and forage reduced him to great distress*.[17] However Camac managed to retreat and recover some supplies. There was then a stand off for a while before Camac managed to make a surprise attack on Scindia's camp taking *thirteen guns, three elephants and twenty-one camels*.[18] The idea of making the surprise attack had been suggested by Captain Bruce, the officer who had led the climbing party at Gwalior. Lieutenant Colonel Muir was then sent with reinforcements from Oudh. He also had orders to replace Camac who was thought not to be up to the task. Eventually a non-aggression treaty was signed with Mahadji Scindia in October 1781.

17. Resident at Baroda : 1781 to 1783

Goddard still had a master plan to advance into the Deccan and pursue the war against the Marathas. This was why he had negotiated more troops from Fatesinghrao. After subduing Pune he then proposed marching into Hydar Ali's territory from the north. But pressure to achieve a peace settlement was increasing and the Council in Bengal ordered him to arrange this as soon as possible.

The treaty with Scindia had opened the way for peace negotiations with Pune. In August 1781 Scindia offered Muir his services as mediator.[19] In November Goddard sent Captain Watherstone to Pune to start negotiations. But no sooner had he arrived than he was recalled by Hastings to be replaced by a civilian negotiator, David Anderson. Anderson arrived at Scindia's camp in January 1782.[20]

It soon became clear that the principle difficulty with negotiating a peace treaty with Nana Fadnavis arose from the connection of the English to Fatesinghrao. Pune wanted Ahmedabad returned and Fatesinghrao's tribute reinstated. Nana Fadnavis argued that Fatesinghrao was not an 'independent prince' like the Nizam, Scindia, or Hydar, but a 'tributary' to the Peshwa.[21] Anderson replied that, *for the sake of peace,* the English were willing to restore to the Peshwa all territories they had acquired from Fatesinghrao. The response to this was that peace would not be achieved unless Bassein and Ahmedabad were restored. Hastings wrote to Anderson advising him that:

> *Should Scindia continue his demand of our entire cessation of Ahmedabad, and you have no expectation that he will recede from it, do not suffer this consideration to retard the peace.*[22]

Eventually a treaty was concluded and signed by Mahadji Scindia and David Anderson on the 17th May 1782, at Salbai, twenty miles south of Gwalior. The treaty contained seventeen articles,[23] some of which are outlined below:

1. All places and territories taken in the course of the war with the Peshwa were to be restored.

2. Salsette, Elephanta, Karanja and Hog Islands were to be retained by the English.

3. Broach was to remain with the English.

6. Raghunathrao was to be permitted to go wherever he pleased and allowed four months for that purpose. After that he would not get any support from the English.

8. Fatesingh was to retain whatever territories he had possessed prior to 1775. For the future he should pay the Peshwa such tribute as was usual. No claim of tribute was to be made by the Peshwa against Fatesingh during the period of the hostilities.

11 & 12. Navigation and commerce of each State to be opened to the other.

13. No European factories were to be allowed in any of the Peshwa's dominions except such as the Portuguese already possessed.

14. Neither party was to afford any kind of assistance to the enemies of the other.

It was also agreed that Broach would then be conferred to Scindia as a token of his friendly disposition towards the English.

What are we to make of this treaty?

The first thing is that not everyone was going be happy. Our protagonist Fatesinghrao would have to give up Ahmedabad and return to paying a large proportion of his income to the Peshwa as tribute. Bassein would have to be returned. The English would retain places of strategic importance, such as Salsette and Elephanta Island. But the most important advantage of the Treaty of Salbai to the English was that an alliance had been achieved with the most formidable power in India, the Marathas, at a time when the Company's very foothold in the country was under threat.

It took many months before the Treaty was ratified. This was a worrying time for Anderson and Hastings. Mudhoji Bhonsle and the Nizam of Hyderabad were not pleased that they had not been involved with the drawing up of the Treaty. Members of the Bombay Council were unhappy about losing control of Barouch and Bassein. Nana Fadnavis eventually signed it in December 1782, but the Treaty was not formally exchanged until the 24th February 1783. The Anglo-Maratha War was finally at an end.

17. Resident at Baroda : 1781 to 1783

Immediately after the ratification Scindia issued a passport for the safe conduct of Colonel Charles Morgan and the Bengal army from Surat back to Calcutta.

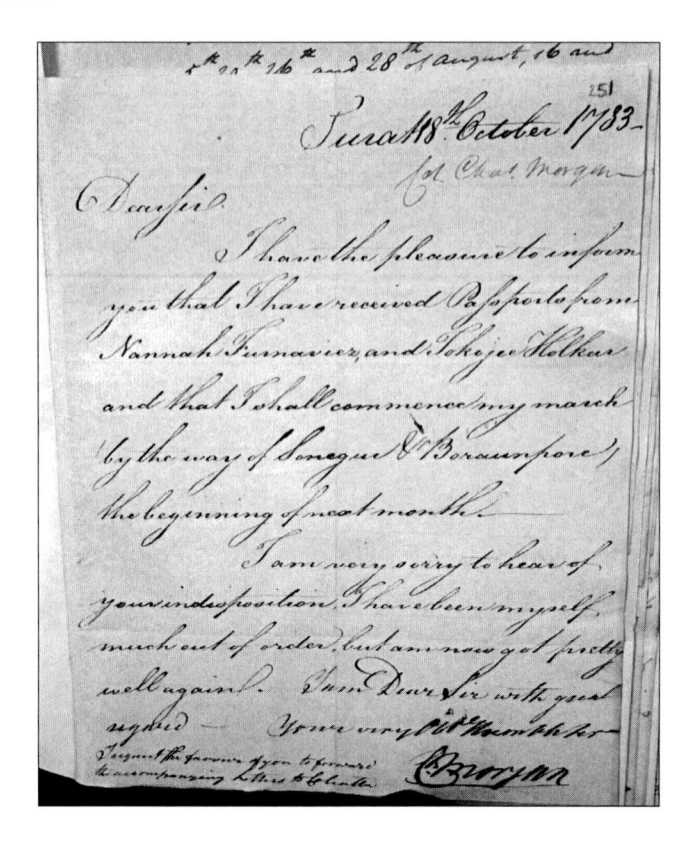

Colonel Morgan's letter to David Anderson giving news of the arrival of the passports.[24]

Transcript of Colonel Morgan's Letter:

Surat 18th October 1783

Dear Sir,

I have the pleasure to inform you that I have received Passports from Nannah Furnavies and Tokoje Holkar and that I shall commence my march by the way of Sonegur and Burampor, the beginning of next month –

17. Resident at Baroda : 1781 to 1783

I am sorry to hear of your indisposition. I have been myself much out of order, but I am now pretty well again.

I am Dear Sir with great regard,

Your very humble servant

C Morgan

But what of events in Baroda?

It is not be difficult to surmise that Fatesinghrao would be a worried man. He had thrown in his lot with the English and they had betrayed him. He would have to give back the city of Ahmedabad and return to paying a huge tribute to his enemies at Pune. And it had been made clear, as the Treaty was being drawn up, that if he failed to give up Ahmedabad the English would no longer offer him protection. At least this implied that the English would continue to offer him protection if he did comply.

Only two letters written by the Resident, Solomon Earle, have survived. Both are letters to David Anderson and both have been preserved as part of the Anderson papers in the British library. The first was written on the 21st October 1782 and concerned the anxieties of the Rajah. It is transcribed below:

Broderah 21st Oct 1782
Mr Earle

To David Anderson Esq.

Sir

By the particular request of the Rajah Futty Sing I take the liberty of enclosing you the accompanying personal letter. He is by no means unacquainted with the nature of your appointment and has often requested me to write to you in his favour which I undoubtedly should have done as I think him very deserving but as I will know the General would not forget to mention him in the most favourable manner to you.

I always declined but he has prompted me so many times within these few days that I would not refuse Him – He wrote you some time ago Himself and was exceedingly pleased with your answer which He communicated to me the moment He received it. You will confer a very particular favour on me by

17. Resident at Baroda : 1781 to 1783

answering this letter as soon as convenient which will ease Him of the anxiety He feels in this particular juncture –.

This uneasiness He must feel as the General going to Europe must be very great but I have not the smallest doubt but He will be perfectly reconciled if made quite happy at the receipt of your answer –

In case your brother [25] should be absent on the receipt of this letter I request you will open it as it contains some news which I have this day received and most probably will be quite new to you.

I have the honour to be with the greatest pleasure

> Sir
>
> Your most obedient
>
> Humble Servant
>
> Solomon Earle

The second letter was written two months later, just after Solomon had received his orders of recall.[26]

25. Dec. 1782

Cap[t.] *Earle*

Sir

I will forward with yours of the 9th *Aug and of the 14*[th] *on my way to Surat to see Colonel Morgan who arrived there with his army on The 5*[th]*. On my arrival at Surat I received my recall as Resident with the Rajah Futty Sing from the Select Committee of Bombay (which I had reason to expect daily since the General departed) as they imagine the business of this Durbar can be carried on as usual by the chiefs of Surat and Barouch.*

When I left Surat (this 19th*…) the accounts we had of Col Mcleod's situation was more alarming than we may have had reason to suppose. He would have been at risk surrounding his whole Detachment and being made prisoners of war, which at that time had little hope of relief. It gave me infinite satisfaction on receiving a letter from Major Corknell a few days after I left Surat an extract of which I have the pleasure to include.*

17. Resident at Baroda : 1781 to 1783

I am this moment returned from the Durbar after having received Mr Hastings letter to the Rajah recalling me from his Court. He was most concerned at the step taken by the Committee.

Situated as affairs are at present I am apprehensive my quitting Broderah will add to suspicions which were ill grounded. The Rajah has lately intimated concerns of the intentions of the English towards him. I made it my particular study during my residence at Broderah to uncover jealousies which were but too often harboured in the breast of the Rajah and had reason to suppose my efforts for that atmosphere were successful.

I am persuaded it will be a most difficult matter to convince surrounded by Indians as He is of the favourable opinion Of the Company towards him, which I have so often advised him in the name of the Government.

I shall use my utmost endeavours during the last few days I remain here to convince Him of the sincere friendship of the English and shall then proceed to join the Army at Surat under Colonel Morgan.

When I left Surat there was talk of a large body of the enemy coming down from the Gauts in order to destroy the Surat Parganahs, but I have every reason to believe the report was without foundation; I cannot find the forces of the enemy have made any movement since the rains.

Col Morgan's Army is laying at the Cantonments near Surat where I imagine they will remain some time, as they have only one batt. of Bombay Sepoys at Surat and another at Barouch, two from which station have been sent to Bombay within the last few days. The whole of the Grenadiers from Bombay Establishment have gone down the coast to attack some Hydar settlements under the Command of General Mathews.

Of the Army under Col: Morgan will be a sufficient protection for the Surat and Barouch Parvagadahs. I therefore imagine it will remain there until everything is finally determined with the Maharatta Government.

By the particular request of the Rajah I beg leave to enclose a letter of His which he tells me is only a complimentary one, and to acknowledge the receipt of your last which seems to have made him exceedingly happy.

I beg to be remembered in the kindest manner to your brother

I am

17. Resident at Baroda : 1781 to 1783

Broderah
25th Dec 1782

Sir

From your obedient
Humble Servant
S Earle

Fatesinghrao must have had a good relationship with Solomon as he was concerned that Solomon had been recalled. However it was not without good reason that Fatesinghrao had his suspicions towards the English and this was no doubt proven when they compelled him to give up Ahmedabad. Solomon clearly had a difficult job persuading him that the English had not completely sold him down the river.

The other part of Solomon's letter refers to some intelligence received about operations in the southwest of the country, from the Malabar Coast. The Bombay Council had sent troops down the coast to support General Matthews in the continued war against Hydar Ali. Solomon also included a transcript he had made of a letter received that gives some reassurance that the situation in the south was not as critical as had been supposed. It was important that David Anderson was kept abreast of all intelligence received, as the treaty of Salbai had not yet been signed and any suggestion that the English had suffered a defeat might prejudice the terms of the treaty. The extract is transcribed below:

Extract of a letter received from Major Corknell dated the 26th Dec (the day after I left Surat)

"The accounts received of the situation of Col: Mcleod's detachment near Callicut, when you set off yesterday, were so alarming that I am happy and anxious to give you the earliest hope that he has been relieved, in order that you may write to Mr Anderson not to give full credit to the critical predicament in which he was reported to be in from the extract of Mr ?Shatlock's letter to me of the 8th Instant.

Mr Drake Arrived at the Bar last night from Bombay in four Days, He says that Col: Macleod's situation was not so alarming as former reports made us imagine, of the certainty of Admiral Hughes' fleet Being upon the Coast, have every reason to conclude and believe that Sir Edward will call at Callicut or Tillicherry to afford Col Macleod the assistance he may want.

17. Resident at Baroda : 1781 to 1783

Mr ?Seallous was arrived from Sir Edward's squadron, and their ships of the fleet were standing with the harbour of Bombay when Mr Drake left it this is certain and the relief of the Southern force in a highly dangerous situation than you heard, is said to be founded by some letters from Col. Macleod himself

I am particular because Col Morgan has enclosed an extract of Mr ?Shatlock's information to Mr Anderson and it may give too great alarm."

SEarle

As mentioned Rear Admiral Edward Hughes had only a small complement of Royal Navy ships to cover the defence of the whole of the Indian Peninsular. The French navy, under Suffren, were supporting Hydar Ali and were planning to land troops in the Carnatic. The British were also at war with the Dutch who held territory along the coast, including the Fort of Galle on the Southern tip of Ceylon (Sri Lanka).

The reassurances passed on by Solomon were only temporary. At the time Colonel Mcleod's forces were pinned down at Panianee by Tipu Sultan's troops, which included French support. The relief gained by Colonel Mcleod's forces only came about as a result of the death of Hydar Ali. In December 1782, when it seemed there was no hope, the English were astonished to see Tipu Sultan striking his camp and leaving. When General Matthews arrived they were ordered to take advantage of this occurrence and advance up the Ghats to Bednore.

However Tipu Sultan soon returned and attacked General Matthew's force. Matthew's force was over-extended and they ended up surrendering. Mathews and several other English officers were taken prisoner and a number of atrocities were carried out. [27] Matthews and his fellow officers were taken to Seringapatum, then on to Kabbal Durga where they were apparently murdered using poison. Tipu Sultan went on to besiege and eventually take Mangalore. As mentioned, the Anglo-Mysore War finally ended with the signing of the Treaty of Mangalore on the 11th March 1784 with terms favourable to Tipu Sultan.

Solomon wrote:

I returned to Surat, and from thence by land to Bombay. The war being ended and my health much impaired, I was advised by the Faculty to return

17. Resident at Baroda : 1781 to 1783

by sea to Bengal. The army returned to Bombay by nearly the same route, now commanded by Colonel C. Morgan in place of General Goddard, who returned to Europe.

The East India Military Calendar (1824) has a postscript:

The following Letter was addressed by this officer to Capt. Earle, at this period.

"It is my particular that the Honorary colours I have ordered to be presented to your battalion may be made up with all possible haste. The Hon. Company's arms are to be represented on the first, the device on the other I have leave to yourself: the motto I have determined on, viz; "Humashah Hauser" (Always Ready) as a compliment I think you truly deserving of, from the very high state of discipline to which you have brought your battalion, and more particularly from my always finding you ready, on all occasions; to execute my orders with the greatest alacrity. It is my particular wish that you adopt the above motto for your own, in remembrance of your sincere friend, (signed) "Thomas Goddard" [28]

A compliment indeed.

Solomon Earle's Seal. Courtesy of Chris Earle

The Bengal detachment was also honoured. The East India Military Calendar (1824) records:

The remains of the gallant Bengal detachment returned by nearly the same route that it went, across the continent of India, and reached the frontier provinces of Bengal, at the close of 1784, under the command of Col.

17. Resident at Baroda : 1781 to 1783

Charles Morgan; reduced by the casualties of the service on which it had been employed, to less than one-half of the original compliment of the corps. Honorary standards were granted to each of the battalions, gold medals to the subadars, silver medals to the jemadars, and likewise to every non-commissioned officer and private sepoy who served with the Detachment from the commencement of the expedition until its return into the provinces. As a further mark of the approbation of government, an additional pay of one rupee per month was granted to each non-commissioned officer and sepoy who had served during the whole period; and the following General Orders were issued by the Com.-in-chief.

Minute by Warren Hastings, Esq. Gov.-Gen.— dated 1ˢᵗ Feb. 1785.

"The Gov. Gen. having been precluded, by the distance of the last station of the Detachment lately returned from Service in the West of India, from making his acknowledgments in person, for their exemplary services, and being now on the eve of departing for Europe, request the Com.-in-Chef to publish to the officers, his countrymen, and to the Native officers and sepoys of the different corps which comprised that detachment, his thanks for the distinguished honour which their gallant and persevering spirit and splendid successes have reflected on the government over which he presided, and on himself in particular. For the share which he had in their original appointment; for having, under that appointment, restored the lustre of the British arms, for having successfully attempted and achieved a long and perilous march through hostile and unknown regions, from the banks of the Ganges to the Western Coast of India, and prove, by their example, that there are no difficulties which the true spirit of military enterprise, under British conduct, is not capable of surmounting.[29]

And what of General Goddard?

He embarked for England, but died just as his ship reached Land's End. He was therefore unable to enjoy his retirement or support his ward, who incidentally happened to be Samuel Taylor Coleridge (see Part 5). Goddard's corpse was embalmed and landed at Pendennis Castle, near Falmouth. He was then buried in the family vault of his ancestors.[30] Another source reveals that this vault was situated at Eltham, in Kent.[31] Eltham parish church has since been completely rebuilt.

18. Return to Bengal : 1783 to 1785

By 1783 Britain's war with America, France, Holland and Spain was drawing to a close. Pressure was building up in the British parliament to take over control of affairs in India. On the 3rd September 1783, the signing of the Treaty of Paris finally ended the war. For the price of peace Britain had effectively lost a major part of North America, but retained some northern states, which later became Canada. The last British troops left New York City in November.

By supporting the American revolutionaries against Britain, France had suffered a huge financial loss. The *ancien régime*[1] tried to claw back its losses by imposing ruinously high taxes. Unrest as a result of these taxes was thought to be one of the causes of the outbreak of the revolution that began in July 1789 with the storming of the Bastille. French support for the revolution in the Americas had sparked a revolution in their own country. As one of the conditions of the Treaty of Paris, Britain had to return all settlements taken from France in India. However, as described in the last chapter, the Anglo-Mysore War dragged on for another six months until hostilities finally ceased with the signing of the Treaty of Mangalore in March 1784.

In Britain there had been political turmoil with many changes of government. The Prime Minister, Lord North, was blamed for the American War and there were strong moves to oust him and end the war. In March 1782 he resigned after a vote of no confidence. The Whigs took power and then, in February 1783, lost it to the Fox/North Coalition. During this time the 'Edmund Burke' Bill, to take government control of affairs in India, got through the House of Commons but was defeated in the Lords with the help of King George III. King George had let it be known that any peer voting for the bill would be regarded as his enemy. But in December the government fell, partly as a result of the failed India Bill. The King then asked William Pitt the Younger to take over as Prime Minister. At the time of his investiture Pitt was only twenty-four, the

18. Return to Bengal : 1783 to 1785

youngest Prime Minister of Britain ever to be appointed. One of Pitt's first actions was to sort out India. This culminated in the India Act that was passed in August 1784.[2]

Pitt's India Act, more correctly known as the East India Company Act, effectively took power away from the Company by setting up a Board of Control, based in London. The Company would continue to be responsible for commerce and day-to-day administration, but any important political matters would be referred to the 'Secret Committee' in London, who would be in direct communication with the Board of Control. For affairs in Calcutta, the Governor-General would have the casting vote over the local Council, something Warren Hastings had wanted for years.[3]

Solomon took passage back to Bengal by sea, due to illness, while his surviving colleagues with the Bengal army marched back overland. Solomon's account makes no mention what was actually wrong with his health. Illness was common amongst the British in India. It may have been a chronic infection, perhaps the same illness that eventually resulted in his return to England in 1785.

Solomon wrote that he had been given letters of recommendation from Colonel Morgan to Warren Hastings and to the Commander-in-Chief, Lieutenant General Stibbert. These letters were instrumental in his promotion to the command of a battalion of sepoys, something in the region of 1000 men. He wrote that he was initially offered the post of aide-de-camp to Colonel Ironsides, but refused as he had been promised the first battalion that became vacant.

In September 1783 he set off for the French settlement of Chandernagore to command the 1st Battalion of the 30th Regiment. As previously described, Chandernagore had been taken by the British in 1778. Chandernagore is situated twenty-two miles north of Calcutta, on the banks of the Hoogli River.

But Solomon did not stay there long as one of terms of the peace treaty, agreed during the same year, was that all French territories had to be returned. In 1784 Solomon left Chandernagore and took his battalion 400 miles up river to Chunar. This was familiar territory to Solomon as he had been previously stationed at Buxar and Benares nearby. Just three years earlier Warren Hastings had sought refuge at Chunar Fort during the Benares Insurrection. Chunar Fort dates from the eleventh century. It was taken by the Mughals, under Akbar, in 1575. The EIC captured the fort in 1764.

18. Return to Bengal : 1783 to 1785

The Benares Insurrection is worthy of further description as it resulted from one of Hastings' attempts to raise money for the war in the Carnatic. Hastings had demanded extra tribute from the Rajah of Benares, Chait Singh. The Rajah ruled as a semi-independent vassal of the Nawab of Oudh, Shuja-ud-Daula.[4,5] After the Nawab died in 1775, the Company decided to take over control of Benares from Oudh, against the wishes of Hastings. A certain amount of autonomy was allowed, but the tribute, previously paid to Oudh, now had to be paid to the Company. With the need to finance the war in the Carnatic, Hastings decided to add two additional requirements; more money and the requirement to supply 2000 mounted soldiers. Troops were also needed to protect the Bihar region from the threat of Maratha invasion. This was negotiated down to 500 troops, but Chait Singh still failed to deliver.[6] There was also evidence that Chait Singh may have been secretly communicating with Company enemies. Hastings decided to pay the Rajah a visit.

In August 1781, Hastings arrived at Benares with a small retinue of 500 soldiers. Further unsatisfactory negotiations took place that culminated in Hastings making the rather risky decision to put Chait Singh under arrest. In retrospect this was unwise as 500 troops were inadequate against Chait Singh's forces and, when two companies of sepoys were sent to Chait Singh's palace to make the arrest, they were not supplied with ammunition.[7]

The result was a massacre. All the sepoys were slaughtered by Chait Singh's palace guard. Chait Singh escaped with most of his fortune, on a rope made of turbans. A major rebellion then took pace in the city, leaving Hastings in dire straits with only 400 men left. The only option was to retreat to the comparative safety of Chunar Fort, losing all baggage in the process.[8]

Rumours then spread that the Governor-General had been killed and his head and right-hand had been suspended over the gateway of Chait Singh's fortress.[9] There was a risk that the rebellion would then spread throughout Bihar and on to Bengal. Hastings decided to sit it out at Chunar for two weeks until sufficient forces had been collected to quell the rebellion.

William Popham, now promoted to Major, took charge and, on Hastings' direction, attacked all Chait Singh's fortresses at once. It took two months before peace was restored. However, in the process, the troops looted Chait Singh's palace and any additional revenue for the war was lost. Chait Singh was then replaced with his nephew, who died a year later to be succeeded by his son, Udit Narayan Singh.

18. Return to Bengal : 1783 to 1785

There was a further incident that occurred at this time that is worthy of mention because it affected the relationship of the British with the Nawab of Oudh and, like the Benares Insurrection, was used against Hastings in one of the indictments at his 1788 impeachment trial. This was the affair of the Begums of Oudh.

The new Nawab of Oudh, Asaf-ud-Daula, has been described as a rather incompetent and extravagant administrator. Both his mother and grandmother, the so-called Begums of Oudh, apparently despised him and had retained a large proportion of the wealth of Oudh, together with jewels (said to be worth two million pounds) in their *zenana* at Faizabad.[10] They had inherited all the wealth, while Asaf had only inherited debts owed to the Company. And what was more there was evidence, albeit circumstantial and based on hearsay, that the Begums had conspired with the leaders of the rebellion at Benares.[11] Mervyn Davies described Asaf-ud-Daula as *a spineless weakling whose fear of his strong-willed and hot-tempered mother was so great that he was unable to pluck up enough courage to take by force what was plainly his by right.*[12] This description seems somewhat unfair, especially as Asaf-ud-Daula is now known as the 'architect general of Lucknow.'[13] Many beautiful buildings were constructed in Lucknow during his reign, including the aforementioned Bara Imambara, where his tomb now lies.

In January 1782 Hastings finally persuaded Asaf-ud-Daula to take action. A detachment of Company sepoys were sent to Faizabad. The palace was taken without resistance and two of the palace eunuchs were incarcerated and kept in irons by the Nawab for nearly a year before the location of a small part of the fortune was revealed. During Hasting's trial the treatment of the eunuchs was added to the list of evidence against him.

Solomon stayed with his battalion at Chunar from 1784 until May 1785 when he was ordered to report with his men to Gazapore (Ghazipur). Ghazipur is a town, also on the Ganges, situated fifty miles east of Benares. It is now famous for its opium factory, founded by the Company in 1820. This factory remains the largest opium factory in the world. It continues to this day to produce opium for the pharmaceutical industry. Lord Cornwallis died at Ghazipur in 1805, during his second tour as Governor-General. His memorial still stands, its Doric columns having overlooked the Ganges for over 200 years

18. Return to Bengal : 1783 to 1785

At this point let us digress a little and catch up with William Hickey's progress on his epic journey back to Calcutta. Hickey and Charlotte Barry finally arrived at Calcutta on the 30th June 1783, *thus terminating as disastrous a voyage as ever unfortunate people made, of exactly eighteen months from the day I left London.*[14] As was common in those days, their ship put in at Culpee. The town is now known as Kulpi. Solomon's ship had put in, at the *pagoda at Culpee,* in 1768. In 1782, Hickey's friend, Robert (Bob) Pott, had a very traumatic time on his arrival there.

Bob Pott had sailed from Madras in May 1782 with his partner Emily Warren. Emily was a beautiful and celebrated society courtesan from London. She had been the subject of a portrait by Joshua Reynolds and was reported by Hickey to have been the daughter of a blind beggar. In India she suffered from prickly heat and was in the habit of drinking vast quantities of cold water, mixed with milk, to help relieve the symptoms. Just off Culpee, after a bout of drinking water and milk, she died suddenly. After her corpse was finally prised from her husband's embrace, it had to be

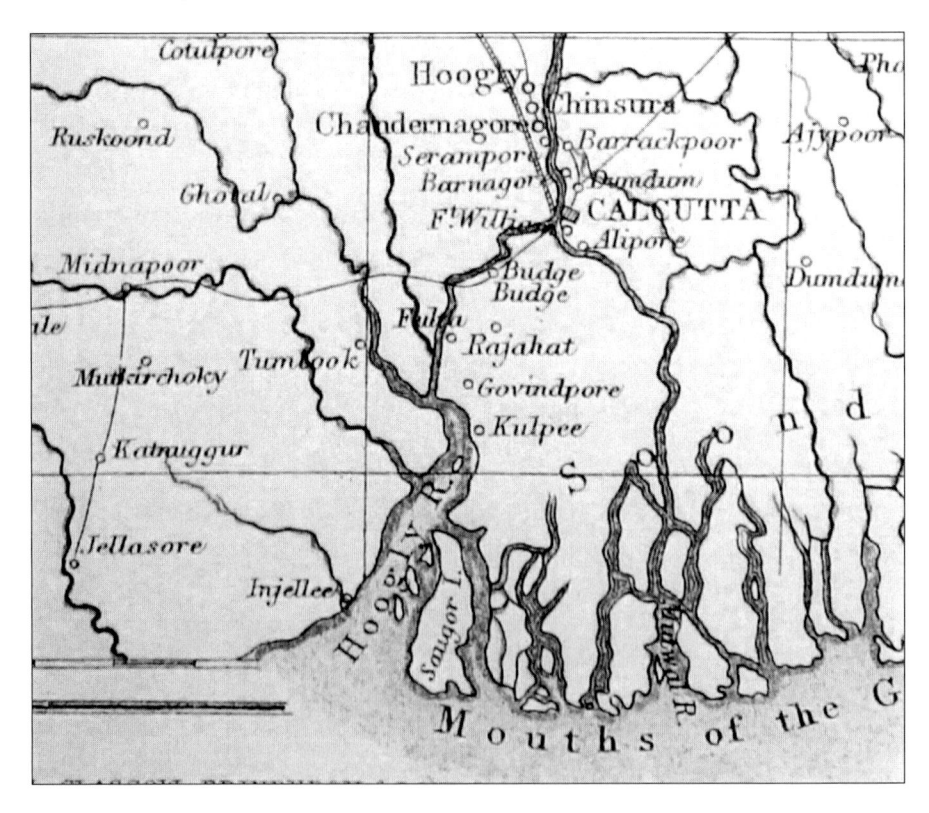

Detail from map of the Ganges Delta. Print from Beveridge History of India. 1862

18. Return to Bengal : 1783 to 1785

transported onwards to Calcutta in a boat tied some way astern of the ship, as her body had *become black and putrid, emitting the most offensive smell*. Pott arranged for a *magnificent mausoleum* to be constructed for her in Calcutta at the cost of *near three thousand pounds*. He also arranged for a column to be built for her at Culpee, *because off that wild, jungly place she breathed her last*. The column cost another one thousand pounds. Hickey wrote that the column was later christened *Pott's Folly* by passing sailors. It apparently served a useful purpose as a landmark for navigation. [15] There is no record of the column having survived.

William Hickey's traumas did not end on his arrival at Calcutta. He discovered that he was no longer on the Court Roll, so could not practice as a lawyer and therefore had no way of earning a living. At the same time he was presented with a demand for repayment of debts and to return an Indian servant. He also received a challenge to a duel. But being William Hickey he did not let these difficulties get the better of him. He personally appealed to Sir Elijah Impey, the chief justice, and managed to get back on the Roll. He ignored the debt demand but did return the servant. The challenge to the duel was from a fellow passenger on the Portuguese ship that had brought them to Trincomalee. While a prisoner of the French, an argument had broken out over Hickey's perceived preferential treatment by their French captors.

The two met the next day at sunrise at the back of Belvedere House, the same place where Hastings had duelled three years earlier. Pistols had been chosen and twelve paces were duly measured out. His adversary, a Mr Bateman, won the toss and took the first shot. Hickey followed. Both missed. They then apologised to each other.[16]

Hasting's wife, Marian, left for England in January 1784. Hastings then started to make preparations for his own return by settling some outstanding matters.[17] One of these was the situation at Oudh. He had received a letter from Asaf-ud-Daula requesting help. There had been famine and the country was in a bad state. Hastings decided to make another trip up the Ganges. He travelled with David Anderson, William Palmer (who stayed on at Lucknow) and the artist, Johan Zoffany,[18] who also stayed on at Lucknow.

Hastings stayed at Lucknow for five months. While he was there the Mughal Emperor's son and heir, who later became Shah Akbar II, arrived

18. Return to Bengal : 1783 to 1785

asking for help. He had fled Delhi as a result of political rivalries and was seeking help from the Nawab and the British. Hastings apparently toyed with the idea of accepting his request and sending an expedition to relieve the Marathas of their hold on the city. But this would have meant starting up the war again, so he decided not to take this course of action.[19] The Mughal Prince accompanied Hastings to Chunar and then on to Benares where Hastings arranged for him to return to Delhi. Back in Delhi the Mughals sought help from Mahadji Scindia instead.[20]

In September 1784 Hastings received news of the triumph of Pitt over the Fox/North coalition. He was actually in Chunar at the time, on his way back to Calcutta, having a two-week break while his wrecked boat was being repaired.[21] He was initially pleased with the news but there was no request for him to stay on as Governor-General. Solomon was stationed at Chunar at the time and it is not known whether Hastings shared his thoughts with the officers of the garrison.

Back in Calcutta there was still no request to stay on as Governor-General, so Hastings booked his passage home on the *Berrington*. When final details of the India Bill arrived in January 1785, he handed in his resignation.[22]

William Hickey gave an account of a meeting with Hastings around this time at an annual gathering of old Westminster schoolboys:

Mr Hastings, who was by nature uncommonly shy and reserved, always unbent upon these occasions and became playful as a boy, entering with great spirit into all the laugh and nonsense of the hour, himself reciting a number of ridiculous circumstances that occurred in his time. His health being precarious, and therefore, when he was obliged to preside and give toasts, had a mixture of weak wine and water prepared for himself, with which beverage he went through all the ceremonies, announcing the standing toasts with great regularity and precision. After filling the chair until midnight, by which time a majority of the company were incapable of swallowing any more wine, he vacated his seat and retired unnoticed, leaving a few of us to continue our orgies until a brilliant sun shone into the room, whereupon we rose, staggered to our palankeens, and were conveyed to our respective homes.[23]

It is worth mentioning that Hastings continued to support cultural and educational activities during his final years in Bengal. For example the

18. Return to Bengal : 1783 to 1785

foundation stone of St. John's Church in Calcutta was laid in April 1784, with the final opening ceremony and unveiling of Zoffany's controversial painting, Last Supper, taking place in 1787. Hastings supported and funded the first translations of *Sanskrit* and founded a Muslim Madrassa in the city. A second expedition was sent to Tibet and the work of Major James Rennell, the founder of Indian geography, continued to receive support.

On the 25th January 1785, Hastings held his last ceremonial duty as Governor-General. This duty was to distribute medals and standards to the survivors of Colonel Pearce's detachment who had just arrived back from the Carnatic. He attended his last Council meeting on the 1st February. The *Berrington* sailed on the 7th February and he arrived at Plymouth on the 13th June 1785.[24]

Solomon remained at Ghazipur for six months. When he returned to Chunar he wrote that, because his health was much impaired, he obtained permission to return to England for three years, *a step judged necessary by the Faculty. Having returned to Europe in a French ship, we reached L'Orient in June 1786, and landed in England the August following.* Note that Solomon used the term we, suggesting that he was not travelling on his own.

Exactly what Solomon was doing taking a French ship back to Europe is an interesting question. Lorient is a French port on the south coast of Brittany. In the eighteenth century it had become the main base of the French East India Company, the *Compagnie Royale des Indes Orientales*. The French company had been wound up in 1769, but was reconstituted in 1785. During the American Revolutionary War, Lorient had become a major base of the French Royal Navy. During the war the British had captured some French shipping, but Solomon's French ship was unlikely to have been a British prize as, if it were, it would not have been sailing to Lorient. What was more likely was there were no places on British ships and a French passage happened to be available. He may have discovered this on his journey back from Chunar, stopping at Chandernagore on his way. He probably got to know some of the French inhabitants during his stay there and would have had contacts in the town. He was also unwell, and Calcutta was not the best place for anyone in a poor state of health. On arrival in Lorient he presumably took passage on a local vessel bound for England, landing at Plymouth or Portsmouth.

Solomon had been away for eighteen years. He had left home as a sixteen year old youth and was returning as a thirty four year old man, an

18. Return to Bengal : 1783 to 1785

experienced soldier. As well as being older and wiser, he had served time as trusted Resident to a Maharaja. He was most likely travelling with his five year old daughter. He would have taken the first available coach to Ashburton to visit his family. He would have had many tales to tell.

PART FIVE : THE COLERIDGE CONNECTION

19. The Coleridge Connection : 1774 to 1783

In Xanadu did Kubla Khan
A stately pleasure-dome decree:
Where Alph, the sacred river, ran
Through caverns measureless to man
Down to a sunless sea.

From Kubla Khan

With sloping masts and dripping prow,
As who pursued with yell and blow
Still treads the shadow of his foe,
And forward bends his head,
The ship drove fast, loud roared the blast,
And southward aye we fled

From The Rime of the Ancient Mariner

Visions of the sea and the wonders of the Orient; where did the poet Samuel Taylor Coleridge (1772-1834) get his inspiration?

When I was searching for letters written by Solomon in the British Library, I came across a letter he had written to Ann Coleridge, Samuel's mother, in 1788. It turned out Solomon had known two of the Coleridge brothers who had both enrolled as cadets in the Company army. And these two brothers may well have inspired some of Coleridge's most famous poems.

Part Five is a small diversion to follow the tragic story of the two brothers, in some ways a parallel story to that of Solomon's, except that they never returned to England. It also provides us with the opportunity

19. The Coleridge Connection : 1774 to 1783

to tie up a few loose ends and follow the story of the British in India to conclude at the end of the first siege of Seringapatum in 1792.

This is best achieved by following the moving letters they wrote home, copies of which are available in the British Library.[1]

Here is the letter that started things. It is from Captain Solomon Earle to Mrs Ann Coleridge:

Stokeley, April 15 1788

Madam

I have lately received a letter from the East Indies, dated in August last from a very particular friend of mine (Capt Archdeacon) who begs me to make application to you to enquire if you received £100 which your son Frank remitted to you (a Bill on Mr Waugh at three months sight) requesting me if the Cash has not been paid to write Mr Waugh on the subject which I will most readily do. I make no doubt that the money will be immediately paid.

Capt Archdeacon gave me the melancholy intelligence of the Death of your eldest Son. He died in April last, at Tillicherry.

I doubt not that your Son Frank has made you acquaint with it ere this. He (Frank) has lived with Capt Archdeacon for several years who is as careful of him, as if he were a Child of His own. He is a very worthy young man and esteemed by every person who has the pleasure of his acquaintance. You would not know him he is so much grown. I saw him on his first arrival in India & two years ago when I last saw him, he was quite a man. He is still an Ensign, but if, please God, he lives I have no doubt but that he will do very well. He is a very different turn of mind from Jack. He, poor lad, was too generous ever to save anything for himself, but if I mistake not Frank will always live and act like a Gentleman, without being too extravagant. I was well acquainted with them both

Frank was at Barrampore about 100 miles above Calcutta last April in very good health.

I am Madam,
Your most obedient Humble Servant
S Earle

19. The Coleridge Connection : 1774 to 1783

My direction is as follows
Capt. S. Earle
Stokeley
Near Dartmouth

Mrs Coleridge
St Mary Ottery

This letter was written two years after Solomon returned to England. We will now turn the clock back fourteen years to 1774, just after brother John's arrival in India. At this time Solomon was stationed at Budge Budge, near Calcutta.

Letter from Ensign John Coleridge (Jack) to his brother William, at Ottery St Mary,[2] near Exeter, Devonshire:

Monghyr Sept 29 1774

Dear Brother

I have embraced with pleasure the first return of the ships of the season to inform you & the rest of my friends of the continuation of my welfare. I left Calcutta about the end of April last, and in a month after arrived here where I have remained ever since. You have no doubt heard of Monghyr, famous for its wild romantic situation, & especially for its being the Mountpellier of the East. About 2 miles from the garrison there is a Hotwell in which the water continually boils, the natives esteem it sacred & flock hither from all parts of the country to receive a holy sprinkling, as they imagine it has the Virtue of cleansing them of their sins. You say my father complains of my not answering his letters, by this time I am sure he is convinced to the contrary.

You desire that I will send you the Persian characters, in answer to which if you want to learn that language you have only to have recourse to Mr Jones' Persian grammar, being much better for your instruction than anything I can write, being at present entirely ignorant, not only of the Persian but of the Malabar language in both which you hope I have made a great proficiency.

We have had a Brigade for some months past up the country with Sujah Dowla for whom it has conquered the Rohillas in a pitched battle in April last, since which there has been no insurrection in their country, for the attainment of their former possessions the Brigade at present is at Pattergur

19. The Coleridge Connection : 1774 to 1783

Fort, near the Thibet Hills. There is likewise an army of Rohillas about 20 miles from them.

By the several ships of the season that have arrived I have not received a single letter.

There has been of late a great reduction in the army, so I don't expect to be a Lieutenant for some years.

Present my duty to my father & mother, my love to my brother and sisters, & I am William with sincere affection your affectionate Bother

—John Coleridge — [3]

John wrote to his father, three years later:

Dear Father,

I had the happiness to get your favour of the 13th of December 1775. Indeed it gives me a great pleasure to be informed of the recovery of our family from that severe disorder which you say reigned throughout England. The death of my grandmother gave me no small uneasiness some time ago, however, 'tis what we must all expect from the ordinary course of nature. I am glad to hear of the success of my schoolfellow Captain Drewe, and more so as to his gallant behaviour.

I hope by the time the rebellious Americans have been totally vanquished by the superior force of His Majesty's arms, & that matters are amicably compromised for the mutual interest of the King and subjects.

I imagine this time you must have received my letter dated about 5 months ago mentioning my being promoted to the Rank of Lieutenant. I must now undeceive you in your opinion that promotion is obtained by interest, one only meeting with Preferment according to the general rise, fixed by invariable rules, upon with some instances of infringement have happened in former times, but in all likelyhood such will never be seen again.

I have the pleasure to inform you that promotion in the army will be quicker now than for many years past as a great many of us officers are appointed by the command of the Troupe of the Nabob of Oude: as I would wish the one of them I have signified the same to some friends in this Country who I believe are about to apply for me; should I succeed you may depend upon

19. The Coleridge Connection : 1774 to 1783

having the most early information of it being an establishment more lucrative than the Company's within the province, so if everything answers agreeable to expectation, I may soon have the happiness to see you reap the advantage as well as myself.

In future should you not hear so often from me as you might expect, I beg you won't impute it to want of duty in me but the casual miscarriages that often attend such long passages.

I now conclude with my sincere wishes for your health and welfare, my Mother's sister & my tribe of brothers (to make of your own phrases) with all other friends & relations

I am dear Father
Your dutiful & affectionate son
John Coleridge

Ramgur, Feb. 25. 1777

The American declaration of independence was signed on the 4th July 1776. Earlier that year the British had evacuated Boston, Massachusetts. In his letter John alludes to one of the advantages of being seconded to the Nizam of Oudh, that of increased pay, or *batta*. As mentioned, advancement in the Company army generally took place in turn, rather than through favour, or money.

The next two letters were written seven years later, in August 1783, when John was stationed near Surat, presumably with Solomon. The first of these is a letter from John to his mother. His little brother Frank (aged thirteen) has just arrived in India.

My dear Madam

I hope long ere this you have received my letter by General Goddard since which I have received your other letter enclosing one from my brother Sam,[4] who I hope General Goddard has inquired after – I am extremely sorry to find the affairs of the family in so bad a situation, but I will endeavour to render you (from time to time) such assistance as shall enable you to put matters upon a much more eligible footing, & to begin I enclose you a draft for the sum of £200 on Mr Watherstone,[5] who was when in this part of the world a very intimate acquaintance of mine, & will be able to give James or whosoever may receive the money from him every intelligence concerning me

19. The Coleridge Connection : 1774 to 1783

I hope, as I can assure you of future remittances, that you will give over all thought of parting with my sister Nancy anywhere out of the family, as it is entirely contrary to my inclination, & I shall take care to provide in such a manner as to render it totally unnecessary –

I have the pleasure to inform you that little Frank is extremely happy in the situation he is in, & I hope that ere long I shall have the satisfaction of writing you of his being an officer, he is writing a small note to you himself.

As I have nothing further to add at present Accept my sincere wishes for your health & happiness. I beg you'll present my love & to my Brothers & Sister and Sam.

Your Dutiful & affectionate son
John Coleridge

Camp near Surat
Aug 1. 1783

NB. Frank will not let me peruse his letter, as the lord knows what he has been scribbling. Be so good as to make Nancy write me.

This is the letter that Frank had 'scribbled':

Dear Mother

You must long ago have heard that I have left my good friend Capt. Hicks for to stay with my Brother in India who is just the same to me as a second Father. I now act as a Volunteer in the Bengal army but I hope before you get this letter I shall be an Officer in the Bengal establishment. I am happy as a little prince and very well. I hope all my good friends in Ottery are well. I also hope that Molly[6] is with you and I desire that you will remember me to her, remember me to M. N.[7] and all my Brothers and Sisters,

And I remain your

Dutiful Son

Francis Coleridge

19. The Coleridge Connection : 1774 to 1783

Ottery St. Mary is a small market town in Devon, situated ten miles east of Exeter. The river Otter passes through the town on its way to the sea, a shoreline now known as the Jurassic Coast. The Reverend John Coleridge settled at Ottery St. Mary in 1760 as vicar of St Marys Church. He was also head master of the local grammar school. He married for the second time and the couple went on to have eight sons and a daughter. Like the Earle family, the Coleridges came from a background of yeoman farmers and small traders.[8] The new station of the family was an example of the rise of the English middle-classes in the eighteenth century.[9]

John, the eldest son, was born in 1754. He left home at sixteen to seek his fortune by enrolling as an ensign in the EIC army, just after his sister Anne, also known as Nancy, was born. You may remember that Solomon enrolled in 1767, three years before John. Five other sons came before Francis Syndercombe (Frank) was born in 1770. Of note James (born in 1759) became a career soldier in England and Luke (born in 1765) trained as a doctor. The most famous son, the poet Samuel Taylor Coleridge, was born in 1772.

Nancy, the only daughter, was described as the beauty of the family and was universally loved by all. John idealised her, although he had only seen her as a baby. Frank, on the other hand, idealised his nurse Molly, who brought up all the siblings. Sam also idealised Nancy and Holmes has suggested that this was really a disguised form of reproach to his real mother.[10] Letters from John to his mother are much more formal than those to his siblings.

Intense sibling rivalry built up between Samuel and his daring, more extrovert brother Frank.[11] This rivalry developed around attempts to gain the affection of nurse Molly and their mother. To begin with his mother doted on little Sam, but things changed as he grew older and he became, in his own eyes, a failure. Eventually, in 1779, a quarrel took place between Sam and Frank over some cheese that resulted in Sam running at Frank with a knife. Sam then ran away. Half the town was turned out to look for him. Eventually it was decided to send Frank to sea. In October 1781 his father took him to Plymouth to enrol as a junior midshipman in the Navy. He was aged eleven. During the night, just after he returned to Ottery St. Mary, Reverend John Coleridge died of a massive heart attack.

This had a devastating effect on the family. Ann Coleridge lost her position and income and the family had to move to temporary lodgings. The family became dependent on brother James, now in the army, and

19. The Coleridge Connection : 1774 to 1783

John in India. There were plans to send Nancy away to work as a shop assistant at a milliner's in Exeter.[12]

Let us return to the letters.

In August 1783, John wrote a separate letter to his brother James:

My dear James

Having just heard of a Packet going to be despatched from Bombay, I thought it would be unpardonable to neglect so fine an opportunity of sending a few lines to you. I have remitted home to my mother by this opportunity the Sum of two Hundred Pounds, and I shall hereafter make such other remittances from time to time as shall enable you to put matters upon a much better footing than they seem to be at present.

I have mentioned slightly to my Mother that 'tis much against my inclinations that my Sister Nancy should be bound to any trade or leave the family upon any account, for you may depend upon it that I will take such steps in providing for her that shall render the scheme of binding her to a trade totally unnecessary. Dear James. Let me request that you will (should my sister be now in Exeter) urge everything that lays in your power for her being recalled back to her mother, where she may improve herself in every accomplishment that ought to adorn the fair Sex. By my honour, James, I would rather live all the rest of my days on Bread and Water than see my Sister standing behind a Counter, where she is hourly open to the insults of every conceited Puppy that may chance to purchase a Yard of Ribbon from her, horrid Idea! chucked under chin, etc. etc. too bad to mention. For God's sake get her back, don't let her go to destruction, as some other has who shall be nameless, but you may guess. Now, James enough of one thing is as good as a feast.

Pray have you been to see General Goddard? I hope you have, as he was a very good friend of mine, & further, he promised to visit my Mother, and provide for little Sam, who, poor little fellow I must write to when I have more time.

I hope that you'll take care that his education is not neglected in any respect whatever, money shall not be wanting, if I can help it. In your next letter you must write me a very particular account of every individual in the Family, that is what kind of men my Brothers are, and do be very pointed concerning

19. The Coleridge Connection : 1774 to 1783

the accomplishments of Nancy, you must tell me how she walks, dances, laughs, sings & converses etc. etc. You know what I mean, don't leave a dimple out of the description.

Little Frank is here with me, he behaves so extremely well that he has gained the love & esteem of every Officer of Rank in the Army, the Commanding officer of the Corps, to which he belongs praises him to the skyes, and says he commands a Division better than most Subalterns in his Corps. He employs his time in improving himself, and I don't doubt that he'll turn out a clever fellow, the young dog is as fond of his Sword as a girl is of a new lover.

I saw one Capt. Biggs aboard the Gibraltar who gave me a most pleasing account of you. And I, true Brother-like, believed every word he said. Let me know how you stand in the Regiment you belong to, and how much it would take to purchase a Captain's Commission for a Lieutenancy –

If you are not in Ottery at the time you receive this, I wish you would hint the attention that is due from all of us to our Mother & the Brothers that may be about her at the time, for I pray to God that the remainder of her days may pass on smoothly and happily, at least 'tis a duty to prevent anything happening to her that may give her the least uneasiness. I must leave off. For I could scrawl all day long, make my Duty to my Mother and love to the family and I remain

<blockquote>

Your friend and Brother

John Coleridge

</blockquote>

Camp near Surat
Aug I. 1983
PS I should like to have Nancy's picture in miniature

Letter to his mother in October 1783:

My dear Mother

I have the extreme pleasure of informing you that my Brother Francis is most elegantly provided for. He is approved to the service to take rank as an Ensign of Infantry from the 15th of October 1782, so the youngest has been an officer above a year & I think if no crosses happen that in a couple of years more he'll be a lieutenant. In future you must direct my letters for me to Bengall, as the Detachment I am with marches for that Country in three days from

19. The Coleridge Connection : 1774 to 1783

this Date. In case of your not having received my letter enclosing a Bill for £200 I send you a Duplicate of it. I have the satisfaction of informing you that little Frank is in fine Health & from all appearances will do very well in this Country, he desires his Duty to you and love to his relatives & friends.

As we are all in a hurry and confusion concerning the march I hope you'll excuse the shortness of this letter, & believe me, my Dearest Mother that you have not a more Dutiful son than,

John Coleridge

NB Make my love to all the Family
Oh! I had like to have forgot. Pray when will my much loved Nancy favour me with a line.

These two letters show the dedication, generosity and caring nature of John in regard to his family, and the fact that he was sending a huge proportion of his income home to support them. Sadly, General Goddard was never able to help to support little Sam because, as previously mentioned, he died just as his ship reached Land's End. The last letter revealed that Frank had achieved the rank of Ensign at the tender age of just thirteen years. As far as can be ascertained, Nancy never did have to enter 'trade'.

John was just about to join the long march back to Bengal with the detachment under Colonel Morgan. They took a similar route to the march out four years earlier. Solomon returned to Bengal by sea.

The story continues in the next chapter.

20. The Coleridge Connection : 1784 to 1792

In next series of letters Frank described his arrival at Bombay, when his shipmates played a trick on him. He also outlined the support he got from Captain Archdeacon, who became a substitute father figure as well as his brother John.

October 1784. Letter from Frank to his sister Nancy:

Dear Nancy

You are very right. I have neglected my absent Friends but do not think I have forgot them, and indeed it would be ungrateful in me, if I did not write them.

You may be sure Nancy that I thank providence for bringing about that meeting which has been the cause of all my good fortune and happiness which I now in fullness enjoy. It was an affectionate meeting and I will inform you of the particulars. There was on our ship one Capt. Mordaunt[1] who had been in India before, when we came to Bombay, finding a number of his friends there he went often ashore. The day before the Fleet sailed, he desired one Capt. Welsh to go aboard with him, who was an intimate friend of your brother. 'I will,' said Welsh, 'and will write a note to Coleridge to go with us.' Upon this Capt. Mordaunt, recollecting me, said, there was a young midshipman, a favourite of Capt. Hicks, of that name in board. Upon that they agreed to inform my brother of it, which they did soon after, and all three came on board. I was then in the lower deck, & though you won't believe it, I was sitting upon a gun and thinking of my Brother, that is, whether I should ever see or hear anything of him, when seeing a Lieutenant, who had been sent to inform me of my Brother's being in board, I got up off the gun; but instead of telling me about my Brother, he told me that Capt. Hicks was very angry with me, and wanted to see me. Capt. Hicks had always been a father to me, and loved me as if I had been his own child. I therefore went up

20. The Coleridge Connection : 1784 to 1792

shaking like an aspin leaf to the Lieutenant's apartments, when a gentleman took hold of my hand. I did not mind him at first, but looked round for the Captain, but the gentleman still holding my hand. I looked in his face, and what was my surprise when I saw him too full to speak, and his eyes full of tears. Whether crying is catching I know not, but I begun a-crying too, though I did not know the reason till he caught me in his arms and told me he was my Brother, and then I found it was paying nature her tribute, for I believe I never cry'd so much in my life. There is a saying in Robinson Crusoe I remember very well viz. 'Sudden joy like grief confounds at first.'

We directly went ashore, having got my discharge, and having took a most affectionate leave of Capt. Hicks I left the ship for good and all.

My situation in the army is that I am one of the oldest Ensigns and before you get this must in all probability be a Lieutenant. [2] *How many changes there have been in my life and what lucky ones they have been, and how young I am still: I must be 7 years older before I can properly style myself a man, and what a number of Officers do I command, who are old enough to be a Father already!*

Nothing gives me such pleasure as to think Molly still continues with my Mother. If God ever puts it in my power I will return some of the numberless favours she has so often done for me when I was at home.

Tell Maria not to marry this sometime, for I am much more likely to make ten thousand pounds in India than one on board ship, so I shall not despair, but still continue her constant lover, for without ten thousand pound I was not to expect her hand, that was the bargain: so you see I am to marry her, and she marries my ten thousand pound, but you may inform her that I should be very happy if she would adorn herself a little, and that if I should be the handsomer for ten thousand pound, she must who has already such a pretty face, look elegantly with five thousand in her pocket, so you see I am very modest.

But we must not forget Miss Sarah Kessell. Pray give my compliments to her, for I am not in love with her, though I do not know where it would not be a good thing to have some strings to my bow, for I believe Maria will soon break. So I am now in a merry state, I will conclude with giving my love to Molly and my Duty to my Dr Mother and I remain in good health

20. The Coleridge Connection : 1784 to 1792

> *Your affectionate Brother*
> *Francis Sindercom Coleridge*
> *3rd Brigade*
> *My Brother is in the 1st Brigade*
> *Cawnpore. October 25. 1784*

Frank had a romantic attachment to Maria Northcote, although he left Ottery St. Mary at the age of eleven. Maria was the daughter of Sir Stafford Northcote, the sixth Baronet, who lived next door. However Maria had prudently stipulated that the price of her hand would be £10,000.[3] But, as you have seen from his letter to Nancy, he had another string to his bow, just in case the attachment did not work out!

November 1784. Letter from Frank to his mother:

> *Camp at Lucknow. Nov. 10.1784*

My Dear and Honoured Mother

My Brother will have acquainted you more than once with the situation and my own since the period of my quitting the Gibraltar. A short time before we left Surat – I gave him a letter to be forwarded with his own, and, such as it was, I hope you have received it.

In future my Dear and only Parent you shall hear regularly and punctually immediately from myself.

Upon the arrival of our Detachment near Bengall, it was broke, and the Battalion that composed it sent the different Brigades. The supernumerary officers of all Ranks were ordered to join the European Regiments. This order affected my Brother and me. But through the Interest of my friends and that good luck which has attended me in general, I was fortunate as to get reappointed to my former station in the 6th Reg^t. of Bengall Sepoys, or Soldiers, in which Corps my Brother served thirteen years.

We are now separated, he to the 2nd Brigade, and I with the 3rd which is now in the Field, however providence has provided me with a Friend with whom I live as I did with him.

My Brother's behaviour towards me has at all time been truly affectionate, indeed so much so that my faults were seldom corrected, nor did I see him in

20. The Coleridge Connection : 1784 to 1792

any other light that that of a fond and indulgent friend, ready to gratify all my little whims and Caprices. However he was not so blind to my interest, but he saw the advantages of a separation, and yet parted from me with great reluctance, tho' he knew I could not be later better cared of by any Person than by the Gentleman in whose charge he left me.

Captain Archdeacon, with whom I live, has promised to assist me, and, by the month of February next I hope to be able to send you a Bill for fifty pounds at least.

The allowances I receive now will enable me not only to remit this sum, but to make a like present to my dear Mother every year while I remain out of the Company provinces, or in the Field.

Nothing will ever afford me more pleasure than contributing everything in my power towards making you and my dear Brothers and Sister happy.

I am studying the Persian Language and already have made some progress in it. Indeed I do not neglect a single opportunity to improve myself, nor would my friends admit of it was I so inclined.

Pray give my love to Nancy and my old nurse and believe me to be

Your affectionate Son
Francis Coleridge

December 1784. Letter from John to brother George:

From Barrampore, near Calcutta
Dec 1. 1784

My dear George

I have received your kind letter of the 20th of March & the 1st April, & the perusal of them gave me more pleasure & happiness than I can find words to express. I thank my God for granting such health & spirits to our dear Mother. May she long continue to possess both, so her latter days may be a scene of tranquillity & happiness. From your pleasing account of the family I think with a little exertion on all sides we may do very well. My little Hero Frank is at present a great distance from me, but his situation is an excellent one, for he is under the command of a very particular intimate & friend of mine & in the receipt of considerable pay & allowances which will in all

20. The Coleridge Connection : 1784 to 1792

likelihood enable him by his time next year to render a considerable assistance to the family, indeed I believe the youngster is considerably above the World already, that is I mean for a lad of his years & standing. He is at present studying the Persian with the greatest attention, & let me assure you, my friend, that he promises as fair for being a good soldier & a sensible man as any boy I ever saw in my life. I have enclosed Nancy's and James' letter to him but have not as yet received an answer from him.

I have since I wrote home last been rather unfortunate. A friend of mine was in distress for Cash to clear himself of a disagreeable business he had got into at Surat, he applied to me for assistance, & I granted him the needful. About 4 months after this affair happened he was taken ill from the severity of a long March, & died, he left me his sole Executor with an idea thus I might repay myself from the sale of his effects. However there has been a Bond debt presented against the Estate that I am very apprehensive will sweep away every farthing of the amount of the Estate. This, George, is an unlucky hit, however don't say anything of it to the old lady as it might make her uneasy. I shall, please God, be able to bring up the leeway in a very few months, the only point that makes me anxious is that 'tis a doubt whether I shall be able to make the remittance that I intended, but rest assured I shall strain every nerve to keep matters in the proper road.

As this letter goes by the first ship of the season, I shall not trouble you with a long epistle, as so many other opportunities will offer during the season for writing you.

I make my duty to my Mother & my love to my Brothers, Uncles, Aunts etc., & further tell my lovely amiable Nancy that I will answer her letters by the next ship; sweet creature; I don't know, George how it is, but that innocent girl takes up more of my thoughts than you can conceive.

Accept of the love & friendship of
Your very affectionate friend & brother
John Coleridge

As is clear from the above letter John had leant money to a friend who had died, leaving him in debt.

In August 1785 John wrote to James (Capt. James Coleridge, 6th Regt. Foot):

20. The Coleridge Connection : 1784 to 1792

Burrampore Cantonments. Bengall

Aug 12 1785

My dear James

I have received yours of the 1st Oct 1784 from Dublin & the perusal of it gave me the highest satisfaction. I thank you for the confidence you have put in me & depend upon it I will remit you the needful by the first opportunity that offers this season. Further I beg that you'll make my best thanks to the Gentleman that may have stood your friends in this business & inform them that I should be happy in an opportunity of returning the obligation.

I should have sent you a very considerable sum a long time ago but was prevented by a Gentleman's death, in whose hands my little all was trusted & who upon enquiry has died Insolvent, so I lost every farthing I was worth; this was rather unlucky as we are circumstanced at present, but as the matter cannot be mended, I must endeavour to extricate myself without repining. I have friends & very sincere ones, who are always ready to assist & support me, by this goodness & my own prudence I hope in 2 or 3 years to be capable of sending that assistance to my own dear Mother & family that is incumbent upon every good man to do.

In remitting this £1000 I think I had better make the Bill payable to our Mother, or her Order, in case you should be absent upon the arrival of the Bill in England; you can mention what is to be done with the Cash on its being received. [4] *Francis writes me that he remitted £80 about six months ago. But you cannot as yet have received it, for the first Bill was lost in an accident happening to the Ashburton Indiaman, but he has no doubt taken care to send a Duplicate of the Bill by the Packet that was despatched since.*

Frank is at present stationed at Cawnpore about a 1000 miles distant from this place, he is under the Guardianship of my friend Capt. J Archdeacon, a man of whose sense & virtue I have the highest opinion; indeed the youngster improves under him ever amazingly, & is beloved & esteemed by every person that knows him. He studies the Persian, & has made some proficiency in it, for in his last letter he says that I should never want a Persian interpreter when he has the pleasure of being with me again, so I think, James, the Boy promises fair to being a Shining Character.

What you mention concerning Luke must be seriously thought of. I cannot at present render him the necessary assistance, but the moment it is within my powers he shall hear from me...

20. The Coleridge Connection : 1784 to 1792

Your description of my dearest Sister, made my Heart palpitate with joy & Affection; may virtue & dignity be her motto & strict honour the guardian of it is my prayer. If ever the Blind Goddess should shower down her favours on me I will endeavour to put that dear, helpless Girl in a line that her virtue intended her to shine in. I received a tender affectionate letter from her, which I have not as yet mustered up resolution enough as yet to answer, but I will do so by the next Ship.

I received letters from Ned, George & Luke which were answered, but the letters were all lost I have been informed since, so I beg you'll inform them that I'm faultless.

Do you know, James, that Nancy has got a kind of a lover in this part of the world? My friend Capt. Meredith is a little touched from the description you have given of her. [5] *We have lived as brothers together for many years, & I may say few Brothers have a more mutual affection for each other.*

I have been thinking for these some days past of getting Sam, a couple of years hence, sent out to me as a Cadet at the India House. Let me know of your sentiments upon this scheme in your next.

Well, James, I will now bid you farewell for a month, when you shall hear from me again. God Bless & protect you.

Your affectionate friend & Brother

John Coleridge

James had borrowed money from his friends to purchase his captaincy on the strength of John's promise of money. John was now sending him money to cover interest on the loan.[6] It is unclear how John had managed to scrape together £1000, a huge sum in those days. Clearly the Nancy fan club had now spread to John's friend, Captain Meredith. It is interesting that John was thinking about getting Sam sent out as a Cadet. Sam would clearly have been an unsuitable officer in the Company army, judging from his volatile character and the later example of his brief career in the 15th Light Dragoons, when he enrolled as a private in 1793. James had to buy him out after a few months. And besides, if he had gone to India he might never have written those poems.

20. The Coleridge Connection : 1784 to 1792

In October 1785, Frank wrote to Nancy:

Dinapore Oct 29. 1785

My Dear Nancy

It is impossible what an addition your letter was to the pleasure of Christmas day, for it happened to arrive on the very day that we were celebrating the Nativity of our Blessed Saviour...

I hope my dear mother will continue to enjoy a good state of health, it my constant prayer to heaven that the remaining part of her life may glide away smoothly and happily and that there may be no more scenes of distress & misery to rack the breast of her to whom I owe my existence.

I have the pleasure of sending home by Captain Waugh a friend of mine a Bill of one hundred pounds as a present to my dear Mother, he will forward it to you as soon as he arrives in England & you will send to your Mother, it is the saving out of my pay since my Brother and I have been ordered to Different Brigades, which has been about these two years. Lately the Corps to which he was in relieved the Regt to which I belong.

We had a meeting. I do not exaggerate, Nancy, when I tell you it was as tender and affectionate as when we first met at Bombay; when we parted tears flow'd on both sides, but we were Soldiers, and as a Soldier I was forced to leave him and march with my Regt; he is in fine health, though the situation of affairs at home has made him rather melancholy.

And now for my good, my dear and faithful Molly (what before Brothers and Sisters? For shame Frank! I think I hear you say: Yes Nancy for I am sorry to say I lay under more obligations to that good woman than I do to all Brothers an Sisters I have got, except my Secundum Pater John) assure her of my unutterable affection and love towards her, that she is still as dear to me as ever, and that I shall ever recollect her Goodness to me when I was at home, for who else would ever wipe the tear off little Frank's cheek, and comfort him in any little distress or sickness? Poor as she was she never refused me any little money that I might have wanted. No. Her generous soul gave even before I asked. Desire my mother to give her five Guineas out of the Hundred Pounds I have sent, that is, if she can conveniently spare them, for when Poor Molly has had but a penny in the world she would divide it with me, and doth not gratitude demand something in return? Certainly. Little as it is, when she knows it comes from me she will think it thousands and when the Recording Angel gives in a list of my crimes, I hope my ingratitude will never be numbered amongst them, for I hold that of all Crimes in the utmost detestation and abhorrence, and the man that can be guilty of ingratitude, let him die the death of a Dog, and even that in my opinion is too good for him.

Remember me to Maria, I ought to say something more but I have not room I hope she will excuse me. Remember me to all my Brothers, Sisters, Uncles, Aunts, Cousins and Friends, and now give me leave to conclude with Being

My Dear Nancy
Your affectionate and Handsome Brother
Francis Coleridge

P.S, Do you now I'm grown very handsome, tell Maria so

There is no record that Frank ever saw his brother again. Earlier that same month, John wrote to Nancy:

Burrampore Oct 2, 1785

My dearest Sister

I had the great pleasure of receiving three days ago your tender and affectionate letter of July 1784 & since that Period I may safely say that I have perused it twenty times, the delicate & soft sentiments that shine through the whole of it added to the justness of your ideas upon your present situation has given me a perfect knowledge of the virtuous mind of the writer. Yes, my much beloved Nancy, your letter has convinced me that you are everything I could wish. I do not flatter you, when I inform you that you have not only made me happy but I pride myself in being possessed of a Sister that bears so beautiful a mind.

You call me in our letter your Brother unknown, & justly so, but in future I must request you'll when you write me, conceive you are personally acquainted with me. Equally as much so as with James or any other of my good Brothers that have the happiness of seeing & conversing with you. When I was about to leave Europe you was an infant, & many is the time, my Nancy, I have had you in my arms & gazed at you with pleasure & affection, tho' at that period people in general thought I was an obstinate, hard-hearted boy that had neither feeling nor affection, but I think I may modestly say they judged without their Host.

20. The Coleridge Connection : 1784 to 1792

I have now one fault to find with you, which is, that you rated every trifling natural act of mine in too high & particular a manner. I have not as yet done anything like what my friends have a right to expect from me, but by the blessing of God if my unfortunate Fates do not always pursue me I will fulfil their warmest wishes .

My late misfortune has thrown me back a little in the world, but my Rank & prospects are such, that I expect to be enabled by this time next year to render my dear beloved Parent & the rest of the family that yearly assistance I intended. What at present troubles me is whether I shall be able to make up this Season the remittance for James for since I wrote him I have met with a disappointment, although no loss in the money way. However I shall exert my best endeavours & if I should in some degree prove unsuccessful, I hope his generous friends will rest contented till next season.

I have sent Frank his letters which will no doubt make him happy, his conduct is so highly praiseworthy that he is an honour to his family, indeed he is beloved & honoured by every person that knows him. I shall have the pleasure of seeing him in about two months, and a joyful meeting it will be; poor little fellow. I have been absent from him now near 14 months; his Corps is coming down to Calcutta, which I am in some degree happy at, although it will be a loss to him as to Cash, but he will have an opportunity of seeing a great deal of the first Company in India, which will polish him and give him a proper confidence, without which nothing is to be got or had in these degenerate days.

O! I had like to have forgot to thank you for your kind & much valued present, it now adorns my bosom, & it frequently, very frequently reminds me of the much beloved person, who was the owner of it.

If you should at any time by accident see my old nurse you must say everything for me to her that you conceive will please her. If it ever should be my fortune to visit my native land, I will, after having received the blessing & embraces of my much honoured parent, go & visit her, be where she will, for I am under very great obligation to her. O! my dear girl, you can have no conception of that woman's kindness & attention to me. I have known her, when some trifling accident has happened to me, show all the tenderness & feeling of a parent & when I have been about to leave her to return to my Parents I have observed the large tear run down her aged face & her countenance too well expressed the pain which she felt at parting from me. O! Butterly! Butterly!

20. The Coleridge Connection : 1784 to 1792

How many were the happy innocent hours I past there; if you shall ever have occasion to pass near the place, visit it for my sake, & if an old large Ash Tree [7] still stands at the bottom of the Green, station yourself under it, & first reflect that you are standing in the spot where I some 20 years ago used to exert all my endeavours to rise the first in the Athletick exercises, while the good old woman used to stand by & shudder for every slight bruise I might receive, & tenderly chide me when I got home for contending with lads above my age & size. I don't know, Sister, whether this subject yields you any entertainment, but the reflections I have on it frequently gives me the most pleasing sensations.

I must now think of concluding for were I go on writing, or rather conversing with you, I should fill more paper than the Post would choose to carry, so make my most dutiful love to my dear Mother, & tell her that the news of her being in health & spirits gives joy & pleasure to my heart, & for a continuation of which she has my daily prayers.

I shall write Luke by the next Ship, this letter goes via the Governor's Packet, no small favour I assure you, & it was by mere accident I heard of the opportunity .

I make my love to my brothers, for God knows I love & esteem them –

Well I must now relieve you from reading this scrawl which I have been forced to run through in a hurry. I have only one more thing to add, which is that I pray that the great protector of Innocence & Virtue will defend & guard you in every situation in life, & I am my much beloved Nancy, your affectionate Brother & friend,

John Coleridge
To A Miss Coleridge At Ottery S Mary, Near Exeter, Devon

This is the last known letter written by John. He was posted to Tillicherry in January 1787 and died on April 7th 1787, apparently of malaria. A Company factory was situated at Tillicherry, protected by a fort, on the Malabar Coast, between Mangalore and Cochin.

Confusingly Bernard Coleridge reported three separate dates of death: May 1786 and April and Dec 1787. [8] Engel's account concludes that John's death was probably a suicide, brought on by debt, depression and illness. [9] His close friend, Captain Meredith had recently died, and when John died he was intestate with his estate recorded as *Insolvent, Rs 2094 being*

20. The Coleridge Connection : 1784 to 1792

aid in part payment of bond.[10] A *correspondent at Tillicherry* had written that, at the time of his last illness, *he was a very gentlemanly-looking man, but his regimentals hung upon him like a sack.*[11]

The suicide verdict looks a distinct possibility when we consider Frank's next letter (1788) to his sister Nancy. As suicide was a criminal offence in those days, suicides were often hushed up by the family and the authorities.

Letter from Frank to Nancy in November 1788. Incidentally Bernard Coleridge did not publish this letter in full in his 1905 account of the Coleridge family.

Camp at Burrawgaum (?Burdwan) Nov: 1. 1788

Perhaps before my dear Sister receives this its office will have been performed or many melancholy Epistles must have miscarried. When I received your very affectionate letter dated Feb: 1788 I was distressed beyond measure at finding it once more necessary to write on a subject in itself how ungrateful to a Brother, in its consequences how afflicting to a Parent, and Sister & thro' every link of our Family Chain. My Nancy, my amiable and all affectionate Sister, if you are in presence of my Mother, retire before you turn the page.

And now know, if unknown before, that you have but one Brother in India & that in May 1786 on the coast of Bombay, the dearest friend of my Nancy terminated his life, & rejoined his more than Brother Capt Meredith to part no more. After whose death he daily declined & was advised by the Faculty to try the Sea air, the result – but I can say no more. If my Nancy has already felt it would be unnecessary, if not 'twould be cruel. And permit me, my dear & only Sister to drop a subject so affecting for me to mediate on & too interesting (?distressing) for your Happiness to peruse.

I still continue with my second father Captain Archdeacon who has been presented by Lord Cornwallis with the command of Sepoy, or Native Battalion, now an independent Command in the interior parts of India. By his interest I have been appointed to his Battalion and through his assistance & Patronage enjoy every happiness this amenity can give. But what can the Son of such a Parent, what can the Brother of such a Sister enjoy, when the eve of the first is darkened by distress & the meridian of the last clouded by misfortune.

20. The Coleridge Connection : 1784 to 1792

My Brothers, have I then no Brothers? Imagination dwells in their once loved features, some have escaped, others have faded, but the forms still exist in my heart, & their memory with unabated love still give delight to my Soul. That they are greatly altered in appearances I can judge from myself, & am certain I could appear without any danger of being recognised before every one of my family. Don't too hastily dissent or deny the possibility of such an occurrence for the reasons, & them glaring ones that I may one of these days bring in support of my supposition.

You mention a letter from Miss Maria Northcott but I have never received any. Present her with the grateful thanks of the poor Exile. Inform Miss how very sensible I am of her kind attention & how very Proud she made me by the few lines her goodness obliged me with.

Assure the amiable & generous Hart family of my most fervent gratitude, nor do I despair of one day seeing them Personally, that out of my own house the world contains none I love so well. I dreamt some time ago of having married, Nancy, & as you know marriages are made in heaven, & dreams are said to descend from above, we are certainly intended for each other, & I have only to find some of the Treasures of Hindoostan to enable me to return home & throw myself at her feet. Pray inform me what reception seriously, Nancy, you think I should meet with.

Desire my dear little Sam (a propos of little I am exactly five feet 11 inches & a half measured yesterday) to write me, & if his Pride enquires why, I don't think it proper to commence a correspondence. Say a great deal in my favour about Duty, business, climate, situation etc.

Great was the satisfaction I received from your account of my dear Luke, may he prosper as he deserves.

The goodness & virtues of my affectionate & dear George's heart with the fine sense & abilities of his head make me drop a tear on reflecting how contracted his sphere is for exerting them.

Were my dear Edward to guard his memory from treachery nor while every one of the family experiences his natural tenderness let an absent Brother sink to oblivion.

Inform my ever honoured Brother James that I still consider that moment the happiest of my life that will present me with the opportunity of draping my

20. The Coleridge Connection : 1784 to 1792

sword to him. And to my mother, my all affectionate, and all tender Parent, tell her I am as I was & ever have been & ever shall be, grateful, affectionate & Dutyfull.

Direct me as follows. Ensg. Francis Coleridge, c/o Capt: John Archdeacon, Bengal Infantry, India.

And now my dear Sister, the last not least in love. Let me implore the favour & blessings of God on you, may he protect you from harm & make you as Happy as the most affectionate Brother could wish.

As you did not mention my Molly, I shall be silent, not indifferent

Your ever affectionate Brother
Francis Coleridge

Our Batallion marches from Burawgaum higher into the Country the 15th of February next.

As outlined in previous chapters, the First Anglo-Maratha War ended with the signing of the Treaty of Salbai in 1783. The Anglo-Mysore War ended in March 1784. After this time, although various battles took place between the Marathas and Tipu Sultan, the EIC kept out of involvement in internal conflicts in India. Warren Hastings had left India in 1783 and Lord Cornwallis took up his post as Governor-General and Commander-in-Chief of the EIC army in 1786. The army was primarily involved in keeping order and peace in existing dominions. There were no plans for any further land acquisitions. But in 1789 Tipu Sultan invaded Travancore.

Travancore was an independent state in Southern India, allied with the British, covering the extreme southern tip of India and present day Kerala. When he heard that Tipu Sultan was building up troops in Coimbatore and was planning to move south, Cornwallis warned him that an attack on Travancore would be a declaration of war with the English. But Tipu paid no head to this warning and invaded all the same.

In 1790 General Medows advanced to Coimbatore while Tipu Sultan invaded the Carnatic. The British established alliances with the Marathas and the Nizam of Hyderabad with a plan to lay siege to Seringapatum. In 1791 Cornwallis took his troops up the Eastern Ghats to take Bangalore. Frank Coleridge and Captain Archdeacon were part of this 'grand army'.

20. The Coleridge Connection : 1784 to 1792

Frank wrote to his mother in September 1791. This is his last known letter.

Sept 20, 1791

My ever honoured, ever beloved Parent–

Your letter has woke me amidst the din of Arms to all the softer feelings of Nature. My Mamma, think not because you have not heard of me that you have not been daily, nay hourly, in my mind. I call my Creator to witness I love you with such affection that does not despair of Equality with my Happier Brothers, but I cannot, like them, tell you so every moment, not always every year.

For these three years past I have been stationed nigh 1,400 miles from Calcutta, and though promoted and ordered to the European Battalion at Bockampore, His Lordship in Council ordered me to succeed to the first vacancy in the Native Battalion up the country. He has since summoned me, with twelve other officers and 800 Sepoys, to attend the Grand Army previous to his laying siege to Seringapatum, the Capital of the Mysore Tyrant. Proud of such an honourable distinction, I join him with ardour, and if Fortune crowns my Wishes, will scatter the Pearls of the Sultan at the feet of my Mamma.

Mr. Tomkins lingers on board for any letter, for we are falling into the Main Ocean from the Ganges. I can detain him no longer, and must be concise. My health has never known disease, my Character has never known a stain. My friends I have never lost. Enemies I have never made, and happy I have ever been, except when, Mamma, you call me across the ocean. God Bless you, best of Parents; tell your children that their absent Brother is what he ought to be, or if he has one fault it is that of being too partial to the banks of the Ganges.

Molly, I kiss you! would you know your favourite boy again; live and you shall see him. My Nancy, would my tears relieve you? I would forget the Soldier, and be more than brother. Amiable Sister, never, never can I forget you.

I have not time to pour out my Heart. I am writing amongst Hundreds of Soldiers...

20. The Coleridge Connection : 1784 to 1792

> *Mamma, receive my Dutyfull, my Eternal Affection. On my knees I call for your blessing on your ever Duteous Child.*
>
> *Francis Coleridge*

After taking Bangalore the grand army marched towards Seringapatum, approximately 100 miles distant, while pursuing Tipu's army. But Tipu's scorched earth policy had made supplying the army difficult and the Maratha army arrived too late to assist.[12] They therefore had to retreat back to Bangalore with the loss of the battering train. Cornwallis then decided to reduce various hill-forts that might cut off his supplies and communication lines. After doing this he planned to have another go at Seringapatum.

The most formidable of these hill-forts, fifty miles north of Seringapatum, was Savandroog (Savandurga), otherwise known as the Rock of Death.[13,14] It must have been a daunting site as Savandroog was an enormous mass of granite, up to 2500 feet in height, with two fortified peaks on its summit, and a *deep chasm* in between.[15] Tipu Sultan had predicted that half of the attackers would die of sickness (malaria from the surrounding jungles) and the rest would be killed in the attack. As a result the defenders were apparently over-confident and did not attack the British as they laboriously cut a *gun road* to bring eighteen and twelve pounders, and two howitzers, within range of the walls of the fort.

Savandroog. Print from Beveridge, History of India. 1862

20. The Coleridge Connection : 1784 to 1792

Frank was present at Savandroog as he wrote a brief 'will' two days before the assault:

Endebted to my God for my life, for everything else to Capt. Archdeacon. I resign to him who made me the existence he bestowed, and every earthly possession besides (except my Gold Ring) I leave to the kind father of my youth. My Gold Ring 2nd L[t.] Conway will favour my memory by accepting. Campbell will not smile over my grave, and Captain A may say, of those who loved me another is departed.

Dec 19. Sewanndroog.
S/. Francis Coleridge[16]

The assault commenced one hour before noon on the 21st December 1791. Lord Cornwallis and General Medows watched anxiously.[17] They need not have worried as the rock fell within one hour with the loss of only one Company soldier and 100 of the Sultan's troops.

On the 5th February 1792 the allied armies finally arrived at Seringapatum. Tipu Sultan's forces were lined up before them, behind the protection of a 'bound hedge' and several redoubts. Behind Tipu's army was a ford over the Cauvery River, and behind that the defensive wall of the fort. Rockets were hurtling in the direction of Cornwallis's army. It must have been a relief for Tipu's surviving prisoners, to hope for release after bring kept in dungeons built into the walls of the fort for so many years.

Taking advantage of the element of surprise Lord Cornwallis decided to embark on an immediate night attack. Tipu had originally planned to hold out until the monsoon, when lack of supplies would force the siege to be lifted.[18] Three columns were assembled, all to attack simultaneously. Frank and Captain Archdeacon were in the central column of 3700 men, under the immediate direction of Lord Cornwallis himself.[19]

What followed was a long night of confused and very hard fighting. Tipu retreated back across the river and only just made the safety of the fort. The central column took the Sultan's Reboubt, afterwards renamed Sibbald's Redoubt, after the English officer who died defending it from counter attack. The forward troops crossed the river and reached the Dariya Daulat Baug, the site of one of Tipu's palaces.[20]

Captain Archdeacon was killed at the bound hedge and for a while his battalion fell into disorder. Later on, probably during the assault on the Sultan's Redoubt, Frank was wounded. Due to his courage in the attack, Lord Cornwallis presented him with a gold watch.[21]

20. The Coleridge Connection : 1784 to 1792

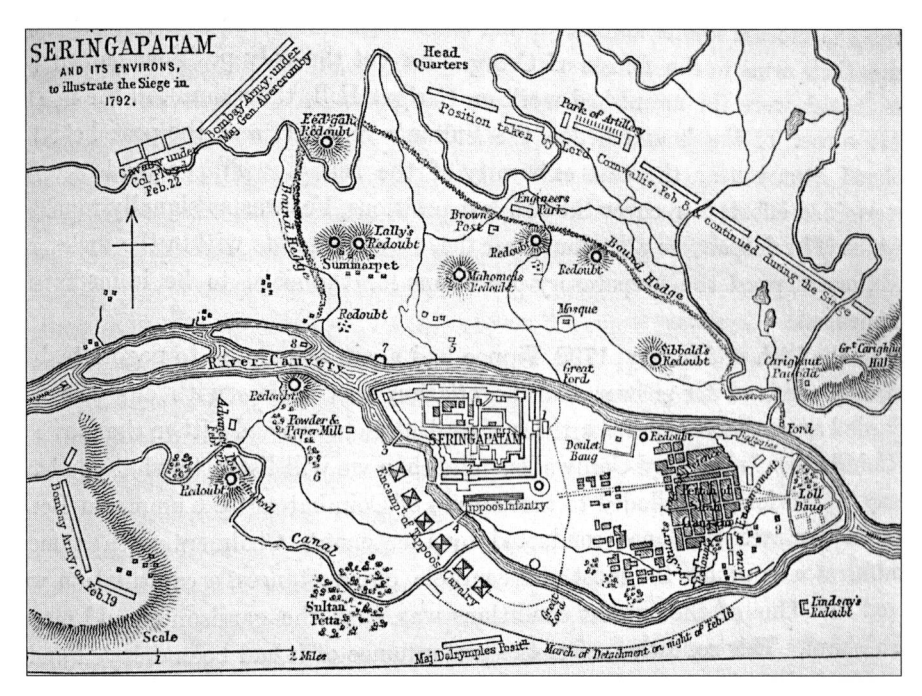

Seringapatum in 1792. Print from Beveridge, History of India

Despite the casualties the initial assault was a success for the allies. Tipu made several attempts at peace terms, at the same time sending out a small group of soldiers on a bungled mission to assassinate Cornwallis. [22] An agreement was finally reached on the 25th February 1792.

In return for peace Tipu agreed to release all his prisoners, lose half his territory, give up two of his sons as hostages, and pay a huge fine. The territory was divided up between the Marathas, the Nizam and the British. The Company troops were upset with the plan for peace as they were then denied the opportunity to gain great riches by taking the city. Instead they were offered a *handsome gratuity* from the financial settlement. [23] Frank would therefore not have acquired any of the Sultan's pearls to scatter at the feet of his mother.

Some time after receiving his gold watch Frank became feverish, perhaps from an infection as a result of his wounds. After the battle the Dariya Daulat Palace was used as a makeshift field hospital. According to most published accounts Frank shot himself while in a state of delirium. The exact date of his death is not known. He would have been aged twenty-one.

20. The Coleridge Connection : 1784 to 1792

This is the story reported in official history. However on looking through many accounts of the battle of Seringapatum, there is no record of a Lieutenant Francis Syndercome Coleridge having been wounded or being presented with a gold watch after the battle. However Sam noted that his mother kept in her possession a gold watch presented to Frank by Lord Cornwallis for bravery at the siege. It does seem rather odd that a delirious soldier would have had access to fire arms. Then there is a rather curious addendum to the Coleridge papers in the British Library, written by Bernard Coleridge in 1905. Coleridge wrote that since writing the book he had received the following information from Sir Arthur Godley, Permanent Under Secretary of State for India:

Francis Coleridge
Cadet 1782
Lieutenant 5Th June 1790
Died 21 Jan 1792 in the Carnatic
No cadet papers, or record of marriage or burial
20 Oct 1792. Administration (with paper writing annexed) granted to Henry Trail.
Estate all paid away.

The document included Frank's 'will,' as transcribed above. It also included the following information:

Capt. John Archdeacon killed at Seringapatum 6th Feb 1992
Probably Capt. E S Conway killed at Benares 10th Jan. 1799

Unless the date is incorrect, this document indicates that Frank may have died at least two weeks earlier, on the 21st January 1792, the date of the assault on Savandroog. And it does seem curious that Frank's death would have been recorded as a suicide, given the great stigma associated with suicide. Lefebrure has theorised that Frank might have been murdered during a raid on the English camp, similar to the raid to attempt to kill Cornwallis.[24] This information could have been kept a secret so as not to affect moral.

The exact cause and date of Frank's death will never be known, but the news of his death would certainly have had a devastating effect on the Coleridge family. In the previous year, 1791, brother Luke, now a doctor

20. The Coleridge Connection : 1784 to 1792

in Exeter, died suddenly of a fever and the fair Nancy died after a long consumptive illness.[25]

Sam blamed himself for Frank's death as he was party to the rivalry that had led to Frank going to India in the first place, and their father died when he returned home from after taking Frank to his ship. News of Frank's death reached Sam just after he found out that he had failed to achieve an important scholarship to support his academic career at Cambridge University. This triggered periods of *suicidal gloom and remorse* which deepened when he received the news of Frank's death.[26] Further drinking bouts and debts followed. In December 1793 Sam enlisted as a volunteer private in the 15th Light Dragoons, for a bounty of six and a half guineas.[27] The name he used, Silas Tomkyn Comberbache, was unlikely to have been a coincidence given that Frank's middle name was Syndercombe.

The Dariya Daulat, Seringapatum. 2017

PART SEVEN : HOME : 1786 – 1824

21. Back in England : 1786 to 1804

It would have taken Solomon a full day to travel the twenty-six miles from Plymouth to Ashburton. He probably hired a private carriage as he would have been travelling with his daughter and belongings. In those days wealth acquired in India was often brought home in the form of diamonds. On his return Solomon was able to support himself and his family for a number of years. He also felt in a position to marry. As far as we know, unlike John and Francis Coleridge, he did not have to send money home.

1786 had been a dry and rather cold year, but weather records show Solomon was lucky he was not travelling in September. During that month a major storm hit southern England. Trees were uprooted and many houses destroyed and ships wrecked.[1]

Solomon's search for a wife lasted almost exactly a year. On the 18th August 1787 he married Rose Rennell, then aged twenty-two, thirteen years his junior. They were married at St. Andrews Church in Ashburton. The church had been restored in 1775 with the addition of a huge, triple-tiered, mahogany pulpit donated by Sir Robert Palk, Solomon's benefactor. [2] Chandeliers were added in 1778. [3] At the time Robert Palk was MP for Ashburton and may well have attended the ceremony if he was in town.

Rose was the daughter of the Reverend Thomas Rennell (1732-1829), vicar of Stokenham, near Dartmouth. Thomas Rennell was born in Bovey Tracey, a village near Chudleigh in Devon, where James Rennell, the father of Indian Geography, was born. [4] They may well have been related. Stokenham is over twenty miles from Ashburton, along typically deep and narrow Devon lanes. There is still a memorial to Reverend Thomas Rennell in the church at Stokenham in what is now a chapel dedicated to the victims of an ill-fated exercise to rehearse for the D Day landings in 1944. Stokenham is about a mile inland from Slapton Sands where the practice landings took place. Live rounds were used, but disaster happened when German E-Boats managed to attack the support ships. In total 740 American soldiers died, more than the actual landings on Utah Beach itself.

21. Back in England : 1786 to 1804

Church of St. Michael and All Angels, Stokenham

Memorial to Rev. Thomas Rennell next to the American memorial. 2017

We do not know where Solomon first met Rose, or how the match was arranged. Solomon would have been a reasonable prospect. He was a Captain in the EIC army and had recently returned from India with an income and means. As far as we know they must have got on well together as Rose went on to have at least ten children. The only cloud on the horizon for Rose was that Solomon was on a three-year furlough and was therefore due to return to India in 1789.

It is likely Solomon spent some of his capital on land and property. He was listed in the Universal British Directory for the period 1793-1798 as being one of two 'gentlemen' resident in Ashburton. He is also noted in land tax records. He rented out fields to his brother John who had stayed on in Ashburton as a farmer.

On April 15th 1788 Solomon was staying at Stokeley, as it was from there that he wrote the letter to Mrs Coleridge expressing condolences for the death of her son. Stokeley consists of a few houses between Stokenham and the sea. They were therefore either staying with, or very close to, the in-laws. Their first child, Elfrida, was born in May 1788. Elfrida was baptised together with Sophia (then aged eight) at Stokenham in June the same year. The next year (1789) Solomon applied for and was granted a further year's furlough in England.

In 1790 he was about to leave to take ship to Bengal when Rose became unwell and he had to postpone his departure. The following year he applied to return to India but his request was denied. It was against regulations as he had overstayed his furlough. Rules are rules and the EIC Council were firm on this matter.

We do not know how Solomon occupied his time over the next few years but we do know where he was living as records show where his children were born. John Lucas was born in 1791 and William Henry and Marianne were both born in 1794. All were christened at Ashburton. The family then moved to Southwark, in London. His third son, also christened Solomon, was born at Southwark in 1797. Daughter Susannah was born there in 1798. There were now seven children in the family. By then Sophia would have been in her late teens.

In London the family were resident at *The Paragon*, a new development on the New Kent Road in Walworth. According to a 1787 map this road was then called Greenwich Road. This part of London was not as built up as it is now. As yet no other developers had built in the area and the Paragon would have stood in glorious isolation, surrounded by market

21. Back in England : 1786 to 1804

gardens, pastures and marshlands. Presumably there would have been an ample supply of fresh vegetables. Just to the northwest were the famous Saint George's Fields and Kings Bench Prison. Saint George's Fields was the site of the 1768 massacre, and also the place where a 60,000 strong crowd gathered in 1780 to march on parliament, the march that triggered the Gordon Riots. There are no sign of the fields now as they were completely enveloped by housing in mid-Victorian times. The only clue to their presence is a road junction called St George's Circus, part of a road system constructed across marshy land to link with the new Blackfriars's Bridge.

The Paragon can be seen in a 1787 map of the area, in the crescent just to the right.

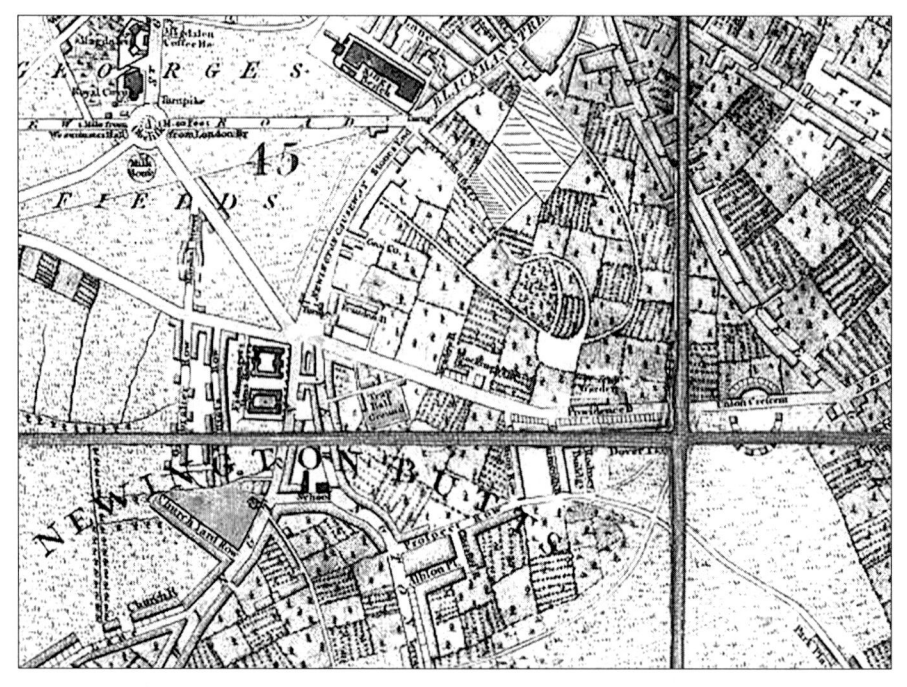

Detail of a 1787 map of the Walworth area

The Paragon was a landmark building in its day. It consisted of a crescent of fifteen pairs of houses linked by lower colonnades. It was designed by the architect Michael Searles [5] and was constructed between 1787 and 1791. In fact it was one of the first semi-detached housing developments ever built. Judging by photos taken in the late nineteenth century, the houses had three stories with attic rooms. The Walworth Paragon was

21. Back in England : 1786 to 1804

demolished in 1898 to make way for a school. In its turn the school closed in 1980 and has since been turned into luxury flats.

All that is left of the site now are a few sections of the crescent-shaped garden that was originally to the front of the properties. A 1970s flyover now transects the site. Michael Searles went on to construct another Paragon on the edge of Blackheath. This latter Paragon has survived and is now a grade-one listed building. Both developments were built to house members of the rising, and moneyed, middle classes. Solomon must have had some funds left to afford to live there.

The Paragon, Blackheath. 2018

The Paragon, Walworth. Before demolition in 1898[6]

21. Back in England : 1786 to 1804

Solomon was clearly looking for some kind of occupation and may have chosen to live in London to be in close proximity to the EIC headquarters at Leadenhall Street. Until the early 1800s ships were still loaded and unloaded in the River Thames at Blackwall. Construction of the East India Docks began in 1803.

There is virtually nothing left of the docks now, apart from a few sections of the import dock. The area would have been a hive of activity with construction work and shipbuilding. There were numerous warehouses holding goods consisting of spices, saltpetre and various cloths. East India Station, on the Docklands Light Railway, is just near to where a huge mast-tower was situated. You can walk across the busy A1261 to Naval Row, past the old wall of the docks, to Poplar High Street, where merchants, tradesmen and shipbuilders lived. In 1654 the Company built a chapel there, the Saint Mathias Chapel, which has since been turned into a community centre. Next to the road is the old hospital for disabled seamen. Poplar was London's first multi-ethnic area.

We do not know whether Solomon was successful in obtaining employment in London but he was eventually appointed as adjutant to the new Company recruiting depot that was being developed on the Isle of Wight. He took up post in 1804.

Earlier that year Sophia Earle married Richard Lipscombe. Lipscombe was variously described as an upholsterer and a yeoman from Hereford. The marriage took place on the 30th January 1804 at Spitalfields, London. At the time Sophia was pregnant with her first child. Richard Earle Lipscombe was born at Rotherhithe on the 21st February 1804. Solomon made separate provisions for Sophia in his will with the effect that Richard Lipscombe was not to inherit any of Sophia's money. Presumably Solomon and Rose did not support the match.

Let us now return to national affairs. During the whole of Solomon's time in India, from 1768 to 1786, the territory controlled by the EIC had barely changed. As part of the Treaty of Salbai, in 1783, Bombay had been made more secure with the annexation of the island of Salsette. As mentioned in the last chapter, hostilities between the English and Tipu Sultan restarted in 1790. After the siege of Seringapatum in 1792, Tipu Sultan had to concede a proportion of his territory along the Malabar Coast, but that was all. At the time it was not policy to acquire any more territory in India.

21. Back in England : 1786 to 1804

During Lord Cornwallis' time as Governor-General (1786 to 1794) the plan had been to reform the government of existing colonies. This was not surprising given the negative feelings in England, and in the British Parliament, towards events in the east. This viewpoint was strikingly illustrated by the great trial of Warren Hastings, which started in 1788.

The trial started with a blaze of publicity that gradually faded over time, although there were further bursts of public interest at points of drama. The trial dragged on for seven years and was in its closing stages when Solomon moved to London from 1794. He may have purchased tickets to attend, particularly when Lord Cornwallis, recently returned to England, was due to testify for the defence. Solomon is likely to have followed the progress of the trial. He knew what had really happened in India at the time and may have been concerned by the attacks on Hastings. After all he had played his own small part in Hasting's plan to consolidate and secure stable government and Company trade. And Solomon would also be classed as a minor nabob, having made his fortune in India.

What is difficult to understand is why the trial started in the first place. Hastings had clearly done his best. He had followed his brief, albeit in difficult circumstances. At the very least he had maintained the territorial status quo and triumphed over many threats, including the powerful Marathas, the French, and the folly of his own side. However he had made a number of unwise decisions and it was these decisions that his enemies singled out. Ackroyd has argued that the trial illustrated the deep uncertainty that still surrounded Britain's imperial status, almost like a momentary spasm of conscience.[7] It can also be argued that the general feeling in England at the time, after the loss of the American colonies, was that someone needed to be blamed for something and Hastings was a handy target. The parodying of the super rich nabobs, returning from India and throwing their money around, would not have helped matters either.

The man who led the plan to destroy Hastings was the philosopher and Whig MP Edmund Burke.[8] One of Burke's close acquaintances was Hasting's sworn enemy, Philip Francis. It was Burke's view that affairs in India had been badly managed. He believed that if a country was to be colonised, then benefits to the people who lived there should be paramount. He supported the American revolutionaries, but not the French, because they attacked the constitutional monarchy. His first action was to try to persuade Parliament to impeach Hastings. In practice Parliament could

21. Back in England : 1786 to 1804

vote for impeachment, but it was the House of Lords that would hear the case and make the final judgement. Burke started by producing a list of charges. Most of the incidents on which charges were based have been covered in previous chapters. There were twenty-two charges in all.[9]

One of the charges put forward that Hastings was guilty of *gross injustice, cruelty, and treachery in hiring British soldiers for the purpose of extirpating the innocent and helpless people who inhabited the Rohillas.* He was also accused of extortion in relation to the affairs of the Rajah of Benares, Chait Singh, and the Royal family of Oudh (the Begums of Oudh). He was charged with *overturning the ancient establishments of the country and extending an undue influence by conniving extravagant contracts, and appointing inordinate salaries.* The inordinate salaries relate to the large sums paid to Elijah Impey and Eyre Coote, to secure their support. There were also many other financial irregularities listed in other charges. One of these included the opium contract awarded to Stephen Sullivan.

Hastings then made things worse by insisting on answering to the charges in person before his accusers, live in parliament. His defence lasted for two days. Hastings was no orator and he should have kept to the point and defended the charges as actions that had to be taken as exigencies of the particular situation at the time. He did not appear to realise the danger he was in and appeared arrogant in his manner.[10] When it came to the vote the Prime Minister, William Pitt, changed sides and voted for impeachment on the matter of the financial demands made on Chait Singh. Then Richard Sheridan, playwright and Whig politician, took to the floor to support the charges against the Begums. Sheridan spoke for five hours with great eloquence. Ackroyd gives us the image of the leading orators of the day, Sheridan, Burke and Fox, launching tirades against an old man in a blue French coat.[11] The end result was that the House voted to proceed to trial. Incidentally the House rejected Philip Francis by a large majority, when he applied for a position as one of the managers of the trial, a blow that Francis would remain bitter about for the rest of his life.[12]

The trial proper started on the 13th February 1788. Westminster Hall was packed, including the Royal Box. Hastings was fighting for his life, literally as the legal system could apply criminal (the death penalty) as well as civil penalties, should he be found guilty. Attendance dropped after the grand opening, unsurprisingly as some of the speeches went on and on. Both Burke and Sheridan spoke for four days each. Sheridan fainted at the end of his highly theatrical performance.[13]

Then the trial had to be adjourned as King George III had his first episode of madness. Some contemporary accounts still put forward the view that King George suffered from the rare hereditary condition of porphyria. This theory was based on one of the symptoms of that condition, notably the passing of blue urine. However it is now known that King George was treated with medicine containing gentian, which has the same effect. The most likely, and more fitting, diagnosis is that he suffered from the far more common condition of bipolar affective disorder. [14] Further analysis of the cause of King George's affliction is outside the scope of this book but, in brief, the King recovered the following year and then remained well for a further twelve years. He had further episodes in 1801, 1804 and 1810. He never recovered from the final episode. He died in 1820.

Hasting's trial resumed in April 1789. In reality the Lord's only sat to hear the case for a few days each year and, over the time of the trial, there were numerous changes of peers. In 1788 the Lords sat for thirty-five days, but only seventeen days in 1789, the year the French revolution started. The court sat for only fourteen days in 1790, five days in 1791 and twenty-two days in 1793, when the prosecution finally completed its case. Marion Hastings attended the trial dressed, according to Fanny Burney, to look like an Indian princess.[15]

The defence extended the trial for another two years. In 1794 Lord Cornwallis gave evidence that the Begums of Oudh were doing very well. He also reported that no Indian subject had complained to him personally about Hasting's actions. Burke's closing remarks lasted nine days. During his speech he compared Hastings to a *rat or a weasel* and described him as a *thief, tyrant, robber, cheat, sharper* and *swindler*.[16]

In February 1795 the jury retired to consider their verdict. Over the course of the trial 87 peers had died, 44 had been newly created and 49 had taken their seats by inheritance. It was pointed out that some honourable members had been schoolboys at Eton at the time the trial started. [17] On the 23rd April the Lords assembled to a packed Westminster Hall to vote on each of the charges in turn. Some of the charges had been lumped together into a general charge of *High Crimes and Misdemeanours*. Although several of the Lords voted for guilty verdicts, the majority found Hastings not guilty. He was acquitted of all charges.

After the trial Hastings retired to his newly purchased family estate at Daylesford in Gloucestershire. His ancestors had once owned the house and Hastings was determined to acquire it, whatever the cost. There is an

21. Back in England : 1786 to 1804

account of a later incident when Hastings bumped into Richard Sheridan at the Brighton Pavilion in 1805. The Prince Regent introduced the two of them. Apparently Sheridan announced that any part he had taken against Hastings was purely political and that no one had a greater respect for Hastings than himself. Apparently Hastings replied, with some gravity, that it would be a great consolation to him in his declining days if that were to be made public. Naturally this never happened.[18] Hastings was never honoured with a peerage and lived quietly at Daylesford until his death in 1818. It was up to Marian to arrange for a bust to be placed in Westminster Abbey in his honour.

Apparently Hastings had a little known link with the family of Jane Austin. Jane's aunt, Philadelphia Austin, went to India and married a surgeon, a Dr Hancock, and they became friends with Hastings. When Hastings' first wife died he sent his son, George, back to England to live with Jane's father. Sadly the boy died, but the friendship between the two families remained. Jane often stayed with relatives at Adlestrop, just a short walk from Daylesford, and was pleased that Hastings admired her books. [19]

In the next two chapters we will cover the final years of Solomon's life, when he moved to the Isle of Wight to take up his new post as adjutant at the Company Depot.

22. To the Isle of Wight

Exactly why the decision was made to establishing a recruiting depot on the Isle of Wight makes more sense when we look what was happening in India and Europe. After the treaty of Seringapatum (1792) had been agreed, Tipu Sultan had been allowed to retain half his territory. Although the Governor-General, Lord Cornwallis, had no plans to take over the government of any more territory in India, he made other changes in Bengal which set the seed for the eventual separation between English and Indians. A civil service was set up in Bengal and the children of mixed-race relationships (known as Anglo-Indians) were banned from service in the civil and armed forces. This decision may have been taken because of Cornwallis' experience in the American Revolutionary War, when the former British colony wanted to govern itself, separate from British rule. Cornwallis did not want this to happen in India. The British and Indians were not to mix. Understandably this seriously affected the career possibilities for the children of mixed-race relationships.

The next Governor-General, John Shore (1793-1798), followed a similar non-acquisition policy to Cornwallis, so much so that the Company stayed neutral during the 1795 war between the Marathas and the Nizam of Hyderabad. With the support of French troops, the Nizam, Ali Khan, believed himself to be in a strong enough position to take on the Marathas. However his forces were routed at the Battle of Kharda and humiliating terms had to be agreed with the Marathas to end the conflict.

But all resolutions by the Company not to acquire any more territory in India ended during the tenure of the next Governor-General, Richard Wellesley, the older brother of Arthur Wellesley, the future Duke of Wellington.

The British had kept a weather eye on the French after the storming of the Bastille in 1789. Three years later Prussian and Austrian armies advanced on Paris. The French rallied against them, counter-attacked,

22. To the Isle of Wight

and pushed them back taking Brussels, Savoy and Nice. The following year Louis XVI was guillotined and France declared war on Britain. Plans were then prepared by the French to launch an invasion. A three-pronged offensive, via Ireland, Bristol and Newcastle, was planned. But the French were not helped by the weather and were only able to land troops at Fishguard, in South Wales (1797). This was the last foreign invasion ever to take place on British soil. It was easily put down. A story circulated that the French surrendered to red-dressed Welsh women, thinking they were British soldiers. The French did manage to land a smaller force in support of the Irish rebellion of 1798. The rebellious Irish were defeated at the Battle of Ballinamuck and further attempts by the French to invade Britain were put on hold.

Following successful campaigns in Europe, the general in charge of the French army, Napoleon Bonaparte, turned his attention to India. His plan was to invade Egypt in order to open up an alternative route to the east. He landed his forces in Egypt in 1798 and quickly took the city of Alexandria. The aim was to invade India with the support of Tipu Sultan and the French troops in Hyderabad.

The British were fortunate that the Nizam of Hyderabad had been persuaded to support the British. French troops were ousted from Hyderabad and the Nizam signed a treaty with the British. This triumph for the Company was made possible by the diplomatic efforts of James Kirkpatrick, the Resident in Hyderabad.[1] In 1799 a huge force of Company soldiers, combined with the Nizam's troops, headed for Seringapatum. This time there was no peace treaty. The fortress was stormed and ransacked and Tipu Sultan was killed. Mysore was given back to the Hindu dynasty, the Wodyars, who had previously ruled that state before Hydar Ali usurped the throne in the 1750s. Naturally the Company remained in overall control. Arthur Wellesley was put in charge of the new arrangements in Mysore.

Back in Europe, Napoleon's plans to invade India never came to fruition because the British fleet, under Admiral Nelson, attacked the French fleet at Aboukir Bay and destroyed it, leaving Napoleon trapped in Egypt. This action was also called the Battle of the Nile (1798).

For a short while there was an uneasy peace between Britain and France. But war broke out again in 1803. [2] From this time the conflict became known as the Napoleonic Wars. Napoleon had become Consul of France in 1799. Napoleon's Foreign Minister was the aforementioned Charles de Talleyrand-Périgord. In 1802 Talleyrand was advised by Napoleon to marry his long-term mistress, Catherine Grand, and it was always good to follow Napoleon's advice. Catherine Grand was of course Philip Francis' mistress in 1770s Calcutta.

Peace was not achieved again in Europe until the final defeat of Napoleon at the Battle of Waterloo in 1815.

Returning to more local matters, due to the Napoleonic wars, the EIC were now in competition with the King's army for suitable recruits. At the time the Company army in India was on its way to becoming one of the greatest private army ever created. By 1803 it had expanded to a total of 260,000 men,[3] of which an increasing proportion were European.

As previously described, officers in the Company army were recruited by patronage, in other words by recommendation from a significant person, together with a second recommendation from a Company director. These officers were the command and control system of the army in India, with the majority of troops being sepoys. Training for officers took place on arrival in India, on an apprenticeship basis. Between 1804 and 1811 a military college was set up at Barasat, near Calcutta. The College at Barasat provided basic training in drill, tactics and Hindustani. But there was little discipline as the commanding officer lived some distance away and the place was eventually closed down.[4] In 1809 a military seminary was opened at Addiscombe, Croydon, near London. In 1806, the Company opened another training college for civil servants (writers), which became Haileybury College. Haileybury is now an independent public school.

In relation to the rank and file, the proportion of European troops in the Company army in 1778 was in the region of fifteen per cent.[5] This proportion gradually increased to thirty per cent by 1805.[6] European regiments were set up to include artillery as well as infantry. In the eighteenth century recruitment in Britain had taken place on a rather haphazard basis using recruiting agents, known as *crimps*. A bounty was paid for each recruit delivered. Given that there was no martial law operating in England for Company recruits, some crimps resorted to using rather dubious methods, including kidnap and confinement, to gain their bounty.[7] After being conveyed to London, recruits were boarded on ships as soon as possible, before they had a chance to change their minds. A Company official described the inspection procedure at Tower Hill:

22. To the Isle of Wight

Last season I generally attended between nine and ten o'clock in the morning and called into a room five men at a time, stripped... I then enquire of them whether they come free and willingly to serve the EI's army in any of their settlements in India, or St. Helena for five years; upon their declaring they do, I pass them on to the Company's inspecting surgeon... those approved are immediately marched to Limehouse and embarked on board the Company's sloop for Gravesend where I supply them instantly with clothing and bedding. [8]

There were frequent complaints about the quality of the men provided to serve in India. Lord Cornwallis described them as *wretched objects* and sent some home immediately.[9] Various attempts were made to improve the recruiting process by establishing a depot, but there was opposition both from Parliament and the Board of Control who were opposed to recruitment into private armies. The management committee at Leadenhall Street also voted against the establishment of a depot as they were concerned that this might give the State an excuse to take over. In 1786 an attempt was made to set up a depot at Carisbrooke Castle on the Isle of Wight.[10] But the castle was found to be unsuitable as it was in too great a state of dilapidation and it would have cost over £8000 to make the necessary repairs. As a result the plan was abandoned.

With the start of the war with France, recruitment became more difficult. Between 1797 and 1799 only eighty-five recruits were sent out and it became imperative to improve matters.[11] A bill was passed in parliament in 1799 that permitted the Company to *train, array, exercise and discipline recruits in England, and also to subject them to martial law prior to embarkation and during the voyage to India*. Recruitment would be on the same terms as the King's troops. Full-time recruiting officers were to be stationed in London, Liverpool, Dublin and Edinburgh.

In 1801 a decision was finally made to establish a depot on the Isle of Wight. There were good reasons for such a choice of location. The Isle of Wight is situated just off the south coast of England, adjacent to Portsmouth Harbour. Company ships were accustomed to calling at the Isle of Wight to pick up supplies and there was a good anchorage just off Cowes, on the Motherbank.[12] The Isle of Wight had long served as a holding point for the assembly of military expeditions and there was a strong military presence on the Island.[13]

22. To the Isle of Wight

Even though Britain had dominance of the seas it was still risky to send ships along the English Channel, across the Bay of Biscay and then south, bound for the east. For example, in February 1804, a convoy of sixteen East Indiaman and other merchant ships nearly came to grief when three French warships attacked them in the Malacca Straits. After firing commenced the French ships withdrew thinking they were up against Royal Navy vessels. This engagement was known as the Battle of Pulo Aura. We will come across one of the Company ships involved in this action, the *Bombay Castle*, later in this account. Because of the risk of attack, ships were therefore sent in convoys, preferably under a Royal Navy escort. These convoys were assembled in the Solent, where they were protected from weather and attack. Recruits were embarked directly from the Isle of Wight. Being an island, it was also much harder for recruits to desert.

The new depot was to be situated at Parkhurst Barracks (now the site of Albany Prison) just adjacent to the town of Newport. This brought the depot into close proximity with the King's troops and their commander-in-chief, General Taylor. There are frequent references to General Taylor in the account that follows, as the Company officers appeared to be rather terrified of him. They were the new boys after all, and the King's army regarded itself as superior, as well as retaining some control over the recruitment process as part of the Act of Parliament.

In 1804 Solomon was appointed as adjutant to the new depot on a salary of £300 per annum (approximately £30,000 in today's money). His salary was increased to £432 in 1814 when he took on the additional post of Paymaster.[14] Solomon moved to the Isle of Wight with his family that same year. At the time the family consisted of his wife Rose (39), Elfrida (16), John Lucas (13), William Henry (10), Marianne (10), Solomon (7), Susannah (6) and Eleanor (1).

In tracing the places where the family lived over the next twenty years, at least five separate addresses have been located. Rosalie was baptised in Newchurch Parish in March 1805. In 1812 the family were living at Lugley Street, Newport, and in 1814, Holyrood Street, just nearby. There is a burial record for a Mary Ann Earle of Nodehill, also part of Newport, who died aged only four months on the 24th March 1816. At the time of Solomon's death in 1824, the family were living at the Mill House at Clatterford, in the shadow of Carisbrooke Castle.

22. To the Isle of Wight

Holyrood Street, Newport. 2017

Lugley Street, Newport. 2017

22. To the Isle of Wight

In the early nineteenth century Newport was a thriving and bustling market town, the capital of the Island. It was renowned for its *handsome shops and good inns* and also for the *ample beauty of the local farm maids who came to town with produce for the bi-weekly markets.*[15] The port of Cowes is situated five miles north, linked to Newport by the River Medina. A mile to the west is the village of Carisbrooke and its famous castle. The castle crowns a hilltop with magnificent views over the surrounding countryside. In 1647 King Charles I was imprisoned at Carisbrooke Castle for eight months before his trial and execution in 1649. During his stay he tried to escape twice, the first time getting wedged between the bars of a window. In the eighteenth century the castle was no longer necessary for defence due to a network of coastal forts and the presence of a strong Royal Navy at nearby Portsmouth. The castle had become a stores depot, then a military hospital, before being allowed to *decay gently.*[16]

Gatehouse of Carisbrooke Castle. 2017

A 'letter book' from the Company depot at Newport, dating from 1804 to 1813, survives at the British Library.[17] What follows in the next chapter is a detailed examination of many of the letters contained therein, some thirty-eight written by Solomon. The letter book consists of transcribed copies of letters sent from the depot by the Commandant, Captain John

22. To the Isle of Wight

Gillespie, the Adjutant, Captain Solomon Earle, and the Surgeon, Thomas Ogle.[18]

The subject matter of the letters gives a fascinating insight into how a Company recruitment depot operated in the early nineteenth century. Some of the problems that the officers had to solve, particularly those related to recruits suffering from mental illness, resemble those faced by today's National Heath Service (NHS). In other words, who pays?

23. The Letter Book

The function of the Isle of Wight Depot was to receive recruits, issue clothing and equipment, and then provide some basic training before embarkation for India. As convoys took time to be assembled, recruits often spent several months at the Depot.

The majority of the letters are copies of reports sent to the Company agents at Leadenhall Street, initially James Coggan, then William Wright. The first letter, by Solomon, is shown and then transcribed in full. After that, for reasons of brevity, letters are transcribed in extracts only.

Transcription of letter:

Newport 11th August 1804

Messrs A & J Lindegren
Gentlemen

I am ordered by the Commanding Officer to inform you that it is his intention to Embark about fifty Recruits destined for the Haven on Monday night, & to request you will be so good as to make it known to Capt. Saunders as soon as possible.–

Capt. Gillespie will esteem himself much obliged by your giving him the earliest intelligence of the arrival of the Unicorn off Portsmouth, that no time may be lost in Embarking the Remainder of the Recruits now at the Company's Depot–

I am Gentlemen

Your very Obed.^{t} H. Servt

S. Earle
Capt:& Adj.^{t}

23. The Letter Book

*P.S. Capt: Gillespie begs to know what
Quantity of Hammocks have been sent
on board the Unicorn, as we shall have
ab^t 50 Recruits on that ship*

Letter by Capt. Solomon Earle. 11th August 1804.
From Newport Letter Book at the BL

The next series of letters relate to the inspection and recruitment of men from the prison ships at Cowes. There was a lack of space in gaols at the time and convicts were often housed in decommissioned naval ships. Agreeing to serve in the Company army may well have been a better option than continued incarceration in a prison hulk. It is unclear whether the prisoners who were recruited were general convicts, or deserters from the King's army. It raises the question whether the King's army had plans to dump its unwilling and less desirable soldiers onto the EIC.

9th August 1805. Captain Gillespie to James Coggan Esq. : ... *it is therefore my intention to embark 100 of the Prisoners with 100 of the Company's Recruits from the Depot on the Britannia as likewise 100 on the Euphrates and Northumberland, deeming it advisable to make this distribution that the deserters may not go all in one ship...*

25th August 1805. Gillespie to Coggan : *Received from Major General Whitelocke twenty nine General Service recruits, and afterwards proceeded with Mr Ogle to inspect the Deserters on board the Prison ship when out of the numbers on board could only Select and Approve of eighty as being fit for the Hon.*ble *Company's Service.*

18th November 1807. Gillespie to Wm Wright Esq. : *Colonel Taylor has received instructions from the Commander in Chief to transfer all the young men on board the Prison Ships at Cowes between the ages of 18 and twenty three to the Company's service. Colonel Taylor and myself have selected 75 from among the Deserters, many of whom will be an acquisition to the Artillery Corps, indeed they are without exception a better description of Deserters than any which have hitherto been transferred under these circumstances...*

The next set of letters relate to the embarkation process itself. Embarkation was often affected by bad weather. In February 1805, five East Indiamen had set out in convoy, with some whaling ships and a Royal Navy escort, from the Motherbank anchorage. One of them, the *Earle of Abergavenny*, hit rocks off the Isle of Portland, further down the coast, and sank with the loss of 283 out of a total of 402 people on board. The ship was carrying 159 King's and Company troops. The Captain, John Wordsworth, brother of the poet William Wordsworth, went down with his ship.

2nd March 1805. Gillespie to Coggan : *Two recruits answering to the description stated in the affidavit ... John and William Summers, finally approved at the Depot for the 30th of October, and transferred with several others to the Hon*ble *Company's Service on the 12th December... were embarked on the Abergavenny. They were afterwards I understand amongst* others saved from the unfortunate wreck and put on board some others of the ships lately sailed … I cannot possibly say on which ship the two lads alluded to are now on board.

The embarkation of other recruits on this particular convoy was not without its problems:

11th February 1805. Gillespie to Coggan : *In reply to your letter of the 6th Instant I have to acquaint you for the information of the Committee of Shipping that from the arrival of the Hon[ble] Company's ships at the Motherbank till the 26th and 7th January it was impossible to embark any troops in such boisterous weather as then prevailed …*

… On the following day, Sunday, I succeeded in getting the number for the Earle of Abergavenny on board and the same day L[t.] Col. Kent embarked the remainder of the King's Troops.

On the next day, viz Monday, I Proceeded early in the morning with the Recruits for the other ships and had them all on board the vessels by 10 o'clock, but unfortunately, as it was then calm and the Tide against us, we could make no way until near three o'clock, so that it was about five o'clock before we reached the Henry Adddington [1] where I left thirty men and lost no time in getting the same number on board the Wexford and Royal George. We afterwards made the best of our way to the Bombay Castle and when near enough hailed her stating that I had Company's troops to put on board. The Commanding Officer answered saying that he would not receive them at so late an hour (then about eight o'clock) saying we ought to have come before dark and that he would fire at us if we attempted to come any nearer. I stated to him the reason for our not being able to reach the ship sooner and that it was late, as it was none of the other ships had made the least objection of their being put on board that evening, at the same time informing him if he persisted in refusing to receive them he must abide by the consequences. He replied saying that he would.

Therefore finding all remonstrations in vain and it was beginning to blow hard, the master of the vessel recommended our putting into Portsmouth as it would be easier to go to the ships early in the morning. To which I consented & we got safely into the harbour by 10 o'clock.

But the next day *no vessel whatever could reach the ships though several made the attempt*. On the following day the weather improved and Gillespie managed to embark the rest of his recruits.

Turning to more mundane matters, there were often difficulties supplying the recruits with the right size and amounts of clothing. Solomon, as second in command, was often delegated to write to the authorities on these matters:

22nd May 1805. Earle to Mr Hunt : *Sir, By Desire of Capt. Gillespie I have to acknowledge receipt of six Hampers of shoes said to contain 550 pr. For the Recruits of the Hon. ble East India Company. If on examination there should be any variation you may rest assured you will be immediately made acquainted with it.*

16th July 1805. Earle to Messrs Welsh and Stalker : *We were totally destitute of jackets … We have now about 100 men arrived over, and not a single jacket in store … Forward as many as you can get made up without waiting for the whole being finished.*

3rd August 1805. Earle to Hunt : *I will thank you to send whatever quantity you may have without losing a moment as we expect to embark a greater number of men than we have shoes in Store. As one of the ships is already arrived and the Tamarind is fairly expected at the Motherbank, it is highly probable we shall embark them the beginning of the ensuing week. Do not neglect to send the shoes by Brookman's Waggon [2] for Southampton. Favour Captain Gillespie your answer by return of post.*

3rd September 1805. Earle to Hunt : *I beg to inform you that we have received from you at three different times (viz) 14th Aug + 200 prs shoes, on the 17th 300 prs, on the 1st Inst. 300. Total 1000 prs according to Invoice. I am very sorry to find the whole of the shoes you have sent are of so large a size that the greatest part of our lads will be deprived of the use of them. I therefore request that you will be particularly attentive in future to send a large proportion of a size for lads from 14 year of age.*

9th September 1805. Earle to Mr Frazer : *I am ordered by Cpt Gillespie to acknowledge receipt of five hundred Caps on the first inst. & also to point out to you that a large proportion of them are of very inferior quality and some of them so very bad we must be under the necessity of returning a great part of them. Had we not been in immediate want the whole would have been sent back.*

Capt Gillespie begs you will give the necessary orders that more care is taken in future.

After this flurry of letters on the clothing front we hear nothing more until:

15th December 1811. Earle to Messrs Stalker and Welsh : Dear Sirs/– I am sorry to be under the necessity of again requesting you will give positive directions to your packets to mark each bale, so that we know the contents without being necessitated to open those we are in no immediate use of, and to include an invoice in a corner of the Bale with a mark thus X where it is to be found.

If each bale is marked as follows I think it will answer.

A for Artillery
I for Infantry

… We have been under the necessity of borrowing 50 Great Coats from the Government lately, having no accounts of those we have long been in expectation of.

The next series of letters refer to the rules regarding the embarkation of women and children, and a man suffering from melancholy. Captain Gillespie appeared to have had a very benevolent and caring attitude to some of his charges, being prepared to go beyond the regulations where necessary.

6th October 1804. Gillespie to James Coggan Esq. : I have the honor to enclose you a letter from Mr Ogle respecting a patient who has been a considerable time in sick quarters and from every appearance likely to continue to be a burden to the Honble Company. I therefore humbly beg leave to recommend that he being discharged for the reasons stated in Mr Ogle's letter.

4th October 1804. Mr Ogle's letter : Thomas Cameron on Highland Bay who was admitted into sick quarters from which he recovered has since been in such a state of Melancholy and Dejection from the idea of being sent away from his home and family that in my opinion he never can be considered useful as a soldier in the Company's Service.

Undated. Gillespie to the Committee : *My reason for permitting an additional woman to proceed on the Albion. I beg to inform you that the Government have on similar occasions granted this indulgence when the strength of the attachment was considerable and the number of women to proceed with their husbands did not exceed more than by one that is allowed by the regulations. The soldier in the present case, having as well as his wife, an excellent character, and there being particular circumstances of distress attending their separation. I was induced for the sake of humanity to step beyond the strict line prescribed when from the hurry of embarkation I had not time to avail myself as was my Duty, of the consent of the Committee.*

I however beg leave to add that in no future instance shall I permit any deviation from the above, or any other Regulation, unless I shall have received the orders of the Committee to that effect.

11th September 1808. Gillespie to Captain Jones of the Walthamstow: *In reply to your letter of the 8th inst. which I received yesterday. I have to acquaint you that the Child of William and Jane Cook (by name Amelia) was inadvertently omitted to be inserted in the Order and as the Children of Soldiers are by the Regulation permitted to accompany their parents permit me to request you will be pleased to rectify the mistake by inserting the Child's name in the Order in your possession.*

The following letters refer to applications by relatives or friends to discharge a recruit known to them. Perhaps the recruit had changed their mind, or, as you will see below regarding Samuel Bethal, they were not seeking discharge, but their family wanted them back. The regulations also made it clear that money would not be accepted to pay for a discharge, but two replacements had to be supplied in exchange. This requirement was presumably virtually impossible to fulfil, given the shortage of recruits. When Samuel Taylor Coleridge precipitously enlisted in the 15th Light Dragoons in 1793, his brother James negotiated his discharge for a fee of more than forty guineas. But Coleridge had joined a cavalry regiment and he was unable to ride a horse. It took several months to affect his discharge. In the end the army dealt with it by declaring him to be insane. But they still took the money.[3]

4th October 1806. Earle to James Humphries : *In reply to yours (without a date) received this morning. I beg to inform you that your son may have his discharge from the Honble East India Company's service on procuring two substitutes properly attested and examined by a surgeon who will give a certificate that they are fit for His Majesty's service – They must not exceed twenty five years of age and stand at least five feet five, if done growing, if under 18 years, five feet three … Every other particular, I beg you to refer to Colonel Robinson.*

3rd January 1807. Earle to James Humphries : *I have been expecting to hear from you for some time past respecting the two substitutes you proposed sending in exchange for your son. As the ships are hourly expected off Portsmouth to receive the troops for the first embarkation, it is desirable we shall send them on board by the end of next week. Therefore unless two good men are here in time, we shall embark him by the first ship as his conduct of late entitles him to no further indulgences from Captain Gillespie who has befriended him very much, and by whose desire I give you this very unpleasant account.*

Solomon was clearly taking a tougher line than the Commandant. Another applicant for discharge, the aforementioned Samuel Bethal, is interesting as no less than five letters were recorded as having been sent. Mr Bethal clearly had friends in high places.

29th April 1809. Earle to Captain French of the Militia, Chester : *I have to acknowledge receipt of your letter of 23rd inst. re Samuel Bethal, a recruit attached to the E. I.C ny service. In answer to which I beg leave to acquaint you that, in order to obtain his discharge it will be necessary to procure two unexceptional recruits for unlimited service who are to go through the usual routine of recruits enlisted for His Majesty's service and sent free of expense to this depot on or before the limitation of his furlough which will be on the 23rd day of May next, unless Brigadier General Taylor recommends my prolonging his furlough for one month.*

23rd June 1809. Earle to Captain French : *I am favoured with yours of the 18th instant and beg to inform you that Captain Gillespie the Commandant has extended (for the last time) Bethel's furlough to the 23rd July, but, in case the two substitutes not being here by that time 'tis the Commandant's positive order that Bethal himself is at the Depot, in order that he may be ready to proceed to India by the first ship after his return.*

If Bethal has been punished it must have been before he was turned over to the Company's service, he never has since, so far from it, has been very much indulged in consequence of yours, and Mr Steane's application in his favor.

15th July 1809. Gillespie to Mr Wright. (At the Shipping Committee): *I send you the enclosed copy of a correspondence on the subject of Samuel Bethal's Discharge, by which you will see that every facility has been afforded him of procuring the necessary substitutes that being the only mode possible of proceeding in this matter and as to the idea of his friends transmitting money instead of Men, it is evident that such a proposal cannot be listened to for a moment, nor, if it could be attended to, would it be of any avail, since substitutes are quite as difficult to be procured in this island as in any other part of the Kingdom, as, however Embarkation is now unlikely to take place for a length of time, I should imagine his friends might still obtain the recruits, for which purpose I would willingly agree to renew his furlough for a longer period.*

19th July 1809. Gillespie to Captain French (in Chester) : *as no embarkation of the Honble Company's troops is likely to take place for some time I have been induced at the request of Mr Robinson, one of the Hon. Directors and Mr Wright of the India House (who it appears are very desirous of facilitating Bethal's discharge) to prolong his Furlough for two months, by which time I trust you will be enabled to procure the necessary Substitutes.*

Both Gillespie and Earle continue to hold their ground.

7th August 1809. Earle to Captain French : *By order of Captain Gillespie* (clearly Solomon needs his sanction in this case) *I beg leave to acknowledge the receipt of your favor to him, of the 21st inst. and to acquaint you that Bethal returned to this place on the 21st, although, that he solemnly declares if substitutes were procured for his discharge, he would enlist again.*

I would therefore strongly recommend that, his friends put themselves to no further expense on his part, for they may rest assured, he will not be prevailed on to remain at home, or any consideration whatever – and at any rate embarkation will not take place for some months.

23. The Letter Book

That was the last latter sent about Samuel Bethal. It would be interesting to know why he wanted to get away from his friends and family, and why these important people wanted him back.

It seems odd that money was never to be accepted, as the following letter did not appear to follow this rule. This letter also outlined the rules for run-away apprentices when, to affect discharge, their master had to register the absconding apprentice with a Justice of the Peace or Magistrate and take an oath, within one month of the disappearance of the apprentice.

19th April 1811. Gillespie to William Wright Esq : *Agreeable to your desire I shall give a discharge to Alex^r Miller. The sum specified by order of the Commander in Chief to be received on the Discharge of a Recruit enlisted for unlimited service (of which description Miller is) amounts to forty-seven pounds and five shillings. The circumstances of Miller's being an apprentice avails him nothing, as his quitting his Master's service was not certified before a Magistrate within one month from his departure, and even, where this had been done, altho' the Recruit must be delivered up to his Master, for the term of his apprenticeship, yet, at the expiration of that time he is again to be claimed by Government as a soldier...*

There is a follow up letter written by Solomon a few days later:

28th April 1811. Earle to George Miller, Nicholson's Square, Edinburgh : *I beg leave to acquaint you your son Alex^r left this place for London yesterday taking his discharge with him directed to you, with every intention of calling on his brother on his way home.*

It may be necessary to mention to you that he was unfortunate enough, the night before he went away, to lose the whole of the money, rather better than £6 intended for his conveyance, so that Captain Gillespie was necessitated to advance him two pounds to enable him to proceed, which I doubt not will be refunded by his brother, as soon as he arrives in London.

They seemed quite keen to get rid of Mr Miller. He may have spent the six pounds on a night out on the town celebrating his release. There are several letters describing episodes of misconduct at the depot in relation to other recruits.

22ⁿᵈ December 1809. Gillespie to Mr Henry Dixon : *I received your letter dated the 16th December, stating the circumstances of your son, William Dixon, obtaining money from you under the pretence of having his discharge being sick.*

In reply to which, I beg leave to inform you the whole is a fabrication, for the purposes of imposition, and procuring money: I also think it necessary to state, your son is not, neither will he be, discharged, therefore send him no more money as he has everything here that can render him comfortable. Not withstanding, he has behaved extremely ill since joining at this Depot, having been frequently confined in the Guard room for irregularities of different kinds, rendering himself not worthy of any indulgence.

PS The £5 you sent him has been made so improper use of, that he expended it in liquor, besides having made away with his Regimental necessaries, which he must be put under stoppage to replace.

It appears that Captain Gillespie was exasperated with having to be a substitute father for this lad. The next series of letters refer to bad behaviour at the depot from veterans from India.

9ᵗʰ November 1807. Gillespie to Wright : *It is with great regret I am under the disagreeable necessity of representing the conduct of the following men of the Bombay Detachment as every way unbecoming the character of soldiers (viz.) William Frazer, serjeant, Martin Rice, Dennis Constantine, James Hamilton – privates.*

These Men after applying for furloughs which they received with arrears of pay, positively refused to accompany the Non-Commissioned Officer who had Orders to see them off the island – and have from that time, and still continue to behave in the most riotous manner.

As we have now a considerable number of Recruits and expect more very soon, the example shewn by those Men has already been attended with much mischief.

Serjeant Frazer, whose time is expired, is every way unworthy of being again admitted into the Honorable Company's service, indeed the other Non

Commissioned Officers are ashamed of his conduct – Rice, Hamilton and Constantine have each two years to serve, the former is reported as fit for Garrison duty only.

I should therefore strongly recommend all these as well as the Serjeant to be discharged, as unfit for continuing any longer in the Service. Some of these Men have an idea they are under no obligation to serve the Company, but in the East Indies and that they are not under martial law in England.

Every indulgence has been given to these men which was in my Power to grant, in consideration of the fatigue they have for some years undergone, and the difference of climate, and every precaution has been taken to prevent their conduct from being taken notice of by Colonel Taylor who I am certain would not suffer such unsoldier-like behaviour to pass with impunity.

Discipline was much stricter in the King's Army. Lieutenant Leslie Charles of the 29th Foot was stationed at Parkhurst in 1807. His regiment was about to embark for Spain to take part in the Peninsular War. He wrote that a *dashingly dressed young man* was brought into the barracks, handcuffed, under a military escort. This man was accused of desertion and court marshalled and sentenced to 500 lashes.[4]

But the story of our four badly behaved veterans was not over yet:

18th November 1807. Gillespie to Wright : *I have been favoured with your letter in reply to your letter of mine of the 9th instant. I am rather surprised to hear of Lieutenant Crofts having given Serjeant Frazer so favourable a Character after his Contemptuous conduct to some of the Officers while on board the Sir Edward Hughes, and I can venture to say 'till within these few days (now the money is all spent) that he has not been sober throughout one day since he has been in this barracks, independently of this he can neither read nor write and is consequently, in my opinion, unfit to be a Non-Commissioned Officer.*

With respect to the other three. I will deal with them as the Chairman has directed – though I have already been under the necessity of confining Rice, and Matthews in the Black-Hole and Guard Room for repeated Drunkenness and Riotous Behaviour – and I beg leave to state the following Report of Serjeant Brennan respecting Rice.

> *"That he has been eight years in the Company's service, during which time he has never done more than two days field duty – That he gets in liquor every opportunity, consequently he is very troublesome and has frequently been confined in the Guard at Bombay, for unsoldier-like conduct, and has not conducted himself a bit better since he left it – and has been more troublesome than all the rest of the detachment, and further says that when in a state of intoxication, he would as soon strike one of his officers, as one of his companions."*
>
> *I shall however do everything in my power to reform them – and as Serjeant Frazer appears now very Penitent, and promises to behave better in future and in consideration of his having two children at Bombay (his wife I understand being dead) I have therefore reprimanded him for his late conduct, agreed to give him anther opportunity of retrieving his Character at the same time informed him that he was not to expect any Bounty, 'till upon the eve of his departure for India.*

Presumably Sergeant Fraser had received his back pay and then celebrated with a drinking binge until his money had all been spent. Drinking was rife at that time, especially in the armed forces, and especially amongst the army in India. Samuel Hickson recorded the reason for death amongst ordinary soldiers as being mainly due to *the climate, intemperance and debauchery*.[5]

You may remember a certain W. Fraser from a previous chapter (15). Fraser, after being dismissed for abandoning his post in the Wadgaon campaign, retrieved his character by volunteering and surviving the storming of the City of Ahmedabad in 1780. He volunteered to be a member of the forlorn hope. Presumably he would therefore have been held in much esteem in the Bombay army, and Solomon would almost certainly have come across him. W. Fraser may well be the Sergeant William Fraser referred to in the above letters.

As mentioned the Company officers at the Depot were rather afraid of General Taylor who comes across as a bit of a martinet. This was evident in May 1809, when General Taylor demanded the immediate presence of the surgeon, Mr Ogle, to check whether a recruit was fit enough for punishment, presumably a lashing:

23. The Letter Book

Sunday 21ˢᵗ May 1809. Earle to Gillespie : *My Dear Sir,*

On Monday last I addressed a letter to you stating General Tayler's particular desire that Mr Ogle should return to the Island immediately as one of the Company's Recruits was then under sentence of Court Martial for Desertion, and he was resolved never more to punish any of our men unless our own surgeon was present.

On Friday the Adjᵗ came to the Office to inquire whether Mr Ogle was returned and yesterday the General sent for me and desired me to write again this day (no post going to London yesterday) to say he should expect Mr Ogle down on Tuesday.

As I have reason to fear something unpleasant may occur to my friend Ogle, unless he can give a very sufficient reason to the General for not being here before this, or more especially if he neglects to comply immediately with the content of this letter; I entreat you will advise him to set off immediately for the Island and report himself immediately to the General on his arrival, if in the evening be sure to be at the Barracks early the following morning.

I shall enclose a few lines to Ogle myself, and beg you will forward them as quick as possible.

Sickness, particularly mental illness, was a common problem amongst recruits at the Depot. This is hardly surprising when so many recruits passed through on their way an uncertain future in India, unlikely ever to see their home and family again. Mental illness appeared to be dealt with in a caring and understanding manner, especially given the lack of facilities. There were few hospitals specifically for mental illness at this time. The hospital used by the Company tended to be the Bethlem Hospital in London. The Company had to fund the cost of transfer and treatment. Confinement in the Company's small hospital in Newport caused no end of problems, examples of which are outlined in the following letters:

31ˢᵗ October 1809. Gillespie to Wright : *In reply to your letter of the 20ᵗʰ respecting John Miller, I am now informed by Lieut. Wilkinson, the officer commanding the Detachment of Artillery from Madras, who arrived yesterday, that the Man in question, was found to be in a deranged state of mind, and otherwise considered unfit for service and it appears for some trifling reason, he changed his name to that of Wright, which was the case, as you observe, that he could not be identified. He now says that he went out in the Essex, commanded by Captain Strover, in the capacity of Seaman, and not as a recruit, as he before stated.*

I have, under these circumstances, added to the information from Lieut. Wilkinson, rejected him as being, in my opinion, unfit for the Service.

8th January 1810. Gillespie to Wright : *I beg leave to inclose you a letter received respecting a Recruit named Thomas Walker, who according to his own account has, at different periods, been deranged, altho' he appears at present, perfectly sensible. If the statement in the letter, which corresponds with that of the Man himself, be correct, the disease is certainly liable to recur, and, under this impression, it is the opinion of Mr Ogle and myself that it would be advisable on repayment of the Bounty and expenses incurred on his account, which amounts to about thirty pounds, to grant him a discharge.*

I shall, therefore, be obliged to you to inform me of the determination of the Committee on this heading.

Thomas Walker was most likely to have been suffering from bipolar affective disorder, like King George III, an illness that can often resolve completely between episodes. Mr Walker may even have been in a manic state when he decided to enlist. People often make decisions they later regret when in such a state. It appears both Captain Gillespie and Mr Ogle had a reasonable working knowledge of mental illness. In 1810 George III had his final episode of mental illness, in this case melancholia, from which he never recovered.

The next two letters were written by Solomon. They concern another case of mental illness, but also a case where Solomon felt unduly criticised by the London office and wanted to set the record straight.

10th July 1810. Earle to Wright : *I have been Honored with your letter of the 9th Inst. enclosing a copy of Captn Gillespie's addressed to you on the subject of Waite, and feel myself much hurt at being supposed to be the cause of keeping this unfortunate Man, after he had been discharged by the Honble Comys service. As Captn Gillespie's explanation to you is by no means so clear as to exonerate me from Censure, I entreat I may not incur the displeasure of the Hon. Court by stating the exact circumstances.*

Waite was received by Captn Gillespie himself on the 1st day of January last, (as Captn Gillespie justly remarks) at which time he had an apparent weakness of intellect, but it was at the time thought to be feigned. However, after a trial of some weeks it was found to be real, and at times appeared totally deranged. On the eve of Captain Gillespie's going to London, he ordered Waite to be detained until a favorable opportunity offered to send him to London, so that he might be enabled to get to his friends in Scotland by sea. The Discharge and money was left in the office as the man was not in a fit state to take care of it.

Captain Gillespie had scarcely left the Island before this unhappy man threw himself into the river, and would certainly have destroyed himself, had I not taken the steps I did to prevent it by placing him in the Hon. C^{ys} hospital, no opportunities having offered to send him to London as recommended by Captn Gillespie, and if there even had, no person would have taken charge of a man so totally deranged.

As you may rest assured the above is the exact sate of affairs of the case, I trust to your goodness in submitting this letter to the Committee, as yours implies a censure on me for receiving this man again into the Company's service, when in fact he never received his discharge being in too deranged a state to be spoken to on Captn Gillespie's going to London.

I shall embrace the first favourable opportunity of sending Waite off, at the least possible expense to the C^{py}.

12th July 1810. Earle to Gillespie : *I received a letter from Mr Wright dated the 9th Ins^t enclosing your explanation to him on the subject of James Waite. As I am very much censured by the Committee for having received this poor unfortunate man, after having been (as the Committee imagined) regularly discharge. I am very sorry you had not informed the Board of the real state of the case and, as Mr Ogle was present, it might have been explained to the satisfaction of the court...*

Solomon then went on to explain how Mr Waite threw himself in the river and how he sent him to the hospital,

(lest General Tayler might see him in that state), with direction to take the proper steps to prevent him from doing an injury to himself in one of the

Detached Offices for fear of him molesting or disturbing the patients. I have consulted Dr Moore who has seen Waite, and assures me he is clearly of opinion that he never will be fit for any kind of duty as a soldier and has given me a Certificate to that effect.

Solomon then outlined that he had consulted the Borough and County Magistrates who had advised that the Company were responsible for Waite and must *keep him confined until I had an opportunity of getting him conveyed, whether to his friends, or to some proper place of custody, nor would he* (the Magistrate, Sir Henry Holmes) *on any account suffer a person in so deranged a state to be at large on the island.*

Solomon then went on to outline that Waite had twenty-eight days pay left in the office, and that the one pound and eight shillings this amounted to, would soon be expended.

Solomon wrote again to William Wright, only three days later. This might seem a bit soon until you examine the contents.

13th July 1810. Earle to Wright : *As I have not been favored with an ans^{er} to my letter of the 10th inst. (either by yesterday or this day's post) – I deem it necessary to inform you that Mr Waite still remains in confinement in a detached office belonging to our hospital in Newport, This is certainly a very improper place being surrounded by dwelling houses, but it is the only place of security we have. The neighbourhood, as well as the patients in the Hospital, are very much annoyed by the noise of this poor unhappy Lunatic, he is kept in a straight jacket but we cannot prevent him from making a noise, which he is constantly doing. The Magistrates insist on keeping him in Confinement, until he can be removed from the Island, and, not withstanding, I stated to Sir Henry Holmes, the County Magistrate, that the man was no longer a Soldier, he told me the Parish could not be burdened with him, and I must be answerable to get him removed as soon as possible, and to keep him in confinement, until he could be sent off the island.*

When similar circumstances occur in His Majesty's Service (which I understand is frequent) it is reported by the Medical Department to General Taylor, when the report is sent to the Commander in Chief, who orders proper people from one of the insane hospitals to come down and convey the patient to London.

23. The Letter Book

In the present circumstances I beg leave to suggest, if an order could be obtained for the reception of Mr Waite at St. Luke's I could get him conducted to London by one of the Non Commissioned Officers, and a private, either on top of the stage or on foot, the former I should conceive the safest and Cheapest – I could send him to Southampton or Portsmouth in the afternoon, and the poor fellow might be placed in Hospital the next morning.

After this the trail goes dead, until James Waite's name comes up in a letter written by Captain Gillespie on September 1811, a full year later:

7th September 1811. Gillespie to J. E. Batter Esq. : *... James Waite was transferred to the Company's service on the 3rd January 1810. In this case no decided marks of Insanity were perceived till the beginning of July in the same year, when his situation was reported to the Committee and on their application was received into Bethlem Hospital.* [6] *His Parish is Dunes, in Berwick upon Tweed.*

From enquiries I have made, I am given to understand that these men are not chargeable to the Parish in which their malady occurred; but, if passed to the Parish in which they were born, they must necessarily be taken care of. If this is the case (which may probably be ascertained by application to the Company's Solicitor) it would certainly be advisable to pass Waite immediately to Berwick. [7]

There are several other letters relating to recruits suffering from mental illness. For example Frederick Walsh was found to be insane in July 1811 and there were plans to transfer him to Bethlem Hospital. But sadly, he never got there:

7th September 1811. Gillespie to J. E. Batter Esq. : *Fredck Walsh, the Insane man at this depôt, was transferred to the Company's service on the 5th July and was at the time in apparently good health. Symptoms of Insanity appeared on the 20th of that month when he was received into the Hospital where he has since been in a state of complete derangement. He was born in the parish of Hardwicke, Warwickshire...*

... In the case of the other man (Frederick Walsh) who has a wife residing in or near London, it might perhaps be agreeable to the Company to get him admitted into Bethlem Hospital, at the same time discharging him from the

Company's Service, and obliging his friends to receive him on his removal from Bethlem whether cured or incurable.

13th November 1811. Earle to Mrs Walsh of 21 York St., Westminster: *I am sorry to acquaint you that your husband Frederick Walsh departed this life in the Company's Hospital on the 29th October. The arrears of Pay due to him at that time is about one pound Sterling which I herewith enclose you, and request you will acknowledge the receipt thereof.*

6th October 1811. *Return of men unfit for service in consequence of disease incurred since their being attached to the Honorable East India Company.*

1. John Nichols Insane
2. Wm Keating Insane
3. Roger Hoyle Rupture
4. John Kennedy Rupture
5. Wm Morly Defect of sight
6. Wm Cooke Fits
7. … Nelson Fits
8. James Wayley Defective Intellect

Signed by Dr Ogle

The following year the two insane men were apparently still in the Hospital in Newport:

25th October 1812. Earle to Wright : *Dr Moore has again been to speak to me relative to the removal of the two insane men, Nichols and Keating, from the General Hospital. I beg you will urge the Committee to finally decide on them as soon as possible and favour me with the result.*

12th November 1812. Earle to Wright : *I am sorry to trouble you again, to know whether the Committee has yet determined on the cases of two insane men, Nichols and Keating, in order to point out the necessity of as speedy a decision as possible. I enclose which I yesterday received from the Principle Medical Officer of the Depot, by which you will perceive how anxiously their removal is sought for.*

How little things change. These matters are familiar to the author who used to work as a consultant psychiatrist for the NHS.

23. The Letter Book

The remaining letters (not quoted) cover a number of matters including: returns on the numbers of recruits embarked, a plea for charitable funding for a widow and payment of expenses. An idea of the numbers embarked each year is evidenced in the final letter transcribed in this account. This is a letter signed by both Captain Gillespie and Mr Ogle, and addressed to William Wright, about the desperate need for a new hospital. This letter was sent on the 10th April 1812.

Dear Sir,

You will recollect that some time ago, Ogle and myself, both in conversation with you, and by letter to the Chairman, urged the necessity of providing an Hospital on a larger scale than the present one for the accommodation of the sick at the Company's Depôt on the Isle of Wight. He also hinted that a grant of land might possibly be obtained in the neighbourhood of Parkhurst Barracks for the erection of one suited to the purpose. However strong our reasons then were for this representation they are now still more forcible in consequence of the very considerable increase in number of our recruits.

From the Christmas of 1810 to the following one of 1811 we had under our charge above 1500 men, of which number between six hundred and seven hundred men in Barracks at the same time, and that, too, at a very sickly period of the year.

The premises we now occupy as an Hospital are not capable of affording suitable accommodation to scarcely more than one third of the sick, which must necessarily exist under so extensive an establishment.

Add this that the House is situated in midst of a very populous town, into which, by its means, infectious disease are liable to be continually brought, a circumstance which has repeatedly called forth the remonstrances of the Magistrate of the place, and which unfortunately we are conscious being founded in truth.

The cause of our representing this matter at this present moment is that a bill is now in Parliament for the "Disafforesting the Forest of Parkhurst", in consequence of which a large portion of the Land will be vested in the Crown; and a considerable grant from it is as we learn, to be allotted to the present Barracks.

23. The Letter Book

There is little, or perhaps, no doubt, but that on the proper application by the Court of Directors to the Secretary of State, or President of the Board of Control, a similar grant could be made to the Company of a proportionate quantity of Land for the site of an Hospital and Barracks if at some future period it should be thought advisable to erect the latter.

Should this application be judged expedient, which we most earnestly hope will be the case, the most convenient spot of ground in our opinion, would be that piece which joins the present Barracks enclosure on its south side, and which lies between the present Barracks enclosure and the lands belonging to the corporation of Newport consisting of about five and twenty or thirty acres.

Carisbrooke Church with Parkhurst Forest behind. From the Castle. 2017

It is not known whether the hospital was ever built but we do know that the Depot was transferred to Brompton Barracks, Chatham, in March 1815. Thankfully Parkhurst Forest was never completely 'disafforested'.

It is unclear why the Newport Depot was transferred to Chatham but on the international scene the allies had entered Paris in 1814 and the war was thought to be over with Napoleon safely ensconced at the island of Elba. Protected convoys were therefore no longer essential and the King's army was in the process of being disbanded. It must therefore have been easier to recruit troops for India. Maybe the Depot was becoming too expensive to run and a cheaper option, the barracks at Chatham, had become available.

23. The Letter Book

Napoleon, of course, escaped from Elba and landed at Cannes in March 1815. He then followed what is now known as the Route Napoleon, up the east side of France, to meet his Waterloo the following June.

In the final part of this chapter we will catch up with what was happening to Solomon's family.

In the early nineteenth century Newport was a small and close-knit community, a town dominated by shops, various tradesmen, the military and the church. Solomon and Rose would have socialised with colleagues in the military, and of course with Solomon's friend, Dr Ogle. The Earle daughters, to a large extent, ended up marrying military men.

Marianne was the first Earle daughter to make a match. She married Doctor William Lempriere in 1810. William Lempriere (1763-1834) was an interesting character remembered to this day on the Isle of Wight. While an assistant surgeon at Gibraltar in 1789, he volunteered to attend one of the Sultan of Morocco's sons and ended up travelling around the country and treating the Sultan's harem. He wrote about his experiences in a book that became a best seller.[8] He then joined the Jamaica Light Dragoons and spent some time in the West Indies. He obtained his MD at Aberdeen in 1799 and was then appointed Inspector General of Hospitals before retiring to the Isle of Wight. He was a prolific writer and also published research.[9] He must have been aged forty-seven when he married sixteen-year-old Marianne at Newport. At the time he had a twelve-year-old son who died of TB in 1819. His death is commemorated by a plaque in All Saints Church, Newchurch:

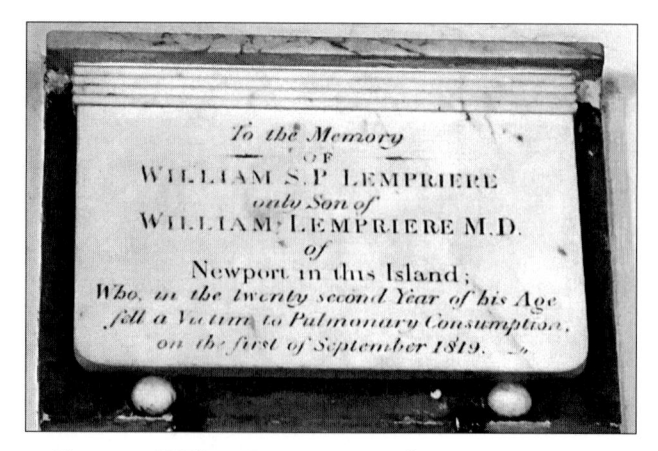

Plaque to William Lempriere in All Saints, Newchurch

The Earle family must have had a close relationship with the Lemprieres as John Lucas also married into the family, marrying Mary Lempriere in 1817. In 1813 Elfrida married Lieutenant Gabriel Matthias, from the artillery, and in 1824, Eleanor married his brother, Edward Coleridge Matthias, an ensign of the 44th Regiment at Carisbrooke.

We know that Solomon's son, also called Solomon, attended the Academy of Monsieur L'Abbe de Grenthe, a French refugee, situated in Quay Street, Newport, as this fact is recorded on his original application to join the East India Company in 1813. Charges for a day pupil were one pound and one shilling per term, although extras, including French, geography, drawing and dancing were also available. [10] Solomon Junior then joined the King's German Legion and fought at the Battle of Waterloo (1815) at La Haye Sainte, a crucial part of the battle. He re-applied to join the EIC as a Cadet in 1818 and spent the rest of his life in India.

Rose had three more children while resident in the Isle of Wight: Rosalie (1805), Emily Susan (1807) and Mary Anne (1816). Rosalie went on to marry another soldier, William Sheaffe, in 1825. Emily married Frederick Ranie, a bachelor of Woolwich in Kent, in 1823. As mentioned Mary Anne died at the age of four months.

In total Rose gave birth to ten children of which nine survived, a good survival record in those days. At least four ended up in India. Rosalie accompanied her husband to Australia in 1833.

When the Depot was transferred to Chatham in March 1815, Solomon was transferred with it, together with Captain Gillespie and Mr Ogle. As far as we are aware his family stayed behind in Newport.

24. Coda

INDIA

At the end of Chapter 17, we left Fatesinghrao in charge at Baroda but, under the terms of the Treaty of Salbai, he had to give the City of Ahmedabad back to the Peshwa and return to paying large amounts of tribute. Although Fatesingh had received reassurances of support from the English, his alliance with them had brought him little more than the greatly intensified enmity of the Peshwa, or more particularly of Nana Fadnavis, who dominated the Pune court.[1] A new obligation had been added, he had to provide the Peshwa with troops whenever called upon to do so.

But this never happened as infighting broke out between the principle noblemen and courtiers at Pune with the result that there was no question of the Peshwa's army immediately demanding a supply of men.[2] Fatesingh was therefore able to live out his remaining years in comparative peace. Being the shrewd operator that he was, he did not pay all the taxes demanded by Pune. We know this because when he died, the arrears were huge. The government in Pune demanded that all debts be paid before agreeing to promote his successor.[3]

But Fatesingh did not have long to enjoy the peace. He died on the 21st September 1789 and did not leave an heir. He apparently died as a result of an accidental fall from the upper story of his palace.[4,5] Intriguingly no other information is available. Fatesingh was succeeded by his younger brother Manajirao. Govindrao, his older brother and rival, had failed to gain support from the Peshwa and Mahadji Scindia supported Manajirao. Manajirao also promised to pay all of Fatesingh's arrears.[6]

But Govindrao did get to be Maharaja in the end. Manajirao died in 1793 and Govindrao again pushed forward his claim. The Pune government detained him until he agreed to pay an even greater sum of money and, in addition to this, all the jewels, money and clothes that could be found in the Baroda palace. He also had to supply elephants, land and his share of custom revenue from Surat.[7] A Pyrrhic victory indeed.

It seems that Nana Fadnavis was intent on ruining the Gaekwad family and breaking up their government in Baroda. And he would have succeeded but for the intervention of the English. When Govindrao appealed to the EIC for help they supported him by pointing out that it was against the Treaty of Salbai to demand land. Duff wrote that Govindrao became *Regent* in December 1793.[8] This suggests that his mentally disabled brother, Sayajirao, may have still been alive.

After this the Gaekwads continued to hold on to power in Baroda right up to Independence in 1947. This was not easy as, when they sought help from the English to resolve disputes with Pune, there were of course conditions. These conditions usually included an acceptance of increased control from the Company. After the demise of the Maratha Politic in 1818, Baroda was maintained by the EIC as a semi-independent Princely State.[9] Despite this, and perhaps because of it, Baroda State became rich, especially during the American Civil War in the 1860s, when cotton prices went through the roof. Various political shenanigans followed, including an incident when one of the Maharajas, Malharrao, was deposed by the British after being accused of attempting to poison the then British Resident, the detested Colonel Robert Phayre. The Maharaja was accused of administering ground glass to the Resident. Following this incident a decision was made to appoint a new Maharaja, a boy who would be sent to Britain for his education and therefore would, in the eyes of the British, be more controllable. Sayajirao was adopted as the new Maharaja in 1875.[10]

Maharaja Sayajirao III turned out to be a wise choice. He took Baroda on *a forced march from its feudal past towards a rich and elegant future.*[11] Many reforms were made in public services, finance and agriculture, and in the emancipation of women. A park and zoo were built next to the river and many public buildings were constructed, including the university and a hospital. A new palace was planned. The ill fated architect, a proponent of the 'Indo-Saracen' style,[12] Major Charles Mant,[13] was chosen to design the palace. But poor Mant did not live to see the completion of his masterpiece. He committed suicide in 1881 due to worry that he had got his calculations wrong and his buildings would collapse. However the Laxmi Vilas Palace still stands today and remains the residence of the current Maharaja, Samarjitsingh Gaekwad. There are plans to convert it into a luxury hotel.

24. Coda

Laxmi Vilas palace, Baroda. 2016

After being abandoned by the British at the signing of the Treaty of Salbai, Raghunathrao surrendered, with all his family, to the Peshwa. He was sent to live at Kopargaon and underwent penance in the Godavari River. But his penance did not last long, as he died in December 1783, at the age of forty-eight.[14] Shortly after his death his widow Anandibai gave birth to a son, Chimaji. At the time of his father's death, the older son, Bajirao, was aged nine. Bajirao was destined to become the last Peshwa of the Maratha Politic.

Tukoji Holkar continued to keep the peace in Indore until his death in 1797. He was described as a plain, unaffected man and a loyal and good soldier. Mudhoji Bhonsle of Nagpur died in 1788.

In 1783 Mahadji Scindia was fast emerging as a major power in the Maratha Politic. He employed Count Benoit de Boigne[15] and other military adventurers to train his army in European ways.[16] He retook Gwalior and increased his hold over Delhi. At the time (1784) the Mughal State was in chaos and the Emperor, Shah Alam, invited Scindia to help him suppress

Muhammad Beg, the governor of the province of Agra. It was at this time that the Emperor's son travelled to Oudh to seek help from Warren Hastings (see Chapter 18). After support was refused (for good reason) Mahadji Scindia became the main ally of the Emperor. The Emperor then appointed him as Vice-Regent of the Empire, such as it was.

Mahadji Scindia   Nana Fadnavis
Prints from Beveridge, History of India 1862

In 1788, while Scindia was busy attacking Agra, Delhi was raided by a Rohilla chieftain, the psychopathic Ghulam Qadir. Qadir drove out the small Maratha garrison and had the Emperor and his family at his mercy. He then *committed a systematic train of violence, rapine and barbarity, almost without example in the annals of the world.*[17] Without going into detail Shah Alam and his family were treated with great cruelty and the Emperor was blinded. The Marathas returned in force to Delhi two months later and Gulam Qadir fled. He was eventually captured trying to get away from Meerut. Duff wrote that Qadir *suffered a dreadful mutilation which he did not survive.*[18] According to Montgomery Martin his nose, ears, hands and feet were cut off and he was placed in an iron cage to be transported back to Delhi.[19] Not surprisingly he did not survive the journey.

24. Coda

Mahadji Scindia restored Shah Alam to the throne and managed to keep the peace thereafter. Scindia further secured his power by defeating the Rajputs of Jaipur at the Battle of Paton (1790). At the time of his death in 1794, his power was at its peak. There is a tomb in honour to him at Pune called the Shinde Chhatri. He left a powerful Scindian army that, in 1803, gave Arthur Wellesley's force a major challenge when they came head-to-head at the Battle of Assaye. In fact Wellesley later said that Assaye was the battle in which he was most tested, more so than Waterloo.

Nana Fadnavis continued to dominate the Maratha Politic until his death in 1800. After the Anglo-Mysore war ended in 1784, Tipu Sultan wanted to regain territories held by the Marathas. He took Kittur and forcibly circumcised his Hindu captives – not for the first time. [20] This atrocity spurred the Marathas into action. With support from the Nizam of Hyderabad, they took on Tipu's army. Peace with Mysore was finally achieved in 1787. As mentioned in Chapter 22, there was a further significant campaign a few years later when the Nizam of Hyderabad, Ali Khan, decided to send a huge army into the Deccan to take on the Marathas. The two armies met at Kharda, in Maharashtra, in March 1795. The result was a decisive victory for the Marathas and turned out to be the last battle the Marathas ever fought together as a united confederacy. During both these campaigns the English remained neutral.

Nana Fadnavis was now at the height of his power. But a catastrophe occurred later that year. The young Peshwa, Madhavrao II, now aged twenty-one, had never been allowed by Nana Fadnavis to take full power. A *fixed melancholy seized his mind* and he threw himself from the terrace of his palace. [21] The injuries sustained resulted in his death two days later. During the consequent dispute for succession Nana Fadnavis struggled to keep power. He got involved in various subterfuges concerning which of Ragunathrao's sons, Bajirao or Chimajirao, would take over as the new Peshwa. This earned him the nickname the *Mahratta Machiaval* by his European contemporaries. [22] After his death in 1800, things got much worse. There was no stopping various rival groups fighting each other. At the Battle of Pune (1802), between the Holkar and Scindia clans, Bajirao II fled the capital and sought help from the English. This turned out to be the beginning of the end for the Maratha Politic.

Nana Fadnavis was another great Maratha leader, probably the greatest since Shivaji. He was a clever statesman who, as Regent, was able to keep rival factions together through many difficult times. His house, the Nana Fadnavis Wada, at the village of Menavali, has been preserved as a memorial to him.

During this account we have followed the deeds of three significant Maratha leaders: Mahadji Scindia, Tukoji Holkar and Nana Fadnavis. It was unfortunate for the Marathas that these great leaders all died within a short time of each other. None of them left strong or resourceful successors and consequent infighting left the Marathas open to divide and rule tactics. Unfortunately for the Marathas, the British were masters at that game.

It is beyond the scope of this book to describe the events that led to the final defeat of the Maratha Politic. In brief, the greatest territorial gains that set the scene for the future British Raj were the wars prosecuted by the EIC under the Governor-Generalship of Robert Wellesley (1797 to 1805). During this period Seringapatum was taken and Tipu Sultan killed. It was then the turn of the Marathas. During the Second Anglo-Maratha War (1803-1805) the supposedly impregnable fortress of Asirghar was taken for the first time. The British were soon to become the dominant power in India for the next 142 years.

SOLOMON AND HIS FAMILY

If Solomon had been allowed to return to India he would have found it to be a very different place. Gone were any ideas of an equal relationship between English and Indians, and certainly any acceptance of intermarriage. The British were there to rule. However, as we shall see, four of Solomon's children settled in India, perhaps inspired by his stories.

We left Solomon employed as adjutant and paymaster at the new Company depot in Chatham. The year was 1815. Brompton Barracks had been completed in 1806 and consisted of a huge set of buildings capable of housing up to 1300 troops, with associated stables and gun carriage sheds. It was the home of the Royal Engineers. Presumably the EIC shared the facility with the King's troops.

In 1817, at the age of sixty-six, Solomon applied for a pension. We know this because a debate took place at the Court of Directors at Leadenhall Street about whether to award this pension. An account of the debate was published later that year.[23] In the chair was John Bebb Esq.

24. Coda

At a previous meeting the Court of Directors had recommended that a pension of £300 per annum be granted as being *sufficient for the maintenance of his large family* and, taking into consideration his *long service,* and *the situation of his wife, who had for twenty years been afflicted with illness.* We have no information as to what sort of illness Rose was meant to be suffering from. Rose had not been so unwell that she was unable to give birth to ten children.

A Mr Hume then opposed the motion citing the short length of Captain Earle's employment, twelve years, and the high amount proposed. Mr Hume argued that the total expense of the Depot was too great (£2300 per year) to supply an average of 800 men per year. He argued that *no man, in his common senses, capable of performing the trivial duties of paying a few soldiers, would give up such a situation, unless obliged to do so; and Captain Earle must be in a deplorable state indeed if he were unable to perform that duty.* He went on to ask where the reports of medical men were that proved Captain Earle's incapacity. He argued that when he himself was paymaster for 20,000 men, he was able to carry out his duties, almost without moving from his chair. He remarked that *if Captain Earle was so gouty and infirm as not to be able to move from one room to another, still, if he could sit in his chair, he might not be capable of performing the duties of his office.* Mr Hume then completed his case by advising that the amount of the proposed grant should be lowered.

Things were not looking good for Solomon.

But Solomon had powerful supporters in the court, including the Chair, who rose and *begged leave to offer a few words on the merits of Captain Earle's case.* Mr E. Parry then pointed out that Captain Earle had actually served a total of thirty-two years, including nineteen years in India. He further stated that Solomon had served the Depot for many years *as faithfully as any individual could do, and, I am sorry to say, he is not likely to live a twelvemonth longer.* Mr D. Kinnaird said that he was *quite sensible that a case was made out to convince the proprietors of his being well worthy of their humane consideration. When he saw a gentleman who had served the Company in so deplorable a state as not to be able to sign his name, he would not hesitate a moment to grant him a pension, which was only to afford him the common comforts of life.* R. Pattison argued that he was actually being paid £432 and ten shillings, so the amount of pension was reasonable.

Mr Hume's amendment was then voted against by a large majority and Solomon was granted the £300 per annum.

24. Coda

After Solomon retired, Captain Gillespie stayed on at the Depot. In September 1817, Major Gillespie, superintendent of the Company Depot, Chatham, was promoted to *Lieut. Col. in the East Indies Only*.[24] Doctor Thomas Ogle died around 1822. His mother outlived him and was awarded a pension of eighty pounds per annum, *in consequence of the destitute state in which placed by her son's death*.[25]

The reviving sea air at the Isle of Wight must have proved beneficial to Solomon's health as he actually lived another seven years. In 1818 both he and Rose were well enough to make the long journey to Greystead in Northumberland so their daughter Emily could be baptised by her uncle, George Rennell, who had been newly appointed as vicar to St. Luke's Church. Both Solomon and Rose were on the baptism register, their address at the time being given as Hackney, Middlesex. The assumption is they made the journey by ship to Newcastle before taking a coach the forty odd miles to Greystead. Quite a trip in those days.

In the final chapter of his life Solomon lived with his family at Mill House, Clatterford, Newport. There were many mills along Lukely Brook, which runs east from the chalk hills, passing between the village of Carisbrooke and its castle. The brook joins the River Medina at the 'new' port, just north of the town. If you walk along Miller's Lane, you can still find the remains of mill-leats and ponds. Following the road down from the castle you cross a ford and just to your left stands an eighteenth century mill, perhaps the one where Solomon lived out his last days. Crossing the ford and ascending the hill to the north, you arrive at the medieval church of Saint Mary's, Carisbrooke. The church originally formed part of a Benedictine Priory. This is where Solomon's bones were laid to rest on December 4th 1824. He was seventy-four years old. A photograph exists of his grave but the actual grave is no more, perhaps removed to make way for others.

On the 4th February 1824, seven months before his death, Solomon made out his last will and testament.[26] His executors were to be his son-in-law, William Lempriere, and his daughter Marianne. The structure of the will was quite complex. It started with Solomon bequeathing one share in the Great Western Canal to each of his children.[27] However his *plate, books, silver and family pictures* were to be left to all his children, except Sophia. As mentioned Solomon no doubt had concerns that Sophia's husband, Richard Lipscombe, might misappropriate the money to pay off his debts.

24. Coda

St Mary's from Lukley Brook. 2017

Solomon's Grave. St Mary's Church, Carisbrooke.

24. Coda

The will does not give any details regarding estate or lands except for the *Whiddon farm and estates, near Ashburton*. As mentioned in Chapter 1, the Whiddon estate was put up for sale in 1828. There was still a reference to a *Captain Earle's Field* on an Ashburton tithe map of 1840.

The estate was to be offered for purchase to his sons in succession, starting with John Lucas, then William Henry, and finally Solomon. However they were unlikely to have been able taken up this option as they were only given six months each to arrange the purchase, and all three happened to be in India at the time of their father's death.

Any benefits from the sale of the land were to be used to buy shares in *Government East India* or *Real Surities*. Dividends and interest that accrued would go to *my dear wife Rosa, for and during her natural life,* taking into account any allowance she might get from the EIC. Rose was actually awarded an allowance of £100 per year from the Company in 1825. An entry in the East India Accounts of 1825 records that the award was given in *consideration of the unfortunate situation in which she finds herself and her two daughters are placed by his decease.*[28]

Each time one of his unmarried daughters was to marry (there were three at the time) they would be given the sum of £400. Any money that remained would be divided up. Money accruing to Sophia had special conditions. It was to be invested in securities and only the dividends would be paid to her. There were also special conditions that money would be paid to daughters rather than sons. The Lemprieres were nominated as guardians for his three unmarried daughters.

This will is interesting as Solomon was clearly very careful that his daughters would benefit. This was of advantage given the lack of financial and property rights that women had in those days.

We can assume that the key attendees at Solomon's funeral would have been his wife Rose, daughters Susannah, Emily and Rosalie, and Marianne and her husband William Lempriere. His three sons were all away in India forging their own careers. John Lucas had been the first to leave, signing up as a cadet in 1806. William Henry followed in 1808. Solomon junior had re-applied to be a cadet in 1818 and, given his experience at Waterloo with the Kings German Legion, would have had no trouble getting accepted. He left that year.

24. Coda

It is probable that Rose lived out her remaining days on the Isle of Wight, in close proximity to her daughters. She would have been around sixty years of age at the time of her husband's death. It has not been possible to find out when she died.

It would have been surprising if Sophia (44)* had attended the funeral. She was living in London at the time and had at least two young children, Emma (1) and William (3), as well as Lucas (16). Richard (born in 1804) had died two years previously. It seems unlikely that her husband Richard would have been keen to attend his father-in-law's funeral.

Elfrida (36) had married Lieutenant Gabriel Matthias, an artillery officer, in 1813. Her husband had been posted to Saint Helena in 1815 and she had accompanied him, although she returned to the Isle of Wight in 1821. They sailed on the same ship as Napoleon Bonaparte, the *Northumberland*. Family anecdotes passed down the story that Gabriel actually played chess with Napoleon. This may well have been happened as Napoleon did play chess during the voyage and would have been introduced to all the officers on board (there were at least twenty eight) during the two month voyage. The *Northumberland* sailed with two other ships and a complement of 2000 troops. The British were taking no chances that Napoleon might escape again.

By coincidence George Rennell, Elfrida's uncle, was also present on the ship, as its naval chaplain.[29] There is evidence that he too spent time with Napoleon discussing religious matters.[30] Elfrida was the only officer's wife on that famous voyage.[31] I wonder if it was ever mentioned to Napoleon that Elfrida's brother, Solomon, had had a small part to play in the great man's downfall during the action at La Haye Sainte earlier that year. Napoleon had many visitors during his remaining years at Saint Helena as the island was a regular stopping place for ships to and from India. Napoleon died in 1821.

Susannah (26) stayed single until 1840 when she married a Company officer, Louis Bird in Meerut, India. The couple were living in Bath in 1851. Eleanor eventually came to live with them. Eleanor (21) had married her brother-in-law, Edward 'Coleridge' Matthias, earlier that same year. Edward's middle name had come from his father's admiration of Samuel Taylor Coleridge's brother James, who he knew well. Eleanor and Edward went to India in 1824. After Edward's death in 1839, Eleanor married a Major Charles O'Neil. In the 1850s she was in Bath living with her sister Susannah. There is no information available as to what happened to Major

O'Neil. Marianne (29) also eventually ended up living in Bath. After her husband died in 1834 she returned to Newport and successfully applied for a widow's pension from the army.

Just five months after her father's funeral, Rosalie (19) married Lieutenant William Sheaffe at St Mary's church, Carisbrooke. Dr William Lempriere gave her away. After giving birth to three children she eventually left for Australia in 1834 with just the youngest, then a baby. Her husband had been appointed to guard 200 convicts on board the *Surrey*. Their son went on to found a Sheaffe dynasty in that country. However Rosalie eventually returned to England in 1863 after her husband died. She died in 1883 and was buried at Adelstone, in Surrey.[32]

Emily had married Frederick Ranie the previous year. At the time she needed permission from her father, as she was only sixteen. She later gave birth to six children, who all died at birth. The couple eventually went to live in Birmingham where Frederick worked as a 'barrack master' for the military. In her later diaries, Harriet Tytler (the aforementioned daughter of John Lucas Earle) had a lot to say about her time with this family. She was sent from India as a child, with her sister, to stay in Birmingham for several years. She did not find it a pleasant experience. She described her aunt as 'strict and really cruel'. She wrote that she was forced to eat mutton fat and described the death of a servant girl for want of medical attention.[33]

This leaves the three sons who went to India.

John Lucas (33), the eldest son, further secured the link with the Lempriere family when he married William's sister Mary in 1817. He was on furlough from India at the time. The couple returned to India in 1819 when, coincidentally, John was appointed as adjutant to the garrison of the fortress of Asirghar. Mary gave birth to at least nine children, including Harriet. John died in 1845 just as Harriet was on her way back to India to join the family. He died at Hoshangabad where Solomon had spent several weeks with the Bombay army, sixty-five years earlier. Harriet stayed on in India and married Robert Tytler and wrote her famous diary.[34] She and her husband were also pioneering photographers.[35] Mount Harriet, the highest mountain in the Andaman Islands, is named after her. Harriet's mother Mary returned to England with her younger children after her husband's death, missing her daughter on route. She died in Somerset in 1890.

24. Coda

Harriet and Robert Tytler

William Henry (30) left for India in 1808. He married Jane Shadwell at Meerut in 1821 and the couple had four children. William rose through the ranks of the Company army serving in Nepal and Burma. He was wounded at the Battle of Punniar (1843), a final push by the Marathas to gain independence after the failure of the British Afghanistan campaign. William died in 1846 having gained the rank of Lieutenant Colonel. He is reportedly buried at *Berhampore*. It would be another coincidence if this was Burhanpur, another place that Solomon passed through on his march across India with the Bengal Army. However there is a similar named town in West Bengal.

This brings us to the final member of the diaspora of the Earle family, the youngest son, Solomon's namesake. Solomon Junior's participation in the defence of La Haye Sainte at the Battle of Waterloo must have left horrific memories. Out of nearly 400 men, only 32 *remained effective*.[36] This action has been described as the pivotal episode of the whole battle – the *400 men who decided the Battle of Waterloo.*[37] As mentioned Solomon Junior joined the Company army as a cadet in 1818 and went out to India. He married for the first time to Elizabeth, but both wife and firstborn son died. His second wife was called Bridget Maples. She went on to give birth to four children.

24. Coda

Solomon was invalided out of the army with the rank of lieutenant in 1828 and spent the rest of his life in Calcutta. According to family stories he lost an arm. He died in 1858 and was buried at the Lower Circular Road Cemetery. His grave is still there. Bridget was buried with him.

Grave of Solomon Earle (1797-1858) Lower Circular Road Cemetery, Kolkata

His Waterloo Medal – (Thanks to Chris Earle)

24. Coda

One of Solomon Junior's sons, Edward William, a silk merchant, had three wives. His third wife was called Mary Amanda Poulson, daughter of an indigo planter, Henry A. Poulson. Henry is also buried, not far from Solomon and Bridget, in the Lower Circular Road Cemetery. One of Mary Amanda's children, another Mary, married Arthur William Nix-James. Their daughter, Edith, is my grandmother.

Mary Amanda and Edward Earle

Grave of Henry A. Poulson, Indigo Planter. Lower Circular Road cemetery, Kolkata

Edward and Mary Amanda's youngest child, Edith Anne, married a steam-engine driver, William Edmund Desmier. Their son Terence is the father of Rick Earle Desmier, who's investigation of the Earle family inspired this book.

On tracing the children of Sophia and Richard Lipscombe, an interesting story emerged. In 2017 a George III Cartwheel Twopence, dated 1797, came up for sale by auction and sold for £110. The inscription *Lucas Earle Lipscombe, Born May Day 1807* was engraved on it. The sale documentation recorded that Lucas *had appeared in the Poor Law Removals and Settlements on 7th January 1832, in which he and his family are noted for being transferred to the care of the parish of St. John's, Hackney.*[38] They must have fallen on hard times.

24. Coda

Entrance to Lower Circular Road Cemetery. Kolkata. 2016

Another son of Sophia and Richard, William George Lipscombe, married Emma Morgan and emigrated to Australia on the *Dawstone* in 1855. They travelled in steerage with their daughter Susannah Sophia Elizabeth (13). In October 1890 Susannah was arrested and put on trial for the murder of a baby. [39] At the time Susannah was working as a midwife. The local newspaper reported that it was alleged that Susannah had produced a false medical certificate. She had organised the burial of a supposedly stillborn baby. The dead baby was actually aged between eleven and fourteen days and appeared starved. At the trial it came out that Susannah had been asked to source an unwanted baby for adoption. However the baby that had been brought to her was unwell and had died a week later. Susannah's daughter, Clarissa Spencely, then sixteen, gave evidence for the defence. The jury found the accused not guilty.

Susannah was married twice and her surname at the trial was Burke. Her daughter Clarissa married Charles Titterton in 1895 and the couple had seven children.

24. Coda

Finally, as William Hickey has featured so much in our story living a parallel, but very different, life to Solomon, it is worth mentioning what happened to him. He stayed on in Calcutta and eventually became clerk to the Chief Justice. His partner Charlotte Barry died soon after their arrival in Calcutta in 1783. He then took an Indian partner, Kiraun, who gave birth to a son. Soon after this he discovered her in bed with her boyfriend. He ejected her, although paid for the upkeep of the boy who was unlikely to have been his son. He then lived for many years with Jemandee, a beautiful and lively Indian woman. [40] Jemandee died in childbirth in 1796 and their son died a few months later. William retired in 1808 and returned to England the following year. He settled with his two unmarried sisters in Beaconsfield, Buckinghamshire, where he wrote his memoirs. He died in Camden Town, London, in 1830.

*Ages in brackets are the age each daughter or son would have been at the time of Solomon's death in 1824.

25. Conclusions

A shortened version of Solomon's account of his military service was published in the East India Military Calendar of 1824.[1] In his introduction the Editor noted that he had included an account of the services of *two distinguished officers of the rank of captain*, implying that officers of such a low rank would not normally have been included in the publication. He went on to state that *had Captain Earle continued on the strength of the army, he would now have stood among the Lieut. Generals of the Bengal establishment.*

What sort of a person was Solomon Earle? Although no personal letters survive the more formal letters reveal a little about his personality. His account of his time in India is largely factual. It is clear he was a stable and reliable Company officer. This is evidenced by the moto that General Goddard awarded him; *Humashah Hauser,* always ready. But he was also a man with a few faults, just like all of us. He clearly had a slight tendency to exaggerate. For example he gave his age as *only fifteen* when he was really seventeen. And it is likely he rather overemphasised his level of disability when applying for a pension. He was also a man who was very careful to preserve his reputation. Evidence for this are the letters he wrote to the EIC Council when he felt he had been unfairly criticised. Reputation was perhaps more important in those days than it is now. He was without doubt a family man and had an impressive record of supporting nine children to adulthood at a time when infant and child mortality was great – not to mention supporting his wife throughout that time.

Solomon just happened to be around, and played his part, when momentous world events were taking place. Some of these events have now been largely forgotten, like the march of the Bombay army across India. Other events were perhaps more purposefully forgotten in Britain, like the defeat of the Bombay army at Wadgaon.

Like Solomon, some of his children went on to become witness to major events too – notably his son's participation in the Battle of Waterloo,

25. Conclusion

and his daughter sailing to Saint Helena on the same ship as Napoleon on his last voyage to exile.

Solomon's experiences bear witness to the early years of the establishment of the British Empire and how it affected others, particularly the people of India. From a limited trading company the EIC developed into a behemoth, the first truly global company, providing a model for the multinationals of today. In 1773 the EIC was a company 'too big too fail', so the government bailed it out, just like the events of 2008, when a similar thing happened with the banks. And, like most multinationals, the push for profit often took precedence over common humanity and the duty of an organisation to provide nurture and care for its dependents.

The history of the EIC has another lesson for today, particularly in relation to the tendency for Britons to hark back to past glories of the Empire, to a time when Britain ruled one quarter of the world. But that particular set of circumstances will not return again. Today's world is very different, particularly in relation to advanced technology and the speed of communication.

Looking back over the history of the British Empire there is a tendency to denigrate and deny its achievements. Although it cannot be refuted that the establishment of empire resulted in the exploitation of others, it was not all bad. Profits could not be maintained at times of instability and disorder and there is no doubt that the foundation of the British Empire did result a long period of stability, the *Pax Britannica*. All that changed when the First World War broke out in 1914. In general a relatively fair and incorrupt legal system and civil service were created in those countries taken over.

During this account, I have tried as far as possible, to give the point of view of the Indian people and their leaders. I have tried to show that, with the collapse of the Mughal Empire, anyone could have come out on top. In the mid-eighteenth century the Marathas were still in the early stages of establishing government in the states they had taken over from the Mughals. They were in competition with Mysore and Hyderabad and this resulted in instability and war. On the boundaries of their territories they were still very much raiders, pillaging and demanding tribute when they could. Without competition from the French it is unlikely that the British would have pushed as far as they did to dominate India.

I have also covered the early stages of the development of the State of Baroda (Vadodara) under the leadership of Fatesinghrao I. With the

25. Conclusion

stability of British rule, Baroda State thrived in the nineteenth century and there is evidence of stability and good provision of public services in the state today.

Perhaps if the British had been more open to the oriental way of doing things, as was the case in the eighteenth century, and if they had played less of the race card, as they did in the following century, things might have been very different today. Despite this there was still a significant mingling of cultures. As we have seen in this account, the British sent their children out into the far reaches of the world: to India, Australia, New Zealand, Canada, America and Africa. In return there has been a significant movement of people of other ethnic origin to our islands, making Great Britain itself a much more cosmopolitan society. This should be seen as a positive thing. Genetic testing has made it possible to see that many British families with an Indian heritage have mixed racial origins. These facts were covered up and erased during the Victorian era.

In regard to the future, with the decision of Britain in 2016 to separate from the European community, there is even more of a need for the British to come to terms with their past and start to re-establish relationships with countries further afield than Europe. As a result of the empire, English has become the language of the world. If history had followed a different course it could so easily have been French.

Notes

1. Introduction

1. Tytler, Harriet (Ed. by Anthony Sattin), *An Englishwoman in India, The Memoirs of Harriet Tytler 1828 – 1858* (Oxford University Press, 1986)

2. Desmier Rootsweb. Trip to India by Bob Adams 2016. Also, *My passage to India*. (York Press 1st February 2017)

PART ONE : BEGINNINGS : 1751 – 1768

2. Ashburton and Gujarat

1. www.oldashburton.co.uk

2. *The Journals of the House of Commons, Vol 27, May 31st 1754 – November 15th 1757* (reprinted 1803) p62

3. Plymouth and West Devon Record Office. Ref 74/733/4

4. Peterloo Massacre. In August 1819, at Peter's Field in Manchester, regular cavalry and armed militia were ordered to charge a 60 to 70,000 crowd protesting about representation in parliament. At least fifteen protestors were killed and hundreds injured.

5. Campbell, Theophilia Carlile, *The Battle of the Press, as told in the story of the life of Richard Carlile, by his daughter* (First Published 1899 by A. & H.B.Bonner, London. Accessed from *Gutenberg.org/files*)

6. Quarterly Review. A literary and political periodical first published in 1809. Continued to be Published until 1967.

7. Gaekwad, Fatesinghrao, *Sayajirao of Baroda, The Prince and the Man* (PVT Ltd. India 1989) p.12

8. Ibid. p.15

9. Ibid. p.17

3. London : 1767

1. Gatrell, Vic, *The First Bohemians, Life and Art in London's Golden Age* (Allen Lane 2013) p.xiv

2. White, Gerry, *London in the Eighteenth Century. A Great and Monstrous Thing* (The Bodley Head, London, 2012) p.xxvi

3. The Gin Act of 1751. This Act was passed by parliament to restrict the manufacture and sale of gin to licensed businesses – see William Hogarth's print 'Gin Alley.' From 1690 onwards England, and particularly London, discovered gin, which was initially imported from Holland at a cheap price. By the 1700s gin had taken over from beer as the nation's most popular drink following a massive rise in consumption. It is estimated that on average Londoners in the 1730s consumed two pints of gin per week. Following the 1751 Act, tea gradually became the nation's most popular drink, a far safer alternative.

4. Roger Hudson, quoted in introduction to *William Hickey, Memoirs of a Georgian Rake* (Folio Society, London. 1995). p.x.

5. The Seven Years War (1756 to 1763) has been described as the first truly global conflict, affecting most European countries, as well as the Americas, India, the Philippines and parts of Africa. There were effectively two sides: Great Britain, Portugal, Prussia and Hanover against France, Spain and the Holy Roman Empire (including Austria). Britain took Quebec and various islands in the Caribbean from the French and was largely successful in India, taking Pondicherry and Chandernagore from the French. Both were returned after the war ended with the signing of the Treaty of Paris in 1763.

Notes

6. From Solomon Earle's journals. From two sources, see Bibliography. NOTE: In future all quotes from Solomon Earle's Journals will be in italics and referred to, but page numbers will not be individually referenced as too numerous.

7. Turnpike Trusts were not-for-profit organisations sanctioned by parliament where a Turnpike Act would authorize the Trust to levy tolls and use the money to repair and improve the road. However this was not without controversy, as the parish also had to pay for the upkeep of roads, resulting in a double payment by locals.

8. Boswell, James, *Boswell's London Journal. 1762-1763* (Heinemann 1950) Introduction by F.A.Pottle. p.22

9. It is difficult to directly compare prices in the eighteenth century to those in the present day, as different products had relatively different prices. Food was, for most people, the largest expense. Up to two-thirds of income went on food and drink (Olsen, Kirsten, *Daily Life in The Eighteenth Century* (Greenwood. 1999)). Only a small proportion of the population (6%) earned £100 or over per annum. A very rough calculator is to multiply by £100. Therefore Boswell's post-chaise could have cost around £1000 in today's prices. Prices were relatively stable until towards the end of the eighteenth century when inflation increased as a result of the war with France.

10. The Lloyds Building, Leadenhall Street, is an example of an 'inside-out' building, or *Bowellism*, where lifts, ducts etc are situated on the outside of the building. The Pompidou Centre, in Paris, is another example. The Lloyds Building was designed by Richard Rogers and partners and was completed in 1986.

11. Boswell, James. From Boswell's London Journal.

12. Boswell, James, *Life of Samuel Johnson* (First published 1791)

13. Hickey, William, *Memoirs* (available from the internet)

14. White, Gerry.

15. Boswell, James, *London Journal*. p. 134

16. Ibid. Introduction p.25

17. Ibid. p.71

18. Ibid. p.86

19. Hickey, William, *Memoirs of a Georgian Rake* (Folio Society, London. 1995) p.43

20. Ibid. p.40

21. Ibid. p.51

22. Ibid. pp.70-71

23. White, Gerry.

4. A Passage to India

1. Sobel, Dava, *Longitude, The True Story of a Lone Genius Who Solved the Greatest Scientific Problem of His Time* (Harper Perennial 2011) pp. 11-13

2. Betts, Jonathan, *Harrison* (National Maritime Museum. Rev. 2007) p.89

3. Wyche, Captain John, *Log of the Salisbury* (British Library Collection)

4. Erikson, Emily, *Between Monopoly and Free Trade : The English East India Company. 1600-1757* (Princeton University Press. 2014)

5. Lind, James, *A Treatise of the Scurvy* (1753. Accessed on line)

6. Hickey, William, From *Memoirs of a Georgian Rake* (Folio Society, London 1995. Hickey's memoirs also accessed via *Google Books*)

7. Parkes, Fanny, *Begums, Thugs and Englishmen. The Journals of Fanny Parkes* (Penguin Books, India 2002)

8. Tytler, Harriet. (Ed.by Anthony Sattin), *An Englishwoman in India, The Memoirs of Harriet Tytler 1828–1858* (Oxford University Press : 1986)

9. A pub called the Three Kings existed, at Sandwich, a few miles from Deal on Strand Street, next to the river Stour. It was built in the 16th Century, closed in 1970 and is now a private house:

From the Dover Express and East Kent News, Friday, 16 April, 1875. Price 1d.

THE THREE KINGS INN, SANDWICH

To be let, a fully-licensed House, close to the Wharves; incoming moderate – Apply to Alfred Kingsford, Buckland Brewery, Dover.

PART TWO : INTRODUCTION TO INDIA

5. Mughals and Marathas

1. Tammita–Delgoda, Sinharaja, *A Traveller's History of India* (The Windrush Press 1994. Second Edition) p.141

2. Reeve, John, *The Lives of the Mughal Emperors* (British Library 2012) p.2

3. Ibid. p.10

4. Ibid. p. 18

5. Ibid. p. 24

6. Tammita-Delgoda. pp. 138-139

7. Gordon, Stewart, *The Marathas 1600–1818*. From the New Cambridge History of India (Cambridge University Press: 1993) pp 1-4

8. Ibid. p. 37

9. Ibid. p. 81

10. Ibid. p. 149

11. Duff, James Grant, *History of the Mahrattas*. 1826. Vol 2. Chapt. 5.

6. The Honourable East India Company

1. Keay, John, *The Honourable Company. A History of the English East India Company* (Harper Collins 1991) p.6

2. Ibid. p.90

3. Ibid. p.151

4. Ibid. p.169

5. Ibid. p.69

6. Ibid. p.289

7. Wilson, Jon, *India Conquered. Britain's Raj and the Chaos of Empire* (Simon & Schuster Ltd, 2016) pp.86-88

8. Robins, Nick, *The Corporation that Changed the World* (Pluto Press, London, 2012) *pp.71-72*

9. Harvey, Robert, *Clive, The Life and Death of a British Emperor* (Hodder and Stoughton 1998) pp 145-157

10. Ibid. p.172

11. Corneille, John, *Journal of my Service in India* (The Folio Society. 1966) pp. 120-125

12. Ibid. p.143

13. Keay, John, *The Honourable Company. A History of the English East India Company.* p.371

14. Robins, Nick, *The Corporation that Changed the World.* p.79

15. Mervyn Davies A., *Strange Destiny, A Biography of Warren Hastings* (G.P. Putnam's Sons, New York 1935) p.61

16. Bankim, Chandra Chatterji, *Anandamath* (First published 1882)

7. The Rise of the Gaekwads and the start of the Anglo-Maratha War

1. John, Paul (Ed.), *Baroda. Know your Roots.* (Times Group Books. New Delhi. 2012) p. 23

2. Gackwad, Fatesinghrao, *Sayajirao of Baroda, The Prince and the Man* (PVT Ltd. India 1989) p.1

Notes

3. Ibid. p.2
4. Ibid. p.8
5. Ibid. p.7
6. Duff, James Grant, *History of the Mahrattas, Vol II*. Chapt. II
7. Ibid. Chapt VI
8. Gaekwad, Fatesinghrao, *Sayajirao of Baroda*. p.15
9. Ibid. p.16
10. Ibid. p.17
11. Duff. Vol. II. Chapt VII
12. Ibid. Chapt.VII
13. Ibid. Chapt VIII
14. Sen, Sailendra Nath, *Anglo–Maratha Relations 1772-1785* (PVT Ltd, India: 1961) p.11
15. Ibid. p.18
16. Navarane M S., *Battles of the Honourable East India Company* (2006. APH Publishing. New Delhi) p.54
17. Sen, *Anglo-Maratha Relations*. p.28
18. Navarane M.S., *The Battles of the Honourable East India Company*. p.53
19. Duff. Vol II. Chapt X
20. Quoted in Sen, *Anglo-Maratha Relations*. p. 46
21. Ibid. p.78
22. Duff. Chapt XII
23. Ibid. Chapt XI

PART THREE : EARLY YEARS IN INDIA : 1768 – 1778

8. Bengal and the Company Army : 1769 to 1772

1. *Newman and Co.'s Handbook to Calcutta.* (Published 1875. Available on line via *Google books)* p. *15*

2. Ibid. p. 24

3. *Mountpellier.* My assumption is that John Coleridge is referring to Montpellier, a town in southern France. However Cheltenham, in England, has a district called Mountpellier well known for its spa, and popular in the eighteenth century.

4. John Coleridge to William Coleridge. September 29th, 1774. From the correspondence of the Coleridge family, 1667 – 1836. British Library.

5. Dalrymple, William, *The East India Company: The original corporate raiders.* Article in The Guardian 21/08/2015

6. Holmes, Richard, *Sahib. The British Soldier in India 1750-1914* (HarperCollins 2005) p.53

7. Bailey, Peter A., *Researching Ancestors in the East India Company Armies* (FIBIS Research Guides. 2006) p.14

8. Ibid. p.14

9. Holmes, Richard, *Sahib, The British Soldier in India 1750-1914.* p.42

10. Ibid. p.328

11. Navarane M S., *Battles of the Honourable East India Company* (2006. APH Publishing. New Delhi) pp. 215-223.

12. Holmes, Richard, *Sahib, The British Soldier in India 1750-1914* p.267

13. Ibid. p.272

14. Holmes, Richard, *Redcoat. The British Soldier in the Age of Horse and Musket* (HarperCollins: 2001) pp. 241-248

15. Mervyn Davies, A., *Strange Destiny, A Biography of Warren Hastings* (G.P. Putnam's Sons, New York. 1935) p.61

16. Ibid. p.62

17. Robins, Nick. *The Corporation that Changed the World* (Pluto Press, London, 2012) p.97

9. Warren Hastings

1. Mervyn Davies A., *Strange Destiny, A Biography of Warren Hastings* (G.P. Putnam's Sons, New York. 1935)

2. Feiling, Keith, *Warren Hastings* (Macmillan & Co Ltd, London, 1954)

3. Bernstein, Jeremy, *Dawning of the Raj. The Life and Trials of Warren Hastings* (Ivan R. Dee 2000. Aurum Press 2001)

4. Harvey, Robert, *Clive, The Life and Death of a British Emperor* (Hodder and Stoughton 1998)

5. Robins, Nick, *The Corporation that Changed the World* (Pluto Press, London, 2012)

6. Bernstein, Jeremy. p.24

7. Macauley, *Critical and Historical Essays*. Quoted in Bernstein. p. 26.

8. Mervyn Davies. p.38

9. Ibid. p.55

10. Ibid. p.56

11. Ibid. p. 70

12. Ibid. p.79

13. Keay, John, *The Honourable Company. A History of the English East India Company* (HarperCollins: 1991) p. 397

14. Robins, Nick, *The Corporation that Changed the World*. p.124

15. Mervyn Davies. p.74

16. Feiling, Keith. p.105

17. Mervyn Davies. p.97

18. Feiling, Keith. p.109

19. Ibid. p.115

20. Bernstein, Jeremy. p.13

21. Markham, Clement R., *Narrative of the Mission of George Bogle to Tibet, and of the Journey of Thomas Manning to Lhasa* (Publ. 1876)

22. Robins, Nick, *The Corporation that Changed the World*. p.123

23. Mervyn Davies. p.163

24. Ibid. p.199

10. India : 1772 to 1778

1. Sal Tree. *Sorea Robusta*. A hardwood tree used in the building of houses and for the manufacture of doors and window. Sal in Sanskrit means house. Sals are native to the Indian sub-continent and grow up to thirty-five metres in height. They feature in the Ramayana, when Lord Rama had to pierce seven sal trees in a row with a single arrow. He succeeded.

2. Bankim, Chandra Chatterji, *Anandamath* (First published 1882. Available on line). First lines of prologue.

3. Lonely Planet Publications, *India* (15th Edition. 2013. PTy Ltd.) p.388

4. Subedar. An Indian officer equivalent to the rank of Captain, but commanded by a British officer.

5. Jamedar. Indian army officer equivalent to lieutenant or platoon commander.

6. Gleig, George Robert, *The History of the British in India. Vol 4*. (1835, from Google books) p.278

Notes

PART FOUR : CROSSING THE PENINSULAR : 1778 – 1780

11. The Crossing I : Antecedents

1. Beveridge, H. *A., Comprehensive History of India. Volume II* (Blackie and Sons, London 1862) p.442

2. Mervyn Davies, A., *Strange Destiny, A Biography of Warren Hastings* (G.P. Putnam's Sons, New York. 1935) p.205

3. Beveridge, H.A., *A Comprehensive History of India.* Volume II, p.443

4. See Desmier Rootsweb

5. Duff, James Grant, *History of the Mahrattas. 1826. Vol II.* Chapter XII

6. Ibid. Chapt XII

7. Beveridge, H.A. Volume II. *p 444*

8. Unknown author, *A Journal of the March of the Bombay Detachment, across Mahratta country, from Culpee to Surat, in 1778* (Printed for W. Faden in ?1779) Available from Hathitrust Digital Library.

12. The Crossing II : Kalpi to the Narmada

1. Unknown author, *A Journal of the March of the Bombay Detachment, across Mahratta country, from Culpee to Surat, in 1778.* (Printed for W. Faden in ?1779)

2. Ibid.

3. Sen, Sailendra Nath, *Anglo–Maratha Relations :1772-1785* (PVT Ltd, India: 1961) p.98

4. Unknown author, *A Journal of the March of the Bombay Detachment.*

5. www.clanmunrousa.org

6. Sen, Sailendra Nath, p.99

7. Ibid. p.100

8. Ibid. p.100

9. Ibid. p.101

10. Letters from Colonel Goddard. 1778, 1779. British Library. Add. 29.119

11. Sen, Sailendra Nath. p. 119

12. Montgomery Martin, R., *The History of the Indian Empire. Volume I.* p.344 (footnote)

13. Khan, Shaharyar M, *The Begums of Bhopal, A History of the Princely State of Bhopal* (I.B.Tauris & Co. Ltd, London, 2000)

14. Beveridge, H., *A Comprehensive History of India. Volume II* (Blackie and Sons, London 1862) p.445

15. Sen, Sailendra Nath. p. 119

16. Unknown author, *A Journal of the March of the Bombay Detachment, across Mahratta country, from Culpee to Surat, in 1778.*

17. Panda, Rajaram, *Khajuraho* (Mittal Publishing, New Delhi. 2010)

13. The Crossing III : Battle of Wadgaon: January 1779

1. Sen, Sailendra Nath, *Anglo–Maratha Relations.* p. 104

2. Duff, James Grant, *History of the Mahrattas, Vol II.* Chapter XII.

3. Ibid. Chapter XII

4. Sen, Sailendra Nath, pp. 106-107

5. Ibid. p. 107

6. Unknown author, *Proceedings of the Bombay Army in their march towards Poonah* (Published as addendum to, *A Journal of the March of the Bombay Detachment, across Mahratta country, from Culpee to Surat, in 1778*).

7. Ibid.

8. Sen, Sailendra Nath, p.112

Notes

9. Unknown author, *General Orders of the Bombay Select Committee. Bombay Castle, 3rd February 1779* (Published as an addendum to, *A Journal of the March of the Bombay Detachment, across Mahratta country, from Culpee to Surat, in 1778*)

10. www.whodoyouthinkyouaremagazine.com Posted in 2011. Ishtur Phakre

14. The Cossing IV : Hoshangabad to Surat

1. Unknown author, *A Journal of the March of the Bombay Detachment, across Mahratta country, from Culpee to Surat, in 1778*.

2. Sen, Sailendra Nath, *Anglo–Maratha Relations*. p. 120

3. Duff, James Grant, *History of the Mahrattas, Vol II*. Chapter XII.

4. Unknown author, *A Journal of the March of the Bombay Detachment, across Mahratta country, from Culpee to Surat, in 1778*.

5. Brierley, Saroo, with Larry Buttrose, *Lion: A Long Way Home* (Penguin Books Ltd. 2017)

6. Sen, Sailendra Nath, *Anglo–Maratha Relations*. p. 121

7. Ibid. p.121

8. Ibid. p.124

9. Ibid. p.122

10. *East India Military Calendar, concerning the Services of General and Field Officers of the Indian Amy. Vol 2*. (via Google books) pp.417-418.

PART FIVE : BARODA AND BENGAL : 1780 – 1785

15. Campaigning in Gujarat : 1780 to 1781

1. Sen, Sailendra Nath, *Anglo–Maratha Relations*. p. 145

2. Adkins, Roy and Leslie, *The Greatest Siege in British History* (Little Brown. 2017)

3. Duff, James Grant, *History of the Mahrattas. (1826) Volume II.* Chapter XIII, p.403

4. Divide and rule/ *Divide et Impera* (divide and conquer). This strategy was not new. It was used extensively by the Romans and recommended by Machiavelli. A less powerful state can conquer, or exert power, over a larger state by breaking up larger concentrations of power into smaller parts that individually have less power than the state implementing the strategy. This is done by breaking up existing power structures, preventing smaller power groups from linking up, and creating rivalry and discord amongst the smaller groups. But things could go wrong. If misjudged this approach can bring a powerful state together. An example of this was the joining together of disparate Maratha groups into a powerful force to defeat the British at Wadgaon.

5. Duff, James Grant, *History of the Mahrattas (1826) Volume II.* Chapter XIII, p.403

6. Sen, Sailendra Nath, *Anglo–Maratha Relations.* p.143

7. Duff, James Grant, *History of the Mahrattas (1826) Volume II.* Chapter XIII, p.403

8. Sen, Sailendra Nath, p. 143

9. Ibid. pp.143-144

10. Ibid. p.144

11. Duff, James Grant, *History of the Mahrattas (1826) Volume II.* Chapter XIII, p.405

12. Yagnick, Achyut and Seth Suchitra, *Ahmedabad, from Royal City to Megacity* (Penguin Books, India. 2011) p.75

13. Ibid. pp.76-77

14. Sen, Sailendra Nath, *Anglo–Maratha Relations.* p. 144

15. Forlorn Hope. This term was first used in the English Civil War (1642-1651) and then frequently in the Peninsular War (1808-1814) to describe a group of soldiers who take part in an attack where the

risk of casualties is extremely high. The term comes from the Dutch *verloren hoop,* meaning lost troop, but the word troop was changed in the English version to mean hope. The forlorn hope was usually manned by volunteers, but occasionally convicts volunteered (as at Ahmedabad). The soldiers were often led by a junior officer who saw this as a way to achieve promotion, or glory. Unfortunately that promotion was often to the next world.

16. Duff, James Grant, *History of the Mahrattas (1826) Volume II.* Chapter XIII, p.406

17. Ibid. p.406

18. Ibid. p.407

19. Sen, Sailendra Nath, *Anglo–Maratha Relations.* p. 146

20. Hickson, Samuel, *Dairy of Samuel Hickson (1777-1785)* (Bengal Past and Present. Jan-March 1935). Hickson escaped from debts and the failure of his business by joining the EIC army in London in 1778. He was immediately put aboard the *Shrewsbury* and taken to Madras where he joined the attack on Pondicherry. In 1780 he was shipped to Surat to reinforce Goddard's army. He was present at the taking of Bassein then returned to Madras to join the campaign against Mysore.

21. Sen, Sailendra Nath, *Anglo–Maratha Relations.* p. 151

22. Duff, James Grant, *History of the Mahrattas (1826) Volume II.* Chapter XIII, p.424

23. Ibid. p.429

24. Captain Archdeacon. We will here more about this gentleman later in connection with the Coleridge family. Captain Archdeacon became a 'second father' to STC's brother Frank.

16. The Duel and the Thunderbolt of Mars

1. Belvedere House, Alipore, is now the home of the National Library of India. It was built by Mir Jafar in the 1760s and was then gifted to Warren Hastings. Hastings sold the house when he left India and

it became the residence of the Lieutenant Governor of Bengal. The house is currently undergoing restoration by the Archaeological Survey of India. During the restoration a hidden room was discovered. All sorts of speculation ensued about what this room was used for, with no conclusion as yet.

2. Mervyn Davies. A., *Strange Destiny, A Biography of Warren Hastings* (G.P. Putnam's Sons, New York. 1935) p.222

3. Ibid. p.229

4. Gordon Riots. Started as a protest march against the Papist Acts of 1778. These Acts were passed in order to reduce official discrimination against Roman Catholics, for example making it unnecessary to swear a religious oath when joining the armed forces. Lord George Gordon led a march on parliament on June 2nd 1780. He had incited the mob to fear that Catholics would support the French and Spanish to invade England. The march turned into a major riot when protestors took over key sites in London. They broke open and sacked Newgate Prison and destroyed property. Chaos ruled for at least five days. The army was then called out and the rioters eventually quelled with considerable loss of life. The riot became a general protest against austerity and the American War.

5. Feiling, Keith, *Warren Hastings* (Macmillan & Co Ltd, London, 1954) p.190

6. Mervyn Davies. p.215.

7. Feiling, Keith. p.201

8. Peculation. To embezzle or steal. From the Latin, *peculari*, to embezzle property. Perhaps the charges against Barwell related to the 'theft' of Clavering's daughter.

9. Feiling, Keith. p.143

10. Ibid. p.202

11. Hickey, William, From *Memoirs of a Georgian Rake* (Folio Society, London. 1995) p.226

12. Feiling, Keith. p.224

Notes

13. Mervyn Davies. p.220

14. Ibid, p. 221

15. Ibid. p.222

16. Feiling, Keith. p.228

17. Ibid. p.247

18. Mervyn Davies. p.229

19. Robins, Nick, *The Corporation that Changed the World* (Pluto Press, London, 2012) p.153

20. Feiling, Keith. p.256

21. Mervyn Davies. p.285

22. Hickey, William. From *Memoirs of a Georgian Rake*. pp.342-354

23. Ibid. p.356

24. Mervyn Davies. p.288

25. Ibid. p.300

26. Hickey, William. From *Memoirs of a Georgian Rake*. p.357

27. Ibid. p.357

17. Resident at Baroda : 1781 to 1783

1. Website www.historyofvadodara.in

2. Weedon, Rev. Edward St. Clair, *A Year with the Gaekwar of Baroda* (Chapel River Press, Surrey 1911. Various digitalised sources)

3. www.historyofvadodara.in

4. Princely States. These states were vassal states during the time of the British Raj (1858-1947) and were governed by a local ruler. Overall there were 565 states covering nearly half the country. Each state received a gun salute, from nine to twenty one, depending on the importance of its ruler. Baroda received a twenty-one-gun salute.

5. Weedon, Rev. Edward St. Clair, *A Year with the Gaekwar of Baroda*.

6. Elliott F.A.H, *The Rulers of Baroda* (Originally published by Baroda State Press 1879. Then Oxford University. Digitalised by Google) p. 19

7. Ibid, p.14

8. Ibid. p.17

9. www.historyofvadodara.in

10. John, Paul (Editor), *Baroda. Know Your Roots* (Times Group Books. New Delhi. 2012) p.23

11. Duff, James Grant, *History of the Mahrattas (1826) Volume II.* Chapter XIII, p.430

12. Ibid. p.433

13. Sen, Sailendra Nath, *Anglo–Maratha Relations*. p. 164

14. Ibid. p.165

15. Ibid. p.166

16. Duff, James Grant, *History of the Mahrattas (1826) Volume II.* Chapter XIII, p. 453

17. Ibid, p.446

18. Ibid. p.447

19. Sen, Sailendra Nath, *Anglo–Maratha Relations*. p.175

20. Ibid. p.181

21. Ibid. p.182

22. Ibid. p.184

23. Ibid. pp.184-5

24. Anderson papers. Volume XIX Add. 45.435. British Library

25. David Anderson's brother James was an officer in the Company army. He was born in 1758, so is likely to have been still an ensign.

Notes

He was clearly known to Solomon. Both brothers were born in Edinburgh, David being born in 1750. David was appointed as a writer and James as a cadet. Both became assistants to Warren Hastings. James acted as a Persian interpreter. David returned to England in 1785 with Hastings and later helped Hastings in his impeachment trial. James returned to England in 1786.

26. Anderson papers. Volume XIX Add. 45.435. British Library

27. Navarane M S., *Battles of the Honourable East India Company* (2006. APH Publishing. New Delhi) p.174

28. East India Military Calendar. Volume II, p.375

29. Ibid. p.425

30. Ibid. p.429

31. Dictionary of National Biography. 1885-1900. Volume 22. *Wikisource*.

18. Return to Bengal : 1783 to 1785

1. *Ancien Régime*. French for 'old regime' – the rule of the Valois and Bourbon dynasties that had ruled France from the Middle Ages and came to an end with the French Revolution (1789-1799).

2. Bernstein, Jeremy, *Dawning of the Raj. The Life and Trials of Warren Hastings* (Ivan R. Dee 2000. Aurum Press 2001) p. 172

3. Keay, John, *The Honourable Company. A History of the English East India Company* (HarperCollins: 1991) pp.390-391

4. Bernstein, Jeremy, *Dawning of the Raj. The Life and Trials of Warren Hastings*. p.138

5. Mervyn Davies, A., *Strange Destiny, A Biography of Warren Hastings*. p 240

6. Bernstein, Jeremy, *Dawning of the Raj. The Life and Trials of Warren Hastings*. p.138

7. Mervyn Davies, A., *Strange Destiny, A Biography of Warren Hastings*. p.247

8. Ibid. p.248

9. Ibid. p.248

10. Bernstein, Jeremy, *Dawning of the Raj. The Life and Trials of Warren Hastings.* p.140

11. Mervyn Davies, A., *Strange Destiny, A Biography of Warren Hastings.* p.252

12. Ibid. p.250

13. Wikipedia.org, Asaf-ud-Daula

14. Hickey, William. From *Memoirs of a Georgian Rake.* p.362

15. Ibid. p.361

16. Ibid. pp. 368-369

17. Feiling, Keith, *Warren Hastings* (Macmillan & Co Ltd, London, 1954) p.311

18. Johan Zoffany (1733-1810) was a German neo-classical painter and a founder member of the Royal Academy. He visited India (1783-1788) and some of his paintings still hang there, at the Victoria Memorial in Calcutta. His infamous 'Last Supper' hangs in St Johns Church. This wonderful painting depicts contemporary members of Calcutta society as Jesus and his disciples, including a transvestite magistrate as St John. [Daily Telegraph 6.3.12] There is also a rather cross looking Judas. The identity of the model for Judas has never been revealed, but caused much controversy in Calcutta at the time.

19. Mervyn Davies, A., *Strange Destiny, A Biography of Warren Hastings.* p.324

20. Duff, James Grant, *History of the Mahrattas. (1826) Volume II.* Chapter XV, p.476

21. Mervyn Davies, A., *Strange Destiny, A Biography of Warren Hastings.* p.331

22. Feiling, Keith, *Warren Hastings.* p.326

Notes

23. Hickey, William. From *Memoirs of a Georgian Rake*. pp.382-383

24. Feiling, Keith, *Warren Hastings*. pp. 327-328

PART SIX : THE COLERIDGE CONNECTION

19. 1774 to 1783

1. Correspondence of the Coleridge Family, 1667-1836. British Library Manuscripts.

2. Ottery St Mary is the village where the Coleridge children were brought up. Their father, Reverend John Coleridge, was rector of the parish and headmaster of the local school.

3. An extract from this letter is quoted in Chapter 8. Solomon was stationed at Monghyr from 1768 to 1772.

4. Samuel Taylor Coleridge. Then aged ten. Samuel never met his older brother.

5. Mr Watherstone, or Captain Watherstone, appears in two previous chapters (14 and 17). He was an officer in the Bengal army and was Thomas Goddard's Persian interpreter. This may explain why he was sent, in December 1778, on a fruitless mission to deputise for Goddard at Mudhoji Bhonsle's court at Nagpur. In 1781 he was again sent to deputise for Goddard, but this time to Pune, to negotiate with Nana Fadnavis. However Hastings had him recalled and replaced by David Anderson. According to the House of Commons records (1754 to 1790), Watherstone became MP for Boston, Lincolnshire, from 1784 to 1790. He was a beneficiary of Goddard's will, together with his illegitimate son. This implies that, like Solomon, he brought a child back with him from India. He apparently turned up in Boston, 'worth millions' and was elected as one of the then two MPs for the town. It is thought he died in 1803.

6. Molly Newbury, the family nurse.

7. Maria Northcote, Frank's childhood sweetheart.

8. Coleridge, Bernard (Lord), *The Story of a Devonshire House* (T. Fisher Unwin, London. 1905) p.11

9. Holmes, Richard, *Coleridge, Early Visions* (HarperCollins 1989) p.3

10. Ibid. p. 15

11. Ibid. p.6

12. Ibid. pp.21-22

20. 1784 to 1792

1. Captain Henry Mordaunt was a contemporary of William Hickey. He features heavily in Hickey's memoirs. He was the illegitimate elder brother of the Earle of Peterborough and a captain in the EIC army. Mordaunt returned to London around 1780 where he got into a dispute with Hickey over a woman, Charlotte Barry, who later became Hickey's mistress. Hickey described Mordaunt as *the surly nabob*. According to Hickey he *usually had a scowling countenance* and was often *grumbling and snarling*. After Hickey stole his girlfriend Mordaunt became violent and on one occasion attacked Hickey with a stick. Charlotte was terrified of him. The account ends with Mordaunt disappearing and Hickey hearing that he had arranged passage back to India on a Dutch ship. In fact he must have arranged passage on the *Gibraltar,* the ship on which Frank Coleridge was midshipman. Hickey returned to India in 1783 with Charlotte as his 'wife.' British India was a small world in those days.

2. Frank was actually fourteen at the time. Hardly old, but he did not make lieutenant until 1790, six years later.

3. Coleridge, Bernard (Lord), *The Story of a Devonshire House*. p.47

4. In nine months John managed to accumulate £1000 to send to James, the amount specified by Capt. Biggs. This exceeded ten times Revd Coleridge's annual salary. From Engell, James, *Coleridge, the Early Family Letters*. (Clarendon Press. USA. 1994) Note 3, letter No. 24.

5. Captain John Meredith. Died in 1786. John was greatly affected by his death. See letter from Francis to Nancy dated Nov 1st 1788.

Notes

6. Coleridge, Bernard (Lord), *The Story of a Devonshire House*. p.37

7. Butterleigh. Bernard Coleridge wrote in his 1905, *Story of a Devonshire House*, that the *old ash tree at Butterleigh is now gone*.

8. Note by Bernard Coleridge (?1907) inserted into, Correspondence of the Coleridge Family, 1667-1836. British Library Manuscripts.

9. Engell, James, *Coleridge, the Early Family Letters* (Clarendon Press. USA. 1994) p.12

10. Note by Bernard Coleridge (?1907) inserted into, Correspondence of the Coleridge Family, 1667-1836. British Library Manuscripts.

11. Coleridge, Bernard (Lord), *The Story of a Devonshire House*. p.44

12. Beveridge, H. A., *Comprehensive History of India*. (Blackie and Sons, London 1862) Volume II, p.603

13. Montgomery Martin, R., *The History of the Indian Empire*. (The London Printing and Publishing Company ltd. 1861) Volume 1. pp.370-371.

14. Beveridge, H. A., *Comprehensive History of India*. Volume II, p. 608

15. Ibid. p. 608

16. Note by Bernard Coleridge (?1907) inserted into, Correspondence of the Coleridge Family, 1667-1836. British Library Manuscripts.

17. Montgomery Martin, R., *The History of the Indian Empire,* Volume 1, p.370

18. Ibid. p.371

19. Beveridge, H., *A Comprehensive History of India*. Volume II, p.613

20. Ibid. p.32

21. Coleridge, Bernard (Lord), *The Story of a Devonshire House*. p.50

22. Beveridge, H. A., *Comprehensive History of India*. Volume II, p.617

23. Ibid. p.619

24. Molly Lefebrure, *Private Lives of the Ancient Mariner; Coleridge and his children* (Lutterworth. 2013) p.83

25. Holmes, Richard, *Coleridge, Early Visions* (HarperCollins 1989) p.38

26. Ibid. p.49

27. Ibid. p.53

PART SEVEN : HOME : 1786 – 1824

21. Back in England : 1786 to 1804

1. Lamb H.H., *Historic Storms of the North Sea, British Isles and North West Europe* (Cambridge University Press. 1991)

2. www.oldashburton.co.uk

3. *A Guide and Short History of Saint Andrew's Church, Ashburton* (5th Edition. 2005)

4. James Rennell (1742-1830), who later became known as the father of Indian Geography was born in Chudleigh, Devon. There may well be a link with Rose Rennell's family as they both came from the same part of Devon and share the same name. James' father, an officer in the Royal Artillery, was killed in action in Belgium just after his son was born. James was then brought up by a guardian in Chudleigh. At the age of fourteen, he was sent to sea as a midshipman. In 1756 he took part in a survey of the Palk Straits, between India and Ceylon. He was appointed Surveyor General in Bengal in 1764, at the age of just twenty-one.

5. Michael Searles (1750 to 1813) was a Georgian architect well known for designing and building large houses, mainly in south London, to cater for the well-off middle classes. His masterpiece was the fourteen-house Paragon development on the south side of Blackheath. The last house was not occupied until 1805, by which time Searle was almost financially ruined. The Walworth was completed some years earlier.

Notes

6. From '*Ideal Homes: A history of South-East London Suburbs.*' www.ideal-homes.co.uk From the Borough archive.

7. Ackroyd, Peter, *The History of England. Volume IV. Revolution* (Macmillan. 2016) pp. 253-255

8. Edmund Burke (1730-1797) was a philosopher, politician, author and orator. His mother was an Irish catholic, and throughout his life he supported catholic emancipation. In London Burke mixed with other intellectuals, most of whom have been mentioned in this book. They include Samuel Johnson, David Garrick and Joshua Reynolds. Burke's principles and convictions all linked to his beliefs in the rights of man. He was against tyranny in whatever form it took, including the power of the British government against its colonies, and those it colonised. This was likely to be the reason he was so tenacious in pursuing his action against Hastings.

9. Bernstein, Jeremy, *Dawning of the Raj. The Life and Trials of Warren Hastings* (Ivan R. Dee 2000. Aurum Press 2001) pp.211-212

10. Ibid. pp.213-214

11. Ackroyd, Peter, *The History of England. Volume IV. Revolution.* p.254

12. Bernstein, Jeremy, *Dawning of the Raj. The Life and Trials of Warren Hastings.* p.221

13. Ibid. p.240

14. Peters, Timothy, *King George III : Re-evaluation of his mental health.* British Journal of Psychiatry. Aug 2013 (2) 83

15. Bernstein, Jeremy, *Dawning of the Raj. The Life and Trials of Warren Hastings.* p.253

16. Ibid. p.257

17. Ibid. p.258

18. Ibid. p.285

19. From an article in the Whitney Gazette, 23.7.2014 and from the book, *Jane Austin and Adlestrop* (Windrush Publishing Services, 2013)

22. To the Isle of Wight

1. Dalrymple, William, *White Mughals, Love and Betrayal in Eighteenth Century India* (HarperCollins: 2002). This book covers the interesting life of James Achilles Kirkpatrick, the Resident at Hyderabad, and his relationship with a highborn Persian lady, Khair un-Nissa.

2. Ackroyd, Peter, *The History of England. Volume IV. Revolution* (Macmillan. 2016) p. 335

3. Dalrymple, William, *The East India Company: The original corporate raiders*. The Guardian 21/08/2015

4. Gilbert, Arthur, *Recruitment and Reform in the East India Company Army 1760-1800* (Journal of British Studies. 1975 pp 89-111)

5. Ibid. p.91

6. Holmes, Richard, *Sahib. The British Soldier in India 1750 – 1914* (HarperCollins: 2005) p.216

7. Cambridge History of India. Vol VI. Edited by H. H. Dodswell. (Cambridge University Press, 1932) p.93

8. Gilbert, Arthur, *Recruitment and Reform in the EIC Army 1760-1800*. p.105

9. Ibid. p.101

10. McAleer, John, *Cesspools, Coal Chutes and Carisbrooke Castle : The East India Company on the Isle of Wight* (British Library, Untold Lives Blog, 9th May 2014)

11. Gilbert, Arthur, *Recruitment and Reform in the EIC Army 1760-1800*. p.107

12. Motherbank. A sandbank off the north east coast of the Isle of Wight, between Cowes and Ryde.

13. Thomas, James H, *The Isle of Wight and the East India Company 1700-1840: some connections considered* (The Local Historian. Vol 30. Number 1. February 2000) p.9

14. Debate at the E.I.H, April 18, on Pension to be awarded to Capt. S. Earle. (Asiatic Journal and Monthly Registers. Vol. IV, July –Dec 1817. Accessed via books.google.co.uk) pp. 490-497

15. Thomas, James H., *County, Commerce and Contacts: Hampshire and the East India Company in the Eighteenth Century* (Hampshire Field Club and Archaeological Society. 68, 2013, 167-177)

16. Carisbrooke Castle. (English Heritage Guidebooks. 2013) p.36

17. Depot Letter Book, 1804-1813, British Library, OIOC L/MIL/9/47

18. Thomas Ogle, surgeon, had been a prolific reviewer for several periodicals of his day. In 1791 he was appointed as Surgeon Extraordinary to George, Prince of Wales, and then Surgeon to the Middlesex Dispensary, before his appointment to the Isle of Wight. He was described, rather bizarrely, as *very well – not too tall*, in an annotated list of members of the Prince of Wales Lodge (10th May 1788). (From *British Freemasonry 1717-1813. Vol 1*). In 1790 he wrote a critique of Gulliver's Travel by Jonathan Swift. (*The Critical Heritage, Edited by Karen Williams. London and New York 1970*). In 1791 he wrote another critique entitled, *A Short Enquiry into the Merits of a "new discovered Fact of a relative Nature in the Venereal Poison."* (The annotated Review. Vol XII. Jan –April 1792).

23. The Letter Book

1. *Henry Addington.* An East Indiaman, also called the *Henry Addington*, ran aground in heavy fog on Bembridge Ledge, off the east coast of the Isle of Wight, just five days into her second voyage in 1798. She left the Downs, bound for the East on the 4th November 1798. Most of her valuable cargo of arms, iron, lead and silver were saved, but a certain amount went missing and the ship had to be guarded by an armed vessel. The wreck lay off the coast for over two years. James Thomas gives an interesting account as to what might have happened to the missing cargo (Thomas, James H, *The Isle of Wight and the East India Company 1700-1840: some connections considered.* pp.12-16). The loss of the ship was put down to pilot error, but both pilot and captain continued with their commands. Captain Wakefield commanded the maiden voyage of the new *Henry Addington*, but not

its second voyage when it took part in the aforementioned Battle of Pula Aura. On its third voyage, the *Henry Addington* sailed in convoy with the fated *Earle of Abergavenny*.

2. Brookman's Waggon. Presumably a haulage company. See Crosby's Pocket Gazetteer of England and Wales, or Traveller's Companion, 1807. The entry for Christchurch, page 125, gives notice that, *a Brookman's Waggon arrives every Thursday from Holborn.*

3. Holmes, Richard, *Coleridge, Early Visions* (Harper Collins 1989) pp. 53-58

4. A Record of the 29th Foot by Colonel Leslie Charles (1807-1813). www.worcestershireregiment.com

5. Hickson, Samuel, *Diary of Samuel Hickson (1777-1785)*. (From Bengal Past and Present. Vol XLIX. Pt 1. Jan to March 1935. Accessed through archive.org). p.37

6. Bethlem Hospital. In 1811 Bethlem Royal Hospital (Bedlam) was still located at Moorfields, just north of the City of London, on the site of the present Liverpool Street Station. At the time the Hospital was in a bad state of repair and funding was being sought to build a new asylum. In 1815 the new Bethlem Hospital opened at St. George's Fields, Southwark. The building now houses the Imperial War Museum.

7. This remains the case in the present day when, if a patient is admitted to an NHS psychiatry hospital out of area, costs are charged to the health authority where the patient previously had residence.

8. Lempriere, William, *A Tour from Gibraltar to Tangier, Sallee, Magadore, Santa Cruz, Tarudant, and thence over Mount Atlas to Morocco*. (London. 1791).

9. For example; Lempriere, William. *A Report on the Medicinal Effects of an Alumnious Chalybeate Water, lately discovered at Sandrocks, in the Isle of Wight*. (London. 1812)

10. Advert for the Academy of Monsieur L'Abbe de Grenthe. Published in *Le Miroir Politique*, a Guernsey paper, in 1815, and also in several English newspapers in 1808 and 1817.

Notes

24. Coda

1. Gaekwad, Fatesinghrao, *Sayajirao of Baroda, The Prince and the Man* (PVT Ltd. India 1989) p.22

2. Ibid. p.22

3. Duff, James Grant, *History of the Mahrattas. Vol III.* (First published 1826. Accessed via Google Books) p.94

4. Elliott F.A.H., *The Rulers of Baroda* (Originally published by Baroda State Press 1879. Then Oxford University. Digitalised by Google.) p.19

5. Duff, James Grant, *History of the Mahrattas. Vol III.* p.93

6. Elliott F.A.H, *The Rulers of Baroda* p.19

7. Ibid. p.22

8. Duff, James Grant, *History of the Mahrattas. Vol III.* p.95

9. Princely States. See note 4. Chapt. 17.

10. Gaekwad, Fatesinghrao, *Sayajirao of Baroda, The Prince and the Man.* pp. 34-50

11. Gaekwad, Fatesinghrao, *The Palaces of India* (William Collins and Sons Ltd: 1980) p.154

12. Indo-Saracen Style. A style of architecture common to British architects in India in the late eighteenth century. It combines elements of Indo-Islamic with Indian, gothic and neo-classical. Examples include the Victoria Rail Terminus, the Gateway of India and Taj Mahal Hotel, all in Mumbai, and the Victoria Memorial in Kolkata.

13. Gaekwad, Fatesinghrao, *The Palaces of India.* p.156

14. Sen, Sailendra Nath, *Anglo–Maratha Relations, 1772-1785.* Op. cit. p.194

15. Count Benoit de Boigne (1751-1830) was born in Chambéri, in the Duchy of Savoy. He led an interesting life, being born as the son

of a fur-merchant and rising to be a count. After many adventures in the French and then Russian army, he was captured by the Turks and made a slave. After rescue by the British ambassador to Constantinople he enrolled as an ensign in the EIC army in Madras. He eventually found his way to Gwalior via Lucknow and joined Mahadji Scindia's army. He set up battalions based on European armies.

16. Sen, Sailendra Nath, *Anglo–Maratha* Relations, *1772-1785.* p. 195

17. Duff, James Grant, *History of the Mahrattas. Vol III.* p.29

18. Ibid. p.29

19. Montgomery Martin, R., *The History of the Indian Empire. Volume I* (The London Printing and Publishing Company Ltd. 1861) p.374

20. Duff, James Grant, *History of the Mahrattas. Vol III.* p.5

21. Ibid. p.126

22. Ibid. p.136

23. Asiatic Journal and Monthly Miscellany. Vol 4. From July to Dec 1817. (Accessed on line) p.940.

24. Blackwood's Edinburgh Magazine. Volume I, April- September. (Accessed on line) p.332.

25. East India Accounts. May 1822-23.

26. Will of Solomon Earle, late Captain and Paymaster of the Honorable East India Company's Depot, of Clatterford in the Isle of Wight, Hampshire, 18. Jan 1825. *nationalarchives.gov.uk* REF : PROB 11/1694/173

27. Great Western Canal. The Grand Western Canal was constructed between 1810 and 1839. Just after completion, competition from the railways began in earnest and its use declined.

28. East India Accounts. May 1825.

29. Chaplin, Arnold M.D., *St. Helena Who's Who, or A Directory of the Island during the Captivity of Napoleon.* (London. 1914)

30. Desmier, Rick, *My relative's Brush with Napoleon*. Personal Collection of Rick Desmier.

31. Chaplin, Arnold M.D., *St. Helena Who's Who, or A Directory of the Island during the Captivity of Napoleon*.

32. Sheaffe, Stephen W., *The Sheaffe Family History* (Published 1988. Available through the National Library of Australia)

33. Tytler, Harriet (Ed. By Anthony Sattin), *An Englishwoman in India, The Memoirs of Harriet Tytler 1828 – 1858,* (Oxford University Press: 1986) pp. 37-46

34. Ibid.

35. There are over 80 photographs by Robert and Harriet Tytler in the British Library Indian Collection.

36. Hanoverian Military Journal Part II. 1831

37. Simms, Brendan, *The Longest Afternoon. The Four Hundred Men who Decided the Battle of Waterloo* (Penguin Books 2014)

38. https://www.spink.com/lot/17007000198

39. Sydney Morning Herald. Friday 17 October 1890. Central Criminal Court. Thursday (Before his Honour Mr. Justice Windeyer and a jury of 12) Central Criminal.

40. See painting of an Indian lady by Thomas Hickey (no relation to William Hickey) which now hangs in the National Gallery of Ireland, Dublin.

25. Conclusions

1. East India Military Calendar Containing The Services of General and Field Officers of the Indian Army. By the Editor of the Royal Military Calendar. Vol II. London. 1824.

Select Bibliography

Principle Manuscript and On-Line Sources

British Library (India Office Records)

Warren Hastings Papers. Letters from Colonel Goddard 1778 –1779. 29.119

Correspondence of the Coleridge Family. 1667 -1836

David Anderson Papers

Ship Logs

Debate at the E.I.H, April 18, on the Pension to be awarded to Capt. S. Earle. (Asiatic Journal and Monthly Registers. Vol. IV, July –Dec 1817. Accessed via books.google.co.uk) pp. 490-497

Newport Depot Letter Book A, 1804-1813, British Library, OIOC L/MIL/9/47

A

Ackroyd, Peter, *The History of England. Volume IV. Revolution* (Macmillan 2016)

Adkins, Roy and Leslie, *The Greatest Siege in British History* (Little Brown 2017)

B

Bailey, Peter, A, *Researching Ancestors in the East India Company Armies* (FIBIS Research Guides 2006)

Bankim, Chandra Chatterji, *Anandamath,* (New Delhi, Orient Paperbacks 2000, 1882)

Betts, Jonathan, *Harrison* (National Maritime Museum. Geenwich, London. Reprinted 2014)

Bernstein, Jeremy, *Dawning of the Raj. The Life and Trials of Warren Hastings* (Ivan R. Dee 2000. Aurum Press 2001)

Beveridge, H. A., *Comprehensive History of India. Volumes 1 to 3* (Blackie and Sons, London 1862)

Black, Jeremy, *Warfare in the Eighteenth Century* (Cassell London 1999)

Boswell, James, *Boswell's London Journal 1762-1763* (Heinemann 1950)

Brierley, Saroo, with Larry Buttrose, *Lion: A Long Way Home* (Penguin Books Ltd. 2017)

C

Campbell, Theophilia Carlile, *The Battle of the Press, as told in the story of the life of Richard Carlile by his daughter* (A. & H.B.Bonner, London 1899, Accessed from *Gutenberg.org/files*)

Coleridge, Bernard (Lord), *The Story of a Devonshire House* (T. Fisher Unwin, London 1905)

Corneille, John, *Journal of my Service in India* (The Folio Society 1966)

Cox, Paul, *Wellington, Triumphs, Politics and Passions* (National Portrait Gallery, London 2015)

D

Dalrymple, William, *White Mughals, Love and Betrayal in Eighteenth Century India* (HarperCollins 2002)

Dalrymple, William, *The East India Company: The original corporate raiders* (The Guardian 21/08/2015)

Dalrymple, William, *The Last Mughal, The Fall of a Dynasty, Delhi, 1857* (Bloomsbury Publishing 2006)

Duff, James Grant, *History of the Mahrattas. Vols II & III.* (First published 1826. Accessed via Google Books)

E

Earle, Solomon, *Leaves from the Journal of my Grandfather's Services in India, by P.H.Sheafe* (J.J.Rutter, at the Times Office, Milton, 1880)

Earle, Captain Solomon, (Bengal Establishment). From East India Military Calendar. Vols I & II. (London, 1824, pp 386-312. Accessed via Google Books)

East India Military Calendar, concerning the Services of General and Field Officers of the Indian Amy. Vol 2. (Available online through Google books)

Elliott F.A.H, *The Rulers of Baroda.* (Originally published Baroda State Press 1879. Then Oxford University. Digitalised by Google)

Engell, James, *Coleridge, the Early Family Letters.* (Clarendon Press. USA. 1994)

F

Feiling, Keith, *Warren Hastings* (Macmillan & Co Ltd, London 1954)

Ferguson, Niall, *Empire. How Britain Made the Modern World* (Allen Lane, Penguin 2003)

Forbes, James, *Oriental Memoirs* (1813. Accessed via Google Books)

G

Gaekwad, Fatesinghrao, *The Palaces of India* (William Collins and Sons Ltd 1980)

Gaekwad, Fatesinghrao, *Sayajirao of Baroda, The Prince and the Man* (PVT Ltd. India 1989)

Gatrell, Vic, *The First Bohemians, Life and Art in London's Golden Age* (Allen Lane 2013)

Gordon, Stewart, *The Marathas 1600–1818. From the New Cambridge History of India* (Cambridge University Press 1993)

Gleig, George Robert, *The History of the British in India. Vol 4.* (1835, Accessed via Google Books)

H

Harvey, Robert, *Clive, The Life and Death of a British Emperor* (Hodder and Stoughton 1998)

Hickey, William, *Memoirs of a Georgian Rake* (Folio Society, London. 1995. Hickey's memoirs were also accessed via Google Books)

Hickson, Samuel, *Dairy of Samuel Hickson (1777-1785).* (Bengal Past and Present. Jan-March 1935)

History of Baroda Website, www.*historyofvadodara.in*

Holmes, Richard, *Coleridge, Early Visions* (Harper Collins 1989)

Holmes, Richard, *Redcoat. The British Soldier in the Age of Horse and Musket* (HarperCollins 2001)

Holmes, Richard, *Sahib. The British Soldier in India, 1750-1914* (Harper Collins: 2005)

J

James, Lawrence, *RAJ., The Making and Unmaking of British India* (Little, Brown and Company 1998)

John, Paul (Editor), *Baroda. Know your Roots.* (Times Group Books. New Delhi. 2012)

K

Keay, John, *The Honourable Company. A History of the English East India Company* (HarperCollins 1991)

Khan, Shaharyar M, *The Begums of Bhopal, A History of the Princely State of Bhopal* (I.B.Tauris & Co. Ltd, London. 2000)

L

Lonely Planet Publications, *India* (15th Edition. 2013. PTy Ltd.)

M

Markham, Clement R., *Narrative of the Mission of George Bogle to Tibet , and of the Journey of Thomas Manning to Lhasa.* (1876. Digitalised copy available as free download)

Mervyn Davies, A., *Strange Destiny, A Biography of Warren Hastings.* (G.P. Putnam's Sons, New York 1935)

Montgomery Martin, R., *The History of the Indian Empire. Volumes 1 to 3.* (The London Printing and Publishing Company Ltd. 1861)

Mount, Ferdinand, *The Tears of the Rajas. Mutiny, Money and Marriage in India 1805-1905* (Simon and Schuster UK Ltd. 2015)

N

Navarane M S., *Battles of the Honourable East India Company* (2006. APH Publishing. New Delhi)

Newman and Co's Handbook to Calcutta, (1875. Digitalised copy available)

Nix-Seaman A. J., *The Afghan War Memorial Church and Historical Notes on Colaba.* (Leslie, Manger & Co., Ltd, India. 1938)

O

Olsen, Kirstin, *Daily Life in Eighteenth Century England* (Greenwood, 1999)

P

Parkes, Fanny, *Begums, Thugs and Englishmen. The Journals of Fanny Parkes* (Penguin Books, India 2002)

Panda, Rajaram, *Khajuraho* (Mittal Publishing, New Delhi 2010)

Porter, Roy, *English Society in the Eighteenth Century* (Penguin Books, 1882)

R

Reeve, John, *The Lives of the Mughal Emperors* (British Library, 2012)

Robins, Nick, *The Corporation that Changed the World* (Pluto Press, London 2012)

S

Sen, Sailendra Nath, *Anglo–Maratha Relations, 1772-1785* (PVT Ltd, India 1961)

Simms, Brendan, *The Longest Afternoon. The Four Hundred Men who Decided the Battle of Waterloo* (Penguin Books 2014)

Sixth Report from the Committee of Secrecy on the Causes of the War in the Carnatic. Vol 8. p.854-859. 1782

Sobel, Dava, *Longitude, The True Story of a Lone Genius Who Solved the Greatest Scientific Problem of His Time* (Harper Perennial 2011)

T

Tammita–Delgoda, Sinharaja, *A Traveller's History of India* (The Windrush Press 1994. Second Edition)

Turnbull, Patrick, *Warren Hastings* (New English Library Ltd, London 1975)

Select Bibliography

Tytler, Harriet (ed. By Anthony Sattin), *An Englishwoman in India, The Memoirs of Harriet Tytler 1828 – 1858* (Oxford University Press 1986)

U

Unknown author, *A Journal of the March of the Bombay Detachment, across Mahratta country, from Culpee to Surat, in 1778* (Printed for W. Faden. In Cornhill, ?1779 Available from Hathitrust Digital Library)

Unknown author, *Proceedings of the Bombay Army in their march towards Poona* (Published as addendum to above).

Unknown author, *General Orders of the Bombay Select Committee. Bombay Castle, 3rd February 1779.* (Published with above)

Unwin, Sir Brian. *Terrible Exile. The Last Days of Napoleon on St. Helena* (I.B.Taurus & Co Ltd. 2010)

V

Vallins, Oishi and Perry. Editors, *Coleridge, Romanticism and the Orient.* (Bloomsbury 2013)

W

Weedon, Rev. Edward St. Clair, *A Year with the Gaekwar of Baroda* (Chapel River Press, Surrey 1911. Various digitalised sources)

White, Gerry, *London in the Eighteenth Century. A Great and Monstrous Thing.* (The Bodley Head, London 2012)

Wilson, Jon, *India Conquered. Britain's Raj and the Chaos of Empire* (Simon & Schuster Ltd, 2016)

Y

Yagnick, Achyut and Seth Suchitra, *Ahmedabad, from Royal City to Megacity* (Penguin Books, India 2011)

Glossary

INDIAN PLACE NAMES

EIGHTEENTH CENTURY	PRESENT DAY
Assurghur, Ashere Gurr	Asirgarh
Ballasore	Baleshwar
Baroda or Brodera,	Vadodara
Benares	Varanasi
Boorampore, Burampore	Burhanpur
Bopaul Tol, Bopoltle	Bhopal
Bombay	Mumbai
Calcutta	Kolkata
Ceylon	Sri Lanka
Chatterpour	Chhatarpur
Chupra	Chhapra
Cooch Bihar	Koch Bihar
Culpee	Kalpi
Dinapur	Danapur
Hoogli River	Hooghly/Hughli River
Husnabad	Hoshangabad
Jumna River	Yamuna River
Madras	Chennai
Mow, Mau, Mhow	Mauranipur
Monghyr	Munger
Midnapore	Medinipur

Glossary

Narbuddah River	Narbada/Narmada River
Oudh	Oude/Ayodhya/Awadh/Avadh
Poona	Pune
Savandroog	Savandurga
Seringapatum	Srirangapatna/Shrirangapatna
Wadgaon	Vadegaon

GENERAL GLOSSARY

Ayah	Nurse maid, nanny or governess. Term used by Europeans in India. Origin, Hindi/Urdu āyā
Banyan	The term now means a type of tree. But the original Gujarati word meant a merchant or grocer. This was picked up by the Portuguese, then the British and used to describe the shade of a tree under which business was conducted. Then the term was used for the tree itself
Batta	Extra money paid to EIC army officers when away from their home base
Begum	Mughal noblewoman. Equivalent to *Nawab* for men
Bibi	Indian mistress or wife of a European
Board of Control for India	British Government office representing Parliament for India. 1784 to 1858
Cantonment	A military station in British India. Also a garrison or camp
Caulking	Sealing gaps between ship's timbers to make them watertight, usually with 'oakum', a mixture of hemp and tar.

Chauth	Tax or Tribute collected by the Marathas. Sanskrit for one-fourth.
Collector	Chief administrator/revenue collector for a district, also known as a District Officer
Concker	Most likely a term for a rocky outcrop.
Coss	An Indian measurement of 1.5 to 2 miles. Literally Hindi for 'to shout or call'.
Country Trade	Private, usually internal trade in India. Not part of export to Europe, which was the monopoly of the EIC.
Crimps	Recruiters
Crossing the Bar	Entering a port or, more specifically to cross breakers to land on the beach at Madras.
Dacoit	Robber/highwayman. After the famine in Bengal some villagers had to make the choice to become a *dacoit* or starve.
Diwani	Persian for revenue administration/accounts. The name given to the document signed by Shah Alam II and Robert Clive in 1765, which gave the EIC the right to collect taxes in Bengal on behalf of the Emperor
Dual System	A dual system of government set up by Robert Clive in Bengal where the local rulers were entrusted to collect revenue, but with overall control remaining with the EIC
Durbar	The Court of an Indian ruler, from the Persian (Urdu) *Darbar* meaning Court.

Glossary

East India Company	The Honourable East India Company. Formed by London merchants in 1599 and disbanded in 1858
East Indiaman	A general name for a merchant ship, usually armed, operating under charter or licence to one of the East India Companies based in Europe.
Factors	Agent of the EIC
Factories	A Company depot, where goods are collected and stored for trade. Not a manufacturing centre.
Ferengi/Firangi	Arabic for foreigner
Firman	An order of the Emperor or Sultan, usually a written document
Furlough	Leave of Absence
Furlong	An imperial measure of 1/8th of a mile. Equivalent to 660 feet, 40 rods or 10 chains. This seems an unusual measurement but it has origins from Anglo-Saxon strip-farming. It is the length of a furrow in one acre of a ploughed field. An acre is one furlong by one chain.
Ghats	Landing-stage or steps to a river or tank
Grenadier	A term used for a soldier who could throw a grenade, used mainly in the 17th Century. By the 18th Century the term was used to denote an elite force with enhanced status and pay.
Jagir	A lifetime annuity from land revenues
Jamidar	Indian officer of rank equivalent to lieutenant or platoon commander
John Company	Name used for East India Company, after the Dutch *Jan Kampani*

Glossary

Killadar	Commander or governor of a fort in India (apparently a valid scrabble word)
Lac/Lakh	One hundred thousand
Loot	From Hindustani *lut*, meaning robbery or plunder
Maidan	Public area or park in a town, a parade ground
Mofussil	The provinces, country districts
Nabob	A conspicuously wealthy man, returned from India having made his wealth there. Anglo-Indian term derived from *Nawab*
Nullah	A water-course, riverbed or ravine. (Urdu)
Nawab	The semi-autonomous ruler of a princely state bestowed by the Mughal Emperor. The female equivalent was *Begum*. The term *Nizam* was only used for the ruler of Hyderabad
New Gentlemen	Mervyn Davies used this term to describe the three Council members appointed to the Bengal Council in 1774 who became Warren Hasting's opponents.
Pettah	A town, sometimes fortified, outside a fort.
P & O	Peninsular and Oriental Steam Navigation Company
Palanquin	Covered litter (cf Sedan Chair in UK). Usually carried by around four bearers. Stages, or *Daks*, were set up so travellers could be transported at long distance, with bearers changing at intervals, resting if necessary at

Glossary

	Dak bungalows. These were spaced about ten miles apart.
Perambulator	A surveyor's wheel. Used to measure distances
Picquet/Picket	A small temporary military post closer to the enemy than the main force.
Pindaries	Wandering bands of cavalry, not under an outside command, who raided surrounding villages and towns for forage and food, cf outlaws.
Pukka	Genuine, proper
Purgannah	Or *Pargana*. A division of land or district attracting a *jagir* or tax
Redoubt	Enclosed defensive emplacement outside a large fort. Usually constructed of earthworks and containing cannon.
Reduce	Term used in the eighteenth century when a town or fort is captured. Nowadays the term means to *make smaller,* but its origin is from the Latin, to *bring back, or restore.* The only archaic meaning of the word in the present day applies to surgery, to *reduce* a fracture, means to return it to its original state.
Residents	Senior officers, acting for the British and responsible for relations with more important Indian rulers
Runs	A word often used to describe sea routes near a harbour.
Ryots	Peasants. Work the land and pay a tax.
Sanskrit	An ancient language of Buddhism and Hindus.

Glossary

Sepoy	Indian soldier in the service of the EIC
Ship's Husband	Managing owner of a ship that could be leased to the EIC.
Subedar	Indian officer of rank equivalent to Captain
Suttee, Sati	Burning of Indian widow on husband's funeral pyre
Tank	Artificial Lake/pond
Tonga	Horse-carriage with two wheels
Tulwar	A sabre or broadsword
Vakeel/Vakil	An agent or representative of a person of political importance
Writers	EIC junior officers. A lesser role than a *factor*
Zamindars	Means 'land-owner' in Persian. In India *Zamindars* had the right to collect taxes from their *ryots* (or peasants) to fund courts and armies. The British adopted the zamindar system in some areas of their jurisdiction. It was abolished at Independence.
Zenana	Part of a house for the sole use, or seclusion, of women. A term used by both Muslims and Hindus.

Acknowledgements

I would like to thank the many people who have provided inspiration and helped me to write this book.

I will start with my mother who was born in India and whose stories of this rich and exotic land inspired me to set off on my first journey there, overland, in 1979. Next in line has to be my mother's neighbour, Helen Moller, who steered me in the right direction by deciphering the mysteries of family history research and who initially discovered the link to the Earle family. Then there is Rick Desmier, from Australia, who published a summary of Solomon's life, including the links to Solomon's own account and his will and testament. Rick and I met up recently in the UK and have since become friends. My good friend Steve Reilly accompanied me on my second journey across India in 2016 and put up with my many visits to graveyards and museums on the way.

I would like to thank the staff at the British Library who helped me find the right documents and to Anne Bligh, local historian at Ashburton, and founder of the website oldashsburton.co.uk. Anne was kind to meet me on my visit to Ashburton and send me off in the right direction researching the town. I would also like to thank Chris Earle who showed me Solomon's seal and his son's Waterloo medal. And Clare Arni who we met by chance in Portugal and who let me use her photograph of the Pollilur mural.

On the writing side I owe thanks to Pat Borthwick, my creative writing tutor, and to the York writing group, the Wordsmiths, for their helpful support and criticism for over the last ten years, and for helping me to hone my prose, cutting out repetition and over-explanation.

I would like to thank Samarjitsingh Gaekwad, Maharajah of Baroda, for graciously inviting me to meet him on my second India trip.

Finally I would like to thank my wife Barbara for accompanying me on my third India trip in 2017, for her copy-editing skills, for putting up with my India obsession and for her general support.

Acknowledgements

The author with Samarjitsingh Gaekwad. 2016